William M. Halsey holds a doctorate degree from the Graduate Theological Union at Berkeley and works in San Francisco, California.

The Survival of
American Innocence

Notre Dame Studies
in American Catholicism

Number 2

The Survival of
American Innocence:

Catholicism in an Era of Disillusionment, 1920–1940

William M. Halsey

UNIVERSITY OF NOTRE DAME PRESS

NOTRE DAME   LONDON

BX
1406.2
.H25

Library of Congress Cataloging in Publication Data

Halsey, William M   1945-
  The survival of American innocence.

  (Notre Dame studies in American Catholicism; no. 2)
  Bibliography: p.
  Includes index.
  1. Catholic Church in the United States—History.
2. United States—Church history—20th century.
I. Title. II. Series.
BX 1406.2.H25   282'.73   79–63360
ISBN 0–268–01699–2

To my wife,
Jill Harcke Halsey

One must know when it is right to doubt, to affirm, to submit. Anyone who does otherwise does not understand the force of reason. Some men run counter to these three principles, either affirming that everything can be proved, because they know nothing about proof, or doubting everything, because they do not know when to submit, or always submitting because they do not know when judgment is called for.

Blaise Pascal, *Pensées*, 83.

Contents

Foreword

WRITING A GENERATION AGO of the faith of American Catholics, George Santayana remarked:

> It confronts the boastful natural man, such as the American is, with a thousand denials and menaces. Everything in American life is at the antipodes to such a system. Yet the American Catholic is entirely at peace. His tone in everything, even in religion, is cheerfully American. It is wonderful how silently, amicably, and happily he lives in a community whose spirit is profoundly hostile to that of his religion.[1]

If this picture has meanwhile notably altered, there still remains a measure of validity in Santayana's analysis, for in spite of numerous and varied factors that have contributed to a less cheerful and happy condition among Catholic Americans as the 1970's draw to a close, their principal anxieties do not spring from the pockets of quiet hostility and suspicion to their faith that are holdovers from Americans' most historic bias. They arise rather from new circumstances that were hidden from view in the confident era in which Santayana wrote.

The unraveling of the thought patterns of a people in any period of history is one of the most formidable tasks to which a historian can direct his or her efforts. It is easy enough to chronicle numerical growth or decline in a religious community, to record institutional expansion or its reverse, and to note the influence of ethnic or social groups whose customs color the decisions and policies of a church. It is quite another matter for the historian to trace a religious community's processes of thought through the labyrinth of its changing moods as reflected in journals of opinion, scholarly publications, and the more revealing personal correspondence of ecclesiastical leaders and ranking figures among the laity. Thus it was the literary expressions in prose and poetry, the productions of the academic disciplines of theology, philosophy, history, and the social sciences, as well as those of politics and journalism, that served to shape and mold the American Catholic mind in the critical decades after World War I. Such an undertaking constitutes an exercise in intellectual history, which by general agreement is the most difficult kind of history to write, but by the same token is often one of the most enlightening and rewarding.

That, in brief, is the nature of the story that Dr. Halsey has so skillfully told in this book, a story based in the main on American Catholics' adherence to their traditional training as seen especially in philosophy (neo-Thomism) and in literature, but likewise revealed in other aspects of their intellectual endeavors. When the general American intellectual climate was showing more and more skepticism about nineteenth-century ideas such as that of unlimited human progress, a world governed by reason, and a moral structure inherent in the universe, Catholic thinkers continued during the "age of innocence" to emphasize the Thomistic approach as it was adumbrated in Pope Leo XIII's encyclical *Aeterni Patris* of 1879. In the meantime the old order was breaking up with less and less certainty on any score. That was what contributed to an air of separateness on the part of the Catholic intellectual community down to and beyond World War II, an attitude of mind that had seemed to continue on a higher level the ghetto mentality that was used to describe Catholics of an earlier age. As the author puts the point, "The aloof quality of Thomism enabled Catholics to be optimistic, even if everything around them was disintegrating." To a reader in the late 1970's the remarkable thing is that it seemed to work for as long as it did, for only about 1966 did the Catholic fixity of aim and purpose, so to speak, give way before the bewildering congeries of new and often radical ideas that deepened the religious doubts, uncertainties, and intellectual confusion that have characterized the Catholics' world since the close of Vatican Council II.

The reader will find here no precise and tidy explanation for the contemporary malaise that afflicts the Catholics of the United States. The author did not set out to furnish anything of the kind. What a reader will find, however, is a thoroughly documented account of intellectual trends among Catholics after World War I that will illustrate the milieu out of which the later uncertainty arose, the steady effort to adhere to old patterns of thought which no longer supported Catholics when the 'age of innocence' had vanished for them, as it had previously disappeared for their fellow citizens of other and of no religious faith. In other words, the present work is a splendid example of how much is to be learned for the present from an objective presentation of the past. It will benefit the reader in the sense intended by Owen Chadwick, Regius professor of modern history in the University of Cambridge, when he declared that history "does more than any other discipline to free the mind from the tyranny of present opinion."[2]

With a confident air and steady step born of a deep and widespread acquaintance with the sources of American Catholic intellectual trends as they emerged after World War I, Dr. Halsey conducts the reader along the road of the ensuing half century. And into the mainstream of the narrative are introduced voices that played a leading role in shaping Catholic attitudes. Here one will meet the ranking laymen, Michael Williams and George N. Shuster, founding fathers of *The Commonweal;* priest professors such as John A. Ryan of the Catholic University of America and Leo Ward, C.S.C., of the University of Notre Dame; noted journalists represented by James M. Gillis, C.S.P., of the *Catholic World;* a commanding figure in the spiritual life in Thomas Merton; and as the procession nears the present day there is heard the arresting voice of Michael Novak on the knotty problems with which Catholic Americans have struggled as they tried to sort out the perplexities of this post-conciliar age.

As Miller and Nowak surveyed the 1950's and Ronald Berman the 1960's,[3] so on a canvas restricted to the interplay of ideas of a single religious group, William M. Halsey has contributed a significant chapter to American religious and social history. It is a chapter that will, I believe, find a warm reception beyond the historians of American culture, for this book has a message for theologians, philosophers, and social scientists, as well as for the wider audience of the cultivated general reader who seeks to know what the largest religious community in the United States was thinking in the years after 1920. If the focus is that of religious thought, the product is that of professional competence and scholarly objectivity. For it may be said that this volume is a notable example of what Peter Gay and Gerald Cavanaugh had in mind when they said:

> Experience shows that just as skeptics and atheists can write bad history, religious men can write good history. . . . If it is the historian's task to discover and transmit the traces of God's hand in human affairs, he must discharge that task with diligence, accuracy, and, as Gibbon said of Tillemont, scrupulous minuteness.[4]

No greater compliment can be paid to Dr. Halsey than to say that he has done just that.

John Tracy Ellis
Professorial Lecturer in Church History,
The Catholic University of America

Acknowledgments

I wish to express my gratitude to the following for their critical and creative insights during the preparation of this manuscript: Monsignor John Tracy Ellis, Eldon Ernst, Samuel Haber, and Joseph Chinicci, O.F.M. I was also fortunate to have the expert talents of Jacquelin B. Pels, who edited and typed the rough drafts of a thankful friend.

I would like to take this opportunity to thank my family, especially my mother whose constant example of patience, persistence, and faith has followed me throughout my life. Finally, to my wife, Jill, who endured the many blank glances of a husband dutifully but unfortunately absorbed in his own thoughts, I can only express my deepest gratitude for her support, encouragement, and friendship and hope that in the future I learn how to write with more ease.

Introduction

The Sad Century

THE WINTER OF 1942 SAW Americans bracing themselves for the second world conflagration of the century. Perplexed by another war and weary from the preceding thirty years of doubt and confusion, John A. Ryan, an activist Catholic social reformer of the New Deal, wrote a revealing letter to Carlton J. H. Hayes, a convert to Catholicism and historian of modern Europe. Ryan had just finished reading Hayes's already popular but controversial study of late nineteenth-century history, *A Generation of Materialism, 1871–1900* (1941). It occurred to Ryan that Hayes should write a sequel, "The Generation of Disillusion." In fact, the historian had already indicated a general approach to this subject in an article for *The Commonweal* in 1934, "From One Age to Another." In that essay Hayes had described the "passing of the optimistic Age of Enlightenment. The advent of the pessimistic Age of Disillusionment." Even though Hayes was critical of the former period's materialism and sentimental optimism, he was attracted to its "high order of civilizing aspiration and achievement" in contrast with contemporary skepticism.[1]

The reactions of Ryan and Hayes toward the world in which they lived were indicative of the Catholic intellectual response to contemporary culture in the years following World War I. American Catholics pictured themselves as living in a "disintegrating world." The twentieth century was a "sad century," according to the Jesuit historian Demetrius B. Zema, because it had reaped "a harvest of dragons" since the thirteenth century. The world was contemplating "the desolating spectacle of human degeneration, of debasement of the arts, of letters, and of education, and the indescribable confusion of thought—indeed, the collapse of a civilization."[2] Having drawn for themselves the bleak outlines of an uncertain world out of joint, Catholics promptly set out to build their own world safe from disillusionment but wavering between the charms of innocence and the grip of paranoia.

The Catholic Church has been no stranger to disillusionment. Over the centuries it had developed a reputation for a realistic assessment of human and social possibilities. In the nineteenth century it seemed to be one of the few institutions in the western world which did not queue behind the

1

banners of unlimited progress and other utopian manifestos. In America, the garden of opportunity for the immigrant Catholic, this sense of realism was tested by an environment of democratic, moral, and material optimism. Struggling to contain these conflicting drives, Catholics were gradually drawn into American idealism. The historical moment when this became most evident was the period following World War I. Since then, while non-Catholic Americans encountered successive "shocks of recognition" against a world view of bright promises, Catholics attempted to construct a world impervious to the disruptions of modernity and determined to preserve the receding boundaries of American innocence. This effort has, to a great extent, dominated Catholic sensibilities from World War I to the mid-1960's. The special concern of this study will be to follow its path until World War II, after which there begins an observable unravelling of the cultural concerns of the Catholic community during the interwar period.

As understood by historians of American intellectual history, innocence described the structure of values which characterized nineteenth-century intellectual and cultural expression and which has increasingly been challenged by currents of thought and the flow of events in the twentieth century. In summary, these values include the following: the belief in a rational and predictable cosmos; the belief in a moral structure inherent in the universe; the belief in progress; and a didactic or "genteel" rendering of cultural, especially literary, art forms. In the years preceeding and following World War I, previous certainties were challenged, producing an intellectual atmosphere where complexity and uncertainty were more prevalent and cultural fragmentation more pronounced.

In this milieu, American Catholics sought, with resources both American and Catholic in inspiration, to hold on to the qualities of innocence. After more than a century of immigration, Catholicism, following World War I, began a process of culturally and socially defining itself in America. While the war was largely a disruptive force in American society for Catholics, especially its growing middle class, it served as a mechanism of collective awakening.

Untouched by postwar disillusionment, Catholics set out as "providential hosts" to defend the values and promises of American idealism which seemed threatened by various forms of irrationalism: probability in scientific thought, the subconscious in psychology, skepticism in literature, and relativism in law and morality. Supporting the aggressive social and intellectual posture of Catholicism was the philosophy of neo-Thomism, which allowed Catholics to maintain a rational and moral universe while it supplied a rationale for optimism.

It was in literary expression that Catholics most consistently upheld the values of nineteenth-century American innocence. Thus, their literature lacks the sense of passion, complexity, and urgency which seemed to pervade twentieth-century creative literature. In both literature and philosophy Catholics sought a meaning and value system which brought stability and a sense of direction to a community otherwise characterized by economic and social restlessness.

This study does not argue that American Catholics were the only citizens attempting to maintain a hold on American moralism and idealism in the twentieth century. Nor does it suggest that American innocence abruptly ended in 1919. Innocence, and the moral and intellectual optimism which support it, continued beyond World War I for many Americans. This was particularly true in the pragmatic and technological communities which have offered an endless succession of slogans and gadgets as the promise of democratic vision. World War I was, rather, the first major shock primarily affecting, it would appear, the literary, religious, and intellectual components of American culture. Since then, the gradual erosion of self-confidence and moral optimism has troubled increasing numbers of Americans, especially in the post-Vietnam and Watergate era. What is significant about the Catholic group is that as a substantial element of the population it managed to withstand the intrusions of complexity and obscurity longer than most other groups of its size in America.

Unquestionably, a form of corporate authoritarianism stunted for many years the possibility of internal self-criticism which might have challenged the monolithic structure of Catholic thinking. More impressive than authoritarianism, however, was the active and enthusiastic manner in which a wide variety of Catholics consciously set out to mold a culture that mingled elements of both American and Catholic traditions to produce in the cultural context of the twentieth century a survival of American innocence. Liberal and conservative alike were conscious of the cultural milieu in which they lived. They sought to create a culture within that milieu which was a kind of reflected image of pre-twentieth-century America.

Catholics were allowed to pursue this quixotic venture largely because of the element of time. Though present in America from the beginning, Catholics were never universally welcomed. Most of the nineteenth century was spent trying to dispel popular notions of the "Whore of Babylon" seducing the American Adam or vice versa. It was not until the period of World War I, when enough people were sufficiently convinced of one another's harmless intentions, that Catholics felt secure enough to claim America. This they began to do while many others were bitterly disclaiming it. Thus Catholics arrived in the twentieth century as latecomers to the promises of America. As a group that was just beginning to taste its material benefits, they were unprepared for, and quite naturally opposed to, patterns of thought which appeared to undermine the promise. There is more than a little truth to the charge that Catholics have always seemed to be fifty years behind.

In the 1890's some Catholics were accused of heresy for espousing the activist individualism, self-confident mystique, and optimistic idealism of American civilization. In the 1920's many more were proclaiming the same things, but there was no charge of heresy. From the cultural and intellectual perspective of the 1920's these beliefs had taken on the scent of tradition. It was then possible for Catholics to defend them without fear of appearing to be revolutionaries. In fact, Catholics defended these beliefs with the help of highly orthodox and quite conservative theological and philosophical premises. The methodology and presuppositions of Scholastic and the neo-Thomistic philosophy provided the intellectual means for Catholics to appropriate large areas of the American experience without threat of appearing radical.

The relationship between Thomism, the American Enlightenment, and the Scottish Common Sense Realism of the early nineteenth century was comfortable enough for Catholics to feel a spiritual and intellectual bond with the thinking of most of the founding fathers and Protestant theorists before the Civil War. After World War I Catholic thought also shared a broad intellectual outlook which resembled the thinking of such liberal humanists as Ralph Barton Perry and Walter Lippmann. Although the latter group was not given to metaphysical investigations, Catholics shared with them a neo-Enlightenment affirmation of reason and a belief in an objective moral order in nature. The common enemy was the instrumentalist and empirical thought that rejected a purposive and rationally predictable cosmos in favor of a relative and contingent structure of reality. If Catholics were close to the liberal humanists in their approach to reality, they were nevertheless more eager to expand the boundaries where reason might venture to dominate. The chief cause for the widespread hostility toward relativism was its vulnerability to end in the disillusionment that characterized the literary and philosophical skepticism of the 1920's.

In the 1930's Catholics were joined in their desire for affirmation by many intellectuals who were fascinated by the grandiose designs of Communist Russia. Catholics and American Marxists shared a common mentality. Lionel Trilling has described it as "an impassioned longing to believe . . . the ready feasibility of contriving a society in which reason and virtue would prevail. . . . Once the commitment to this belief had been made, no evidence might, or could, bring it into doubt."[3] While the mentality was similar, Catholics during the 1930's were absorbed in a vigorous and often self-defeating program of violently opposing this alternative to their own system of certainties. It was, however, a lapse in Protestant idealism after

World War I which provided Catholics the opportunity to think of themselves as the saviors of American ideals.

Historians of American religious life often have referred to the postwar period as the beginning of "post-Protestant America." Robert Handy has described it as the "second disestablishment" and the closing of Protestantism's "special identification with American civilization." Sidney Ahlstrom has written of it as a "time of crisis" when Protestants began to lose their grip, not only on their own religious traditions, but on America as well. Catholics, on the other hand, with the immigrant gates closed, were just entering an era of establishment. The transformation of America from a rural to an urban society abetted the opportunity for Catholics to exert their influence as the same transformation tended to erode Protestant influence. This increased Protestant fears that Catholicism was winning America.[4] To the loss of vision and erosion of Protestant self-understanding Catholics often responded with a disarming sense of superiority. Theodore Maynard concluded his *The Story of American Catholicism* (1941) with a popular Catholic attitude that "Catholicism could cut through Protestantism as through so much butter." Such rhetoric echoed Protestant self-criticism. Indeed, liberal Protestants like Charles Clayton Morrison would bemoan the "slump and confusion and humiliation" of American Protestantism, which, he felt, had lost its relevance for contemporary culture because it had either fled civilization or flattered it. It was now "baffled and tired."[5]

The neo-orthodox movement in the 1930's was an effort to harden Protestant drift. Though the "neo" in this effort was similar to the revivalist mentality of neo-Thomism, the two movements were separated by more than their Catholic or Protestant labels. Part of what was repossessed by the neo-orthodox movement was the classic Calvinist and American-Puritan sense of God's mysterious ways and the unpredictability of nature. Catholic philosophy meanwhile was more inclined toward an Enlightenment view of a rationally ordered universe and a predictable God. While Reinhold Niebuhr viewed reason as an instrument of the self-seeking in man, Catholics proclaimed its natural and supernatural powers. The desire to control and harness nature through reason was an essential element of Catholic thought. Niebuhr, on the other hand, emphasized the ironic quality of this desire, which only bred more wants, struggle, and uncertainty. Man frustrated his own visions by the very nature of his finite condition. The natural law, the linchpin of the Catholic structure of reality, was for Niebuhr a vain rationalization. In short, passion and self-interest confused and made impossible any rational or objective norms for structuring reality.[6]

Niebuhr's thought and the whole neo-orthodox movement contained a very contemporary note of caution and a limited sense of expectation.

Catholic thought threw caution to the wind. Passion was something one dominated; self-interest and community interest could be harmoniously linked. Before the mid-1950's Catholics generally felt more comfortable speaking with Walter Lippmann or descendants of Thomas Jefferson than they did with Reinhold Niebuhr, despite the Christian heritage they shared.

Although Catholics moved in the same cultural context with others of the interwar period, they reacted to the pressures of the times in a distinctive manner. The major difference in the realm of thought was a firm commitment not to succumb to disillusion; not to have their expectations limited while the very possibility of fulfillment seemed at hand. The social substratum which helped to make possible this commitment to optimism was the rapid movement among American Catholics from immigrant poverty to middle class respectability. The first half of the twentieth century was a period of arrival. Since the late 1950's, as more and more Catholics felt increasingly at home, the cultural and thought structure which brought them there has evaporated through revision, self-criticism, and an overall sense of weariness. In the 1960's Catholics became simultaneously troubled with both Catholicism and America. This has resulted in their own sense of disillusion, which has been magnified by the fact that for many years previously they had studiously avoided preparing themselves for it.

Before proceeding to examine the Catholic arrival into innocence and its subsequent survival in America after World War I, some final notes of caution. First, the individuals and sources selected in constructing this study have been drawn primarily from a middle-class group of Catholics who had the time and degree of sophistication to express themselves. Obviously, they do not represent the entire spectrum of Catholic aspiration in America. The large majority of Catholics were mostly caught up in the necessities of living and, indeed, felt little inclination to pursue the niceties of philosophical, literary, and even theological reflection beyond an elementary catechetical investigation. Despite the educational gap, there has been a remarkable unanimity of general outlook between those Catholics who found time to write in journals and those who occupied their time in the automobile factories of Detroit, the steel mills of Pennsylvania, and in the law and medical professions of major American cities. Except in one or two instances, the Catholic intellectual did not feel himself alienated from his own group. While sharing a basic pattern of assumptions, it was the intellectual's role to elucidate them in more sophisticated language. The adversary relationship between intellectual and community which tended to fragment American society at this time was not a factor among Catholics.

Neither was there any significant difference of mind between clerical and lay Catholics, except that the former sometimes understood their hierarchical status as evidence of a more authorized privilege to speak for the group. Despite clerical dominance, it is also true that many of the most effective proponents of Catholicism were laymen like G. K. Chesterton and Jacques Maritain. Finally, the individuals examined in this study were not placed into large, all-encompassing, liberal and conservative categories. In terms of social reform such terminology may be useful, but in relationship to general intellectual outlook it does not accurately describe what Catholics were about. In one sense they were all very conservative and in another they were surprisingly liberal, especially in their optimism.

The second cautionary note concerns innocence itself. There is nothing inherently debilitating in a confident approach to reality, nor in believing that in life there dwells a structure of morality necessary for the common interests of humankind. Equally, it is not necessarily a flight from reality to choose not to carry the weight and complexity of the universe on one's shoulders and into the activities of society. There is nothing wrong with having answers. The survival of these qualities among Catholics and others had its attractions and still does. The close association between religion and American ideals derives in one respect from the fact that both have served as a means for ordering life with the expectation that it is worthwhile to do so. Both have been laden with promises. Each has asked man to be hopeful about his chances and aspirations and to act accordingly. There has always been a quality to innocence which is both refreshing and vital.

The problem with American innocence and the Catholic involvement with it, however, was the tendency to absolutize answers and narrow promises. In cultural forms it tended to repress the possibility of doubt, preventing moments of healthy unease. If reality is not all a dark web of conflicting burdens, neither is it a playground for sentimental romantics or fodder for logicians and engineers. The process by which Catholics became involved in the assumptions of American innocence offers a fascinating example of how the moral idealism inherent in the American democratic experience has affected a large group of people from diverse ethnic and social backgrounds. America did not obliterate Catholic group identity or ethnic diversity; but Catholics did reconstruct elements of their own traditions and mingled them with a cultural and moral outlook they came to appreciate and helped to shape.

Such mingling has not always been beneficial. When Catholic absolutism has merged with American absolutism it has resulted in a very irritating individual and an extremely defensive group of people. Although Catholic involvement with American innocence has had its vital moments, much of the record has been marked by a wearisome formalism and defensiveness.

1. Catholicism

The Return from Exile

Generations have trod, have trod, have trod;
   And all is seared with trade; bleared, smeared with
     toil;
   And wears man's smudge and shares man's smell:
     the soil
Is bare now, nor can foot feel, being shod.

And for all this, nature is never spent;
   There lives the dearest freshness deep down things;
And though the last lights off the black West went
   Oh, morning, at the brown brink eastward, springs—
Because the Holy Ghost over the bent
   World broods with warm breast and with ah!
     bright wings.

Gerard Manley Hopkins
"God's Grandeur"

WORLD WAR I LOOMS LARGE in the portrait western society has drawn of itself. The war has been seen, perhaps too conveniently, as the opening wave of a continuing series of disasters, disillusionments, and dissociations humanity has had to endure in the spiritual, political, and cultural dimensions of life in the twentieth century. It is not without some sense of caution, then, that one would add to this burden. For what Catholics were wont to speak of as their "return from exile" in the twentieth century was carried along, if not made possible, by the Great War itself.[1]

The initial phase of the return, however, was hardly disillusioning. Instead, the war precipitated within Catholicism a new sense of identity, an enthusiasm for ideals, and a rather disconcerting confidence in their beliefs. This hardly coincided with the unsettling spiritual, cultural, and intellectual effects others experienced in the war's wake. Thus the Catholic formulation, development, and recently evident decline of these attitudes would

8

seem to merit some inspection. Before speaking of the return, however, it is first necessary to investigate the general atmosphere of Catholicism "in exile," the manner of its arrival, and, finally, how it has survived. This chapter is concerned with a general consideration of Catholic self-consciousness in the western world during the past century. A more detailed analysis of this consciousness in American Catholicism will occupy our attention in the remaining portion of this study.

Many of the images and metaphors contained in Gerard Manley Hopkins' sonnet quoted above are suggestive of the development of the Catholic imagination. The image of a "bent world" obtruded most conspicuously upon this imagination since the French Revolution. It was in the nineteenth century that the extreme moment of this mutual disaffection was played out. While "the world" celebrated an unabashed confidence in its ability to create progress and prosperity through mingling a liberal faith with scientific technology, the papacy of Pius IX responded with a series of declarations accurately described by E. L. Woodward as "an ultimatum."[2] The definition of the doctrine of the Immaculate Conception (1854), the Syllabus of Errors (1864), and the declaration of Papal Infallibility at the First Vatican Council (1869–70) represented a Catholic revolt against the world of "progress, Liberalism and modern civilization."[3] To a confident world expecting an even brighter future, these declarations were at best shrill denunciations of an institution bent on oblivion. Even many Catholics found them somewhat of an embarrassment.[4]

Such shrillness of tone, however, no doubt contributed to a softening of opposition within Catholicism to everything "modern" when Leo XIII assumed the papacy in 1878. Two of his more famous ventures toward rapprochement were the encyclicals *Aeterni Patris* (1879), on the revival of Thomistic studies, and *Rerum Novarum* (1891), on social reconstruction. With these documents the Church passed beyond the stage of blustering negation. The new program proposed by Leo XIII was to link "the old with the new" even if it meant an ingrained predisposition toward the old.[5]

For the next thirty years Catholic intellectuals set about this task, often with unexpected results. In Europe there was held a series of Catholic International Scientific Congresses (1888, 1891, 1894, 1897, 1900) at which evolution, biblical criticism, social reconstruction, and democracy were debated with increasingly open enthusiasm.[6] The controversy in France and the United States over "Americanisme" revolved around the question of a more purposive and hopeful orientation toward modern society. Following closely upon Americanism came Modernism and a growing desire among Catholics to accept modern scientific methodology in the formulation of the Church's intellectual and theological positions.[7] All these efforts were elements of a change in atmosphere in Catholicism which sought to find a new place in the life of modern civilization. Catholic Modernism, however, represented a serious challenge. To the more conservative, that program was, in effect, the new dominating the old, clearly an aberration of Leo's vision. The reaction was swift in coming and culminated in 1907 with the repressive measures which came in the wake of Pius X's encyclical *Pascendi Dominici gregis*. As a result, internal diversity was cut off, but at the cost of removing the Church once again from a world dancing along the bright road to peace and progress.

The modern's path to glory during this time had, however, entered upon some rocky ways. The mid-nineteenth century version of reality, under the influence of Charles Darwin and Herbert Spencer, held that progress was the inevitable result of an evolutionary process determined by fixed laws inherent in the universe. Man was by nature bound to this system, but all was well because the system was programmed in advance to ensure progress. Modern industrialism, though, was well on its way to creating a society "seared with trade, bleared, smeared with toil," uprooting man from nature and from himself. The disruption caused by the sudden advance of industrial technology set the more critical and impatient men of the time to re-thinking their evolutionary standards. This resulted in a more open but no less evolutionary universe; the difference being that man, through the scientific use of his intelligence, was to participate more intimately in the creation of a better society by reforming the more obvious injustices industrialism had brought with its bright promises. Thus social Darwinism acceded to social engineering.

A new world appeared to be in the making in the years prior to the outbreak of World War I. Even in the midst of war men talked of harnessing the passions the war unleashed to fulfill their prewar expectations.[8] The progressive mind itself was fraught with many contradictory impulses. Progressives talked of instincts, passions, forces, as if these were all capable of intelligent control. They spoke of controlling nature, though nature appeared to be increasingly more immense and indifferent to man's aspirations. The war laid bare these contradictions and unleashed a torrent of cynicism, skepticism, and disillusionment. It broke up a number of prewar "harmonies." Man and nature were now at odds; the intellectual revolted from commonality; realism was at war with idealism; the naturalist opposed the supernatural; and reason was incompatible with instinct. Amid the welter of these disruptions, observing Catholics saw advantages in their previous aloofness and prepared for a return.

Catholics took delight in, and were praised for, standing firm against a now debunked bourgeois world.[9] In 1922, when Pius XI stepped out onto St. Peter's balcony to proclaim his blessing *Urbe et orbe* for the first time since 1870, Catholicism faced a new era and symbolically dropped its self-proclaimed "prisoner" identity. For the next fifty years the Church assumed a new role. It was still "over the bent world" brooding as ever, but now striding confidently with "bright wings."

To the Catholic, the world appeared not only bent but at loose ends; "the last lights of the black west" neared extinction. To protect these last flickers and to rekindle the fires was a deep-felt and nearly universal mission. G. K. Chesterton's immortalization of Don Juan at Lepanto during the high-water point of the Counter-Reformation as "the last Knight of Europe" was even more significant as a characterization of Catholicism itself and of its defenders throughout the western world.[10] Knighthood flourished alongside the more illusive concept of "revival" in the years between the two world wars. The revival fervor touched nearly every aspect of Catholic life: intellectual, literary, liturgical, and social. Catholics everywhere were pleased to hear that they were in the midst of an intellectual and spiritual resurgence. "The Church," the German Romano Guardini felt, was "coming to life in the souls of men."[11]

The intellectual leaders of this revivalist temper of mind were a mixed lot of highly self-conscious Catholics. For a time the group included what was known as the "Catholics without faith," champions of political and intellectual reaction in France who followed Charles Maurras and the *Action Française* movement until both were suddenly condemned in 1926 by Pius XI. Less reactionary, and evidencing a more hopeful response to the modern world, were such figures as Charles Péguy, Maurice Blondel, Karl Adam, Romano Guardini, and Christopher Dawson. In the Thomist revival Etienne Gilson and Jacques Maritain became such internationally known personalities that often many were led to the confusion of identifying Thomism with Catholic thought, which, at least in France and Germany, was never true. In literature a number of Catholic writers, Georges Bernanos, François Mauriac, Sigrid Undset, G. K. Chesterton, Hilaire Belloc, Evelyn Waugh, and Graham Greene commanded an attention to Catholic writing if only because they were all such unusual Catholics.

After World War I the revivalist sensibility firmly rooted itself. The crisis which Modernism introduced to Catholic thought by Alfred Loisy, George Tyrrell, and others fast became a forgotten problem. The Modernist challenge withered within Catholicism first through excommunication, then through intellectual repression, and, finally, because the age which inspired it had passed. Writing in 1928, T. S. Eliot (a non-Catholic but very much a part of this new Catholic awareness) thought the Modernist sensibility dead because it attempted the impossible: "the reconciliation of antagonistic currents of feeling within themselves." Referring to Friedrich von Hügel, who was associated with Catholic Modernism, Eliot believed his sensibility "no longer the order of the day."

He belongs to a past epoch, a period of intellectual indistinctness, in which he moved among a host of half Christians and quarter Christians. The present age seems to me much more an age of black and white without shadows. . . . We demand of religion some kind of intellectual satisfaction—both private and social—or we do not want it at all.[12]

The Catholic intellectual revival, at the flood by 1926, was a new kind of awareness. It was so quickly championed by Catholics that questions posed by the Modernists were forgotten. In the new world "without shadows," troubling queries striking at the heart of one's own position seemed uncalled for and very much a nuisance.

Frank Sheed has recently recounted the striking fact that when men "talked happily of the Catholic Intellectual Revival" between the two world wars, they were concerned with neither intellectual repression nor Modernist problems.[13] Their task, as defined by Eliot, was to reconcile "an ancient feeling with modern thought and science."[14] More specifically for Catholics, Maritain called for

a truly Catholic, that is to say, universal synthesis, to construct, to gather together, to insist everywhere on the positive, and . . . to reconcile . . . aspects which although too long kept apart are in reality complementary, doctrinal absolutism and evangelical daring, fidelity to pure truth and compassion . . . tradition where needed, revolution where needed. . . .[15]

As the Protestant synthesis was found wanting, Catholics were eager to try their hand at refitting the pieces of a broken world.

Other characteristics of the revivalist atmosphere were numerous and equally involved in contradictions. Calvert Alexander, a contemporary commentator, observed a temper of mind universal among Catholic writers, a "sense of conflict, of crisis, of the necessity of working while there is still light."[16] Catholics shared the crisis mentality with others in the interwar years, though their own sense of confidence precluded any complete acceptance of the doom orientation of Oswald Spengler. On the other hand, while others would put forth provisional moral and intellectual positions, Catholics offered full-fledged affirmations. "He who does not bellow the truth," said Péguy, "when he knows the truth makes himself the accomplice of liars and forgers." Catholics arrived on the scene as André Gide once described the appearance of Paul Claudel:

He gives me the impression of a solidified cyclone. When he talks, it is as if something were released within him; he proceeds by sudden affirmations and maintains a hostile tone even when you share his

opinion. . . . His conversation . . . does not improvise anything, you
feel. He recites truths that he has patiently worked out. . . . I try to
discover what is lacking in that voice . . . a little human warmth?
. . . No, he doesn't charm; he does not want to charm; he
convinces—or impresses.[17]

What kept the revival alive for many years was this "frontal sense" and
"hostile tone." It fed on a sense of rivalry and produced the celebrated
debates between George Bernard Shaw and Chesterton, H. G. Wells and
Belloc, Claudel and Jacques Rivière. In some respects the outcome was less
important than the fervor generated by the clash. While many, like Ernest
Hemingway, sought to make a separate peace with the world, Catholics
like Bernanos, Mauriac, Waugh, and Greene would have no part of any
peace treaties. Bernanos' *Sous le Soleil de Satan* (1926) was bred in the
disillusionment men everywhere felt with the hollow victories of World
War I, but its extreme violence of attitude could not tolerate any compromise.[18] There was Truth to be possessed and to be possessed by.

Along with modern writers from Proust to Faulkner, the Catholic
novelist has participated in what Allen Tate has described as the "drama of
withdrawal . . . from the action of society."[19] Jansenist in its moral
foundations, this literature was energized by a rejection of the shallowness
of middle-class civilization. It emphasized grace over nature and faith in
opposition to reason. God's laws appeared as arbitrary commands undetect-
able by human intelligence. Human achievements were suspect, if not
egotistical, and remained always inadequate. As Martin Green has put it,
"only grace-assisted goodness is valid and grace-assisted badness is perhaps
even better." The literary intellectual was bent on expressing in creative
form "the defeat of human virtue" in all its variety.[20]

Another, less violent and perhaps more dominant, aspect of the Catholic
revival in English-speaking countries was an attitude noted in 1940 by
Frank Sheed, who made a career of publishing its various elements. Sheed
was struck by the pervasive role of "wit, humor and high spirits" operating
on the Catholic mind. "You get the impression," he wrote, "that Catholic
authors stride through the land gay and confident."[21] In a world gripped by
economic insecurity, intellectual skepticism, and moral uncertainty, this
gaiety exuded by Catholics was rather singular. It was attractive to some,
repellent to many others; but for the ordinary Catholic it was his badge of
confidence.

The pervasiveness of this state of mind was due in large measure to the
resourcefulness of Chesterton and Belloc, who, if only because of their
oddities, and despite their differences and their faults, commanded a
hearing. Both were in earnest about Catholicism. Chesterton's characteristically irreverent description of the Church as "the thing" was his way of

expressing the ineffable quality of its nature. Belloc, on the other hand, would have no such reticence, as the following passage suggests.

> For what is the Catholic Church? It is that which replies, co-ordinates, establishes. It is that within which is right order; outside the puerilities and the despairs. It is the possession of perspective in the survey of the world. . . . Here alone is promise and here alone a foundation. . . . Our dead are with us. Even in these our earthly miseries we always hear the distant something of an eternal music and smell a native air. . . . You may say, "All this is rhetoric." Have you any such? Can your opinion (or doubt, or gymnastics) do the same? I think not.
>
> One thing in the world is different from all the others. It has a personality and a force. It is recognized, and (when recognized most violently loved or hated). It is the Catholic Church. Within that household the human spirit has roof and hearth. Outside it, is the Night.[22]

Belloc expressed in the most tangible language the intangible instincts of many Catholics in his generation. However triumphalist and utopian it might appear to the present generation of Catholics, such testimony was integral to their view of reality. It happened that it was as real as it was illusionary. Even the most intellectually daring Catholics would quietly submit to authoritarian impulses rather than leave the hearth.[23] For its foundation such sublime confidence rested on faith, a difficult quality to measure. But if there was one thing that united all thinking Catholics it was their view of Catholicism as not only a religion but an important cultural reality.

In the realm of cultural objectives, one of the primary elements for Catholic ebullience was the discovery, or rediscovery, that Catholicism had its own mind. Since the Reformation Catholic philosophy had been swimming in the stream created by Descartes, Leibnitz, Newton, Wolff, and Kant. During the eighteenth and early nineteenth centuries Catholic textbooks of philosophy "were very much up-to-date in the sense of being modern. The latest findings of modern science were incorporated; the Bible and post-Cartesian philosophers were generously quoted while Aristotle and scholastic philosophers were hardly mentioned."[24]

It wasn't until the mid-nineteenth century that alienation from the modern mind took hold. Then, with a swift series of condemnations beginning with the democratic idealism of the Abbé Félicité de Lamennais (1832), Georg Hermes's Catholic Kantianism in 1835, and Anton Günther's Catholic Hegelianism in 1857, Catholicism soon found itself afloat in a sea of negativism.[25] Newman's appropriation of historicism and development escaped condemnation while escaping any widespread Catholic attention as well. As one Roman theologian put it, "Newman miscet eit confudit omnia."[26] By 1870 it appeared that Catholicism affirmed its beliefs on the sole authority of the Pope. Moreover, as the first Vatican Council demonstrated, there were many Catholics hesitant about proclaiming even that. If the Catholic mind knew what it was against, it had precious little means of demonstrating critically what it was for.

Viewed from this perspective, neo-Thomism was a rescue operation. It was that, but more. It became an intellectual phenomenon of the first order. It is a truism that many great men have to die before they become known. In the case of Thomas Aquinas seven hundred years was surely a long death. For Catholics and non-Catholics alike the resurrection of Thomism had all the trappings of "a great historic novelty."[27] Within the Catholic household this novel quality gave to Thomism a certain "providential" aura. Its time had come, both for the Church and for the world.

From *Aeterni Patris* to the fifth decade of the twentieth century, the Catholic mind was absorbed in the task of re-expressing Thomistic principles for the modern world. Without arguing the merits of this effort, what should be stressed here is the importance of the Thomistic revival for the general intellectual awakening of Catholicism in the twentieth century. Thomism supplied Catholics with an ideological leverage wanting in previous centuries. It became for them the intellectual and cultural component of Belloc's reference to a "possession of perspective in the survey of the world." As Thomism increasingly seemed to dominate Catholic thought, Catholics were more willing to believe that there was a uniquely Catholic view of things.

Catholic self-awareness peaked in the years between the two world wars. This process was born in a spirit of negation and alienation. Definition by negation, though never completely absent from the Catholic sensibility, soon made room for what could be called definition by tradition. Here an already present Romantic fervor merged with a desire for self-consciousness. Whatever force Catholicism generated in the twentieth century, it drew its inspiration from an urge to repossess, to purify, and to refound its "mystique."[28] Initially, Catholic introspection was preoccupied with things medieval. The Middle Ages fascinated even the more respected of Catholic thinkers. Etienne Gilson, for example, believed that Catholic interest in medieval civilization was vital to its sense of identity. In the works of Aquinas and Augustine, said Gilson on the occasion of the opening of the Pontifical Institute of Medieval Studies at St. Michael's College in Toronto in 1929:

> Catholic thought has crystalized itself, justified itself . . . that can be considered as definitive. . . . A Catholic thinker should be, as it

were, so wholly permeated with medieval thought that anything he says or does, even though it looks or is new, should be but a natural, immediate, and spontaneous expression of that everlasting tradition itself. This for Catholics is the only possible way to be at one and the same time conservative and creative.[29]

To be both conservative and creative has always been a most tortuous undertaking. For those who have tried, it has been difficult to escape mediocrity. The urge toward repossession, however, was not for its leading exponents a romantic turning back. Its objective, explained Maritain, was "to accomplish a perfect reflexion, the essential thing here being not the turning back, but the grasp, the penetration of the self by the self which is integral to it.[30] Medieval Christendom was the object of penetration but not a blueprint for the new Christendom. The modern "historical sky" was too radically different to entertain a transplantation *en masse.*[31]

Maritain's basic metaphysical insight coincided remarkably with the revival-repossession mentality of twentieth-century Catholicism. Reality, as described by Maritain, was "intelligible mystery." Wisdom and progress were the result of a continuous plunging into the mystery, issuing in a "growing intimacy" with life, but never exhausting its variety or reducing it to immutable constructs.[32] Stability and continuity were achieved by appropriating Thomistic philosophical and theological principles. These guided the penetration but admitted of "many discoveries, renewals and unexpected explanations."[33] The "novelty" of Thomism for Maritain and many other Catholics was its ability to penetrate into the mystery of things while remaining inventive, open to fresh experience, and capable of surprising itself.[34]

This cogent and subtle exposition of St. Thomas by Maritain led a precarious existence throughout the century. It was liable to mishandling by neo-Thomists incapable of surprise, and, on the other hand, susceptible to dissolution by its own success. Maritain himself always feared "a progress by substitution in which the *Neo* would devour the Thomism."[35] Inherent in the neo-Thomistic revival from the beginning, and espoused as its reason for being, was its power to assimilate the best of modern thought. As Thomism fanned out into contemporary thought the power of assimilation was irresistible. It followed a path suggested in John Henry Newman's *Essay on the Development of Christian Doctrine:*

> Sometimes assimilation is effected only with an effort; it is possible to die of repletion and there are animals who lie torpid for a time under the contest between the foreign substance and the assimilating power. . . . This analogy may be taken to illustrate certain peculiarities in the growth or development of ideas . . . doctrines and views which

relate to man are not placed in a void, but in the crowded world, and make way for themselves by interpenetration, and develop by absorption.[36]

It would appear that the fate of neo-Thomism was either death through petrification and repletion, or expansion through absorption, the latter resulting in a transformation so radical as to be outside the definable limits of the Thomistic tradition.

When Catholic thought radiated into Marxism, existentialism, personalism, pragmatism, and the process thinking of Bergson and Whitehead, it did so initially with a "buoyant optimism" that Thomism offered a richness of perspective no less than an orthodox methodology. The technique of baptizing diverse philosophical orientations was observed by Sidney Hook as a perverse corruption by adoption "of doctrines that cannot be refuted or suppressed."[37] Its real effect, however, was quite the opposite. W. Norris Clarke, S. J., in a recent examination of his own development in the Thomistic tradition, noted that "in the experiment of grafting new shoots on my basic Thomistic stock, the question of how much my own resulting synthesis can be called 'Thomistic' must remain enveloped to some degree in a question mark."[38] Thus Maritain's fears proved to be quite real; and in the 1960's, forgetting his own precept of the unexpected surprise, he lashed out at the multiple directions Catholic thought had taken.[39] Thomism in effect had devoured itself.

What happened to the neo-Thomistic revival is similar to the movement of the whole of the intellectual revival, and of Catholicism itself, in this century. Born in a spirit of revolt and negativism, it gradually moved in the direction of self-clarification; of refounding itself in its own deepest traditions. In this, the period of its return, we find Catholics confident of their ability to answer the big questions concerning God, the universe, man, and society. The modern world, it seemed to Catholics after World War I, had lost faith not only in religious beliefs, social customs, and moral certainties, but even in reason itself. Modern man had become prey, in Belloc's rhetoric, to "the vile gods of complexity and weakness."[40] Catholics meanwhile upheld an almost Enlightenment fascination with reason and its powers of construction. Thomism was the ideological vehicle used in the construction of an "objective rational system" in order to save spiritual, intellectual, and human values "in the face of contemporary aspirations and perplexities."[41]

In an intellectual world at first unaccustomed to disillusionment and the uncertainty of all values, but eventually forced to make uncertainty a way of existence, the Catholic was driven by a desire to proclaim and affirm. "To love only to seek—on the condition of never finding—to want only disquietude," replied Jacques Maritain, "that is to hate truth." There was, however, even in Maritain's writing, a tendency to equate truth with certainty. Hannah Arendt, in 1945, observed in referring to Maritain's Thomism that "certainty is not truth, and a system of certainties is the end of philosophy." Arendt's criticism was not without its validity, especially as others less subtle than Maritain were eager to use his thought.[42]

The cultural ramifications of this view of reality were immense. For one thing, it meant the creation of a world within a world. A host of professional, educational, social, literary, and intellectual organizations appeared intent on expressing "the uniqueness, separateness, difference of the Catholic Church from and to all other institutions existent among mankind."[43] For a time, general euphoria reigned, as symposia met to discuss the "Catholic" novel or "Catholic" psychology, history, philosophy, journalism, and even the special attributes of being a Catholic librarian. The cultural outreach was spectacular in its rich diversification, if not always so in creativity. Whatever the result of such activity, Catholics reveled in their newly found possession of perspective. This sensibility was contagious not only among Catholics but among many who peered from without. Walter Marshall Horton, a contemporary Protestant theologian, with obvious sincerity, and long before ecumenical equanimity came to characterize Catholic-Protestant relations, was attracted by this appeal. "But whatever one may think about Roman Catholicism," concluded Horton in his 1938 survey of European theology,

> this tribute must be paid to it by anyone who meets with it in the most casual way: *it knows where it stands, and why, and so holds steady in a world that is being shaken to its foundations.* It may be well that, before plunging into the maelstrom of contemporary Protestant thought—where so many are rapidly changing their stand, or maintaining their position by sheer pugnacity—we have dwelt for a time in the serene light of the Catholic world and acquired (perhaps) a certain sense of perspective.[44]

Such praise was the stuff by which enthusiasm was bolstered and illusions fostered, to become catastrophes when the bubble was pricked. Before the bubble was pricked, however, Catholics enjoyed a period of aloofness in their outlook on the world. With the present-day waning of self-consciousness, and with the growing confusion and anxiety within the Catholic world that has followed in the aftermath of Vatican Council II, the Church has been forced to admit a deeper participation in the world's failures as well as in its desires. In doing so it has had to give up the role of "brooding" over the world as some knight errant of medieval legend. While a sense of color, enthusiasm, and even humor has faded among Catholics in recent years, especially in the United States—and some yearn to find

security once again—Catholics might find some less serene sense of perspective in these words of Jacques Maritain:

> As in each case in which thought attacks a difficult task, it begins in
> the conquering of new domains, and especially the interior domains of
> its own spiritual universe, by bringing on troubles, disasters. The
> human being seems to disorganize itself, and it happens in fact
> sometimes these crises of growth end badly. There are nevertheless
> crises of growth. [45]

2. Michael Williams
The Romance of American Innocence

IN SEPTEMBER OF 1907 PIUS X issued an encyclical, *Pascendi Dominici gregis,* which, in effect, capped a century-long papal effort to banish the explosive threads of nineteenth-century thought from Catholic minds. Evolution, biblical criticism, historicism, progress, Kantianism, Hegelianism, and immanentism all came under the condemnation of Modernism, "the heresy of all heresies." The commanding ideas of a century were officially judged by Catholicism to be a failure and a subversion of Christianity. The Catholic Church continued in its peculiar rebellion from the modern world.[1]

As papal theologians busied themselves with the task of delineating the errors of a century, a young former ex-Catholic was busy with the less sublime effort of producing a short story for *McClure's* magazine. Michael Williams, a struggling young journalist, was also in rebellion. Williams was a fringe voice in an American generation in the throes of a "counter-reformation," a "revolt against formalism" and a "rebellion of intellectuals" encompassing art, politics, literature, history, law, economics, and psychology.[2] If the Catholic rebellion seemed at the time to signal a further retreat, the American revolt was a spirited cry for action, involvement, and engagement with the forces of life. It was a renewal of idealism in spirit even if it denounced idealism, moralism, and formalism in thought. The American counter-reformation Charles Beard spoke of in 1914 was meant to sweep away abuses "while retaining and fortifying the essential principles of the faith." As this process continued, however, more was being swept away than the excesses of capitalism, social Darwinism, idealistic philosophy, or bourgeois respectability. The combined upheaval of ideas in their acceptance of the irrational, the passionate, and the experimental threatened to destroy some long-held principles of American culture: confidence in life, certainty of a moral order in the universe, progress, and optimism. With World War I and a more tragic encounter with life's "poisons," the rebellion turned from vital engagement to disillusioned withdrawal; from community action to a "retreat into privacy"; from a concern for reconstruction to disintegration and more obvious fragmentation.[3]

Williams, a fringe voice within this rebellion in the prewar decades, was to become an active leader in Catholic postwar rebellious resurgence. An ironic reversal had taken place. Catholic retreat flamed into Catholic "action," "resurgence," "awakening." While American prewar vitalism smouldered into postwar blues, Williams managed to be neatly within the upsurge of both movements. In 1934 he was to reflect upon Modernism, which had had little impact upon him in 1907, as an "abortive movement" which threatened to disrupt "the inner peace and harmony of Catholicism." With the defeat of the Modernist challenge, the undisturbed inner peace of Catholicism had escaped the confusion which had disrupted the institutions, political organizations, and social systems of the Western world in their confrontation with new ideologies and war. With everything else in a "condition of flux" since World War I, the Catholic Church, Williams announced, had intensified its activity "to a higher degree and on a broader scale than at any other time since the beginning of the Counter-Reformation."[4] An examination of Williams' activities both in his prewar American idealism and in his postwar Catholic idealism provides a personal instance of the survival of American innocence and also points to the more general ways in which American Catholicism had appropriated and was about to set forth to defend innocence in the decades following World War I.

"A Fight in One Round" was Williams' short story that eventually appeared in the May issue of *McClure's* for 1907.[5] This story is similar to others Williams would write concerning innocent victims caught up by the indeterminate forces of disease, labor-capital strife, or simply by chance itself. These stories hardly set the literary world afire, but they did echo an emerging voice in American life and fiction of the time.[6] Williams was not a muckraking journalist; he concentrated instead on the attitudes and spiritual drive his characters brought to the realities of society. The promise of industrialism had by the turn of the century produced a dullness and heaviness upon the American spirit from politics and philosophy to art and literature. Voices arose calling for an end to a muggy formalism in philosophy, crass commercialism and sentimentalizing in literature, governmental inaction, reckless capitalism, and the general determinism of social Darwinism.

There was excitement in the general effort of progressive America to create the humane society, be it the Kingdom of God of the social gospel ministers or the value-centered humanism of social scientists and socialists. The new idealism drew its power and force from the spiritual and intellectual vision of power and force itself. If nature appeared suddenly wild and dangerous, as in the Jack London stories, then man must be equally strong. If the forces of capitalism were exalted, then a new power was demanded by men to assert the spirit and break its bonds of oppression. If the universe appeared mysterious rather than coherent and man the victim of its indifference, then an activist and adventuresome engagement with the universe was celebrated.

In Williams' "A Fight in One Round" Nick Snyder, after a moderately successful boxing career, marries and retires from boxing. While settling into a comfortable new job, Nick finds his life suddenly coming apart. His wife is struck down with tuberculosis. He loses his job as a result of a prolonged strike. He becomes a victim of labor unrest and capitalist intransigence. He is forced by his wife's illness and the birth of their baby to hire on as a scab; but his rig is destroyed by rioting teamsters and he is fired by his boss for letting it happen. Driven from the city, he takes his family to a cold shed in the hills, where he chops wood to keep them alive. The forces bringing Nick down are beyond his control. Now he is not fighting with a visible opponent in the ring, but with something more implacable. He is being defeated by "pugilist Fate."[7] As Williams was to say in another story, only the defeated perceive how "Life" makes smooth paths for the "fortunate of Fate" while others are brought along into the "gins and pits and snares and swamps, the roads to Nowhere."[8]

Williams' pessimism was never complete. There remained the opportunity and moment "to do the really important deed."[9] Nick Snyder feels this moment one evening after returning from his chores when his wife reveals to him a growing strength in her physical condition. Nick goes out of the shed, and, as Williams recorded the scene:

> Below them, far below in the valley, the lights of the city were spread and Snyder thrust out his fists toward it—the amorphous monster below there, crouching in the valley of the shadow.

The story concludes here with Nick wildly punching out into the darkness at the invisible foe that has plagued him: "He boxed with amazing swiftness, strength, ferocity, persistence."[11]

Despite the apparent sentimentality of the story, Williams was able to bring together some important themes in American culture of the time. First, there was the perception of American society being covered by the shadows of despair. Industrial conflict and personal fate combined to obliterate the cliché of success rewarding the virtuous or fit. The growing awareness of the dangerous texture of reality could not be reconciled with naive hopes for a harmonious world. Rather, the menacing forces would only be opposed by an ever-greater exertion of personal force, strength of will, and ferocious persistence. If man could no longer perceive the universe to be purposeful, he must will it to be so. Man must assert his values even while his reasons for believing in them are losing their effect.

The literary efforts of Michael Williams were the result of a life-long struggle in which he alternately moved between enthusiastic expectancy and immobilizing doubt, as the spectre of deathly tuberculosis haunted his movements. In the midst of a new enthusiasm, in 1918 he wrote of his adventures in his *The Book of High Romance.*[12]

Williams had been born in 1877, the son of a roving sea captain of Halifax, Nova Scotia.[13] At the age of thirteen years Michael left the Jesuit boarding school when his father failed to return from a voyage, and he was forced to seek work in a warehouse. Amid the dusty crates Williams was nagged by continual bouts of coughing and bleeding, the effects of tuberculosis. For relief, he turned to writing, plunging himself into "all life that I could enter." As he rushed into new areas of experience, the young man lost interest in the faith of his childhood and any concern for religious beliefs of whatever variety.[14]

When he was nineteen, he moved to Boston. While working in a department store he continued to write stories and poems—all of which were rejected for publication because of their generally depressing and morbid character. His literary heroes were Stephen Crane and Frank Norris. From these authors, and from his own early experiences, Williams was learning that in the face of professional failure and the ever-present spectre of death, ego assertion was what counted.[15]

Philip Hale of the *Boston Journal* gave Williams his first break by publishing a number of his shorter pieces. Williams then embarked on a nomadic career in journalism which took him from Boston to New York City, to North Carolina, to Texas, and eventually to the city editor's desk of the San Francisco *Examiner* in 1906, with only a brief pause to marry Margaret Olmstead in 1900. During these years he was little concerned with social criticism or reconstruction. What he perceived most acutely was the "cold carelessness" of life itself and the "shapeless dead" he reported on in the major cities of the nation.[16]

As city editor of the *Examiner* Williams became attracted to the "frankness" of San Francisco "even in her sinning." He was also jolted by the more disrupting frankness of the earthquake of 1906. Williams was both elated with the spirit of united action following the disaster and disillusioned with the evanescence of this altruistic concern as greed and corruption followed the clearing of the ashes. While in San Francisco, Williams was struck by a new impulse. He wanted to transfer his ego-centered struggle and energy into the struggle for the "kingdom of peace and brotherly love."[17]

A comfortable environment to begin this work offered itself within the bourgeois garden colony of Upton Sinclair's experiment in middle-class radicalism, Helicon Hall, in Englewood, New Jersey. Amidst this congenial assemblage of intellectual anarchists, vegetarians, spiritualists, devotees of free love, and aging single-taxers, Williams was to explore the many and singular "vistas of adventure" propagated by the prophets of strange ideas and life systems budding the American landscape. From the Palisades of New Jersey he would watch the millions of souls in New York swirling upon themselves in "interweaving currents of destiny" which brought the strong upon the weak and mixed the "noble" with the "base." The greater number of these souls, he felt, were "doomed to suffer, were sentenced to ignoble and endless toil and were banished from beauty." But human brotherhood and freedom were man's destiny. The will of man Williams described was like a lighthouse whose light could flash like a sword into the oppressive darkness around him. He would recall H. G. Wells's prophecy in *Modern Utopia* that "the Will of Man can make a world fit for man."[18]

At Helicon Williams was made aware that his quest was not singular but part "of a great group movement" in thought and literature. The multitude of voices, many of them out of tune, but all striving "to find unity and harmony as the Voice of Man," confronted the "ineluctable mystery" of life. Sinclair and Williams planned to take "Helicon on the hoof," wandering in tent and wagon in the West in preparation for the new civilization that seemed sure to dawn. As this plan died before they could hitch their wagons, they settled instead for a less ambitious cooperative venture—a book, *Good Health and How We Found It* (1909), which described the path to the good life and alert thinking through proper hygiene, a healthy diet, and correct breathing.[19]

As a result of his experiences at Helicon, Williams allowed his long-submerged spiritual cravings to come to the fore. Rejecting a materialist version of life, he began, with the help of William James, reading in the varieties of modern mysticism; and he even mellowed his "hot-hatred" of the Puritans, for "they, too, were pilgrims of a quest."[20] After thirty-three years of "Romance" he formulated a book of canons which described his philosophy of "affirmative egotism":

> I believe in Love. . . . I will the brotherhood of man. . . . Mutual aid among men I hold (with Kropotkin) to be the chief factor in evolution, and I deny that the dominating factor is the false idea of the "survival of the fittest," or the "struggle for existence," which are merely excuses for crime, cruelty and stupidity. Mankind is progressing constantly towards a condition of life-in-love, and Art must be made the ruling influence of all things.

Art, thought Williams, was creating a "new dynamic religion" which was based on the "mystical recognition" of the power of beauty itself and the desire to be free in human life. The quest for art and reform was turning the

United States into "a psychic battlefield" where new rules demanded "absolute liberty of expression."[21]

The search for the divine eventually led Williams back to California and to reading the mystics of the Catholic Church, especially the autobiography of Sister Therese of Lisieux and the works of St. John of the Cross. These mystical tracts he found compatible with his growing spiritual desires and his idealism. Upon visiting a Carmelite monastery and having several discussions with Edward I. Hanna, Archbishop of San Francisco, he returned to Catholicism in 1913. Afterward Williams continued his career as a journalist (he covered the Mexican Revolution), and also as a writer of special features for the Panama-Pacific Exposition of 1915. He became organizing secretary for the San Francisco Institute of Art, campaigning for funds to keep the Palace of Fine Arts as a permanent museum for the city.

Williams' experiences in this country from the year he moved to Boston in 1896 to his reacceptance of Catholicism in 1913 placed him within a period of cultural upheaval and intellectual rebellion that marked the prewar decades of the century. From his own personal struggle with depression and pessimism he came to transfer his energies into the passionate intellectual and artistic effort to reform American life. The "rebellion of the intellectuals," as Henry May has described it, was an effort by a small but articulate group of Americans to break out of the cultural confines indelibly dubbed the "genteel tradition" by George Santayana in 1911.[22]

The "genteel" quickly lost some sharpness of definition and came to stand for an array of values, customs, and ideals attacked by the new rebels. In social philosophy it was the seemingly weary determinism of social Darwinism. In philosophy it was the formalism and abstract quality of the academic mind musing on Kantian idealism, Hegelian universalism, or the logical abstractions of Scottish realism. In politics it was the emphasis on moralism, definitions of right and wrong, and the attempt to order society according to abstract ideals, or timeless verities. In literature the genteel was conventional respectability, uplift, sentimentality, didacticism, and the general refusal to admit or succumb to the unpleasant and harsher realities of life.

The values of the insurgents were as pervasive and as indistinct as those they attacked. At center, the whole effort was to break loose from the boundaries cramping the spirit in America. Emphasis was placed on emotion, change, vitality, and experience. They followed William James into the irrational, John Dewey in his conception of an active and molding intelligence; and they delighted in Henri Bergson's metaphysics of motion and organic relationship. The thought of Herbert Croly and Walter Lippmann called for a politics of passion wherein an aristocracy of talent would give to democracy a new destiny. If moral categories were shunned as a vehicle for judging political life, they were even less welcome in literary circles. There a vigorous experimentation in language and theme was the order of the day.

While H. L. Mencken bristled with contempt for sham and the mediocre, Van Wyck Brooks revealed an "insurgent conception of American culture," and a call for literary reconstruction of the American spirit. Little theatres and little magazines came forth with visions of the future as well as critiques of the past. The promise of the future (with James Harvey Robinson, even history became an instrument of the future) lay everywhere.[23] Indeed, the social, literary, and political critics subsumed all of culture under an aesthetic consciousness which had, as Alfred Kazin noted, a vision "of a universal craftsmanship and fellowship in which art would give meaning to community life and society would live by the spirit of art."[24]

Williams saw these insurgent pressures as the "voice of man" erupting into what Santayana had perceived in 1913 as a "new civilization" quite distinct in thought and spirit from traditional Christendom.[25] The guiding spirit was optimistic and idealistic even if rebellious. The pervasive optimism was the one link that tied the rebellion to the culture it was rejecting. That culture rested on a series of assumptions which in their general effect provided the nineteenth-century American with something approaching an ideology. The contour of this ideology took form around three patterns of thought. The first and most sturdy of these, according to Henry May, was the belief in "the reality, certainty and eternity of moral values" which were imbedded in the fabric of the universe and made available to man through reason, intuition, or conscience. Certain of a coherent and friendly universe, the American was able to judge his progress in politics, literature, and every area of his life according to firm moral categories. Evolutionary thought, though capable of threatening the certainty of an harmonious universe, was generally moralized by Americans. Struggle and conflict were but momentary means to an eventual society based on brotherly concern, order, and peace. Materialist implications were glossed by a concerted effort to see God's hand immanent within the movements of the material.[26]

By the end of the nineteenth century a growing number of Americans had grown restive for the good society and were increasingly impatient with labor conflict and capitalist intransigence. Liberal Christians identifying with the Social Gospel called for an end to conflict and unrest by the immediate insertion of the moral categories familiar to the Christian tradition and Protestant America. This quickening of moral fervor produced a ground swell of reformist activities associated with the progressive era.[27] A much smaller group associated with the party of rebellion discounted moral categories as a means to reform and chose instead to value the power of the creative intelligence, technological efficiency, an ethics of experience, or the pure assertion of the passionate will to master the social, political, and emotional forces of life. These attitudes, combined with an increase in more radical Socialist and Communist activities, produced an opening rift in the American belief of the necessity if not the certainty of a moral universe.[28]

The second assumption of many Americans in the nineteenth century was the belief that progress was both inevitable and beneficial. In creating a society that accepted change as necessary, Americans, nevertheless, believed that changes in society were simply the gradual movement of life toward the eternal morality which underlay the universe itself. As May summarized it: "Good was eternal, but yet developing." The reformist temper during the progressive years was simply an effort to speed up the process. But within the progressive group there was an insurgent quality of mind which believed in progress but had little inclination to fetter this movement with what James Harvey Robinson called the obsolete ideals of "sound doctrine, consistence, fidelity to conscience, eternal verities, immutable human nature and the imprescriptable rights of man."[29]

The third article of the American faith, according to May, concerned the ideal of culture itself. Culture in America in the nineteenth century was largely derivative of European, especially English culture. In the United States it came to mean a pattern of thinking and judgment in literature and the arts, for example, which emphasized how men "ought" to behave rather than what they actually did. Culture was supportive of the ideals of a morally responsible man and of his role in the moral system of the universe and society. Literature as a mechanism for the transmission of culture should therefore ennoble and give vision to the moral ideals of society. The harsher aspects of life were minimized and always played off against the ideal. Literature must uphold the distinctions between right and wrong while presenting good and evil in their proper roles. The desire to have literature firmly rooted in a moral vision often led to an easy didacticism and vapid sentimentality. The growing dissatisfaction of American writers with these literary conventions and others regarding language and sex precipitated a literary rebellion which Randolph Bourne thought was symbolized by a new "healthiness' that had "no sense of any dividing line between the normal and the abnormal, or even between the sane and the insane."[30]

The cumulative effect of these upheavals within the various disciplines of society was to hasten, for many, the disintegration of traditional American patterns of judgment. The "new civilization" was more richly complex and more deeply skeptical. The certainties of a morally responsible agent confidently controlling his destiny within a comfortable universe were the first to feel the touch of doubt, then outright rejection, especially as these realities were transmitted in literature and the arts.

The pragmatist attack on idealism and rationalism was spiritually suited to a time when spontaneity and experimentation were creating exciting possibilities. But pragmatism itself was an admission of a loss of confidence in man's grasp of the totality of things. Reason was, at best, an uncertain instrument for solving short-term problems. But even as reason displayed prowess in technological efficiency it seemed to be creating even heavier burdens for the soul. The mysteries concerning man, nature, and the universe were seemingly inaccessible to rational systemization and control. Instead, as Joseph Wood Krutch interpreted the arrival of the "modern temper" in the late twenties, the world appeared "an unresolvable discord."[31]

The optimism that linked the rebellion with the old culture it rebuked received its most crushing blow when the peace negotiations failed to achieve some justification for the bloodletting of the war. After the armistice, cynicism in the intellectual ranks combined with a withdrawal from crusading idealism among the general population to make talk about progress in terms of universal ideals and values seem hollow, even disrespectful. When the rebellion itself lost confidence in its ability to reconstruct American culture, another blow was dealt to the stability of American innocence:

> Innocence, the absence of guilt and doubt and the complexity that goes with them, had been the common characteristic of the older culture and its custodians, of most of the progressives, most of the relativists and social scientists, and of the young leaders of the pre-war Rebellion. This innocence had often been rather precariously maintained. Many had glimpsed a world whose central meaning was neither clear nor cheerful, but very few had come to live in such a world as a matter of course.[32]

Michael Williams, however, continued his precarious romance with innocence in the decades following the armistice. His own picture of reality sharpened in clarity and provided for cheerfulness. He was to lead, and be caught up in, a determined cultural movement to maintain innocence within the Catholic community and to battle for its survival without.

Returning to New York from San Francisco in 1919, he began working for the press department of the war-inspired National Catholic Welfare Council. In 1922 he left that agency to begin preparations for the founding and editing of *The Commonweal* magazine, the first issue of which appeared in November 1924. He was on his way to becoming the "happy warrior of Catholic action."[33]

The direction of his own thought hinged on two perceptions. The first was his comprehension of the leading ideas swirling about him in New York, and the second was his enthusiasm for a "resurgent" Catholicism. As regards the first, Williams saw, particularly in literature, that the insurgent group with which he had identified as a young writer in the years before World War I had, after the war, all but assumed leadership in the literary life of the nation. The older group of "conventional respectability" who had revered as heroes Emerson, Holmes, Lowell, and Longfellow, and magazines like the *Atlantic Monthly, Century, Scribner's,* and *Harper's,* had relinquished their dominance to the group which was in revolt against "the safe and the sane." The younger intellectuals and their organs of expression, *The Smart Set*, *Dial*, *New Freeman*, *American Mercury*, *New Republic*, and *The Nation,* had established themselves on the ruins of the older group.

According to Williams, the "common philosophy" behind this successful revolution in American intellectual life took shape around two outlooks. The first was a view of American life as failure. The social customs, morals, and traditional tools of intelligence had "stunted" human life in an "ugly and narrow" society. This pervasive pessimism and cynicism emerged forcefully in magazines like the *New Freeman* and *Dial,* whose readers and followers were distrustful of any formulas and lived aloof in aestheticism or joined in the attack of Sinclair Lewis and Sherwood Anderson on American symbols of mediocrity—Rotary clubs, Main Street, Babbittry, and Puritanism. This attack was joined, in Williams' estimation, with H. L. Mencken's and the *American Mercury's* campaign for an "aristocracy" to deliver America to a new culture.

The second division of the "common philosophy" was a view of "universal life" which Williams thought to be the "opposite and the nullification of the Catholic view." Here God was seen to be, at best, a pantheistic participant in the evolutionary process. As science and art were raised up as religious forces, religion itself became a department of aesthetics or psychology. The popularity of the Freudian gospel was evidence that man wanted some sort of religion but one that was "de-supernaturalized."[34]

Williams identified this "common philosophy" for his Catholic readers in the twenties as the "new paganism." He first used this phrase in a 1919 article for the *Catholic World.* The heart of the "new paganism" in art, politics, and literature, Williams said, was "an interior, an occult force" which in the most original of its artistic creations was spiritual, though dangerous, because "beauty can be corruptive."[35] The inward-turning mind of contemporary man was fraught with forbidding consequences. Williams found it moving toward state socialism, cults of the strongman or the mass movement. Religion itself was becoming only "the deification of natural forces and of human instincts."[36]

The renaissance of paganism Williams linked with the insurgent intellectual revolt of the pre- and postwar periods. In the "psychic battlefield" which followed the armistice in America the new paganism was already becoming "ritualized" and entering the mainstream of the common life of man. It was "vocalized in poetry, adorned in sculpture, and justified by philosophy." The artistic celebration of this revival disturbed Williams, for in it he found the common trait of withdrawal which marked the whole movement. In his estimation, the arts, in seeking out the "exotic" in a bewildering variety of "psychic aberrations," disjointed itself from the people. In the United States art was fast becoming the province of the few and the eccentric. It offered little consolation to those who believed in democracy. While the commercial, hurly-burly, industrialized society confined art to museums, the more sensitive contemporary artists confined it to the solitary horizons of their own egos.[37] Catholics, Williams believed, were more able than most to perceive the intensity and the spiritual thirst which motivated this "strange ferment" in thought and art. He thought the movement was operating with disguised or twisted Christian insights. But Catholics were also more likely to see the dangers and the corruptive influences at play.[38]

In his own personal quest for the mystical, Williams had exposed himself, as had his one-time mentor William James, to the many curious and extreme expressions of mysticism available to the seeker in American society at the turn of the century. The ideal of endless possibility enlivened his imagination as it seemed to be the motive power behind all the attacks on formalism and tradition. For a while, even as Williams read Catholic mystics like Saints Teresa and John of the Cross, he remained aloof from the institutional Church because he found it too restricting.[39] But the desire to protect the ideal of possibility eventually led him to the conclusion that some all-embracing institutional support was necessary. The Church, Williams eventually accepted, satisfied his desire for utility and communal possibility. By first sanitizing the spontaneous and singular visions of its mystics, it prevented their promptings from becoming aimless and disconnected. Individual insights were, through the Church, rationalized, organized, and made available to all, rather than either remaining the preserve of the individual or developing into eccentric curiosities without communal meaning and tending toward fragmentation. The Church institutionalized mysticism, giving it an "open-air" flavor and communal vitality. The pragmatic use of personal intensity by the Church in its long history saved the individual mystic from personal disenchantment as it brought the entire community into participation with the mystic's spontaneous and singular visions.

In Catholicism Williams found the link between personal intensity and community enrichment. This bond not only protected the individual from disillusionment but made possible the close association between the genius of the mystic or the intellectual and the poorest worshipper at Mass. The Church as a historical institution and cultural reality became an all-important factor for Williams' own life and social outlook. His vision of the Church solved the pressing problems with regard to the artist and the people, art and democracy, the intellectual and the community. Catholicism represented for Williams:

> the synthesis of the result of all human gropings after truth, all human adventures on the paths of the human quest. Hence, the humblest Catholic is by right a philosopher: one, that is to say, who takes a rational view of life. The humblest Catholic is a partaker of the fruits of the "science of the totality of things" [Mercier]. . . .[40]

The wedding of individual ego with the institutional egotism of the Church provided protection from any threat of disillusionment. As others of Williams' generation felt the sting of defeat when the war only heightened doubts and fragmentation in American society, Williams found a vehicle to continue his philosophy of "affirmative egotism" in a Church which he perceived, especially in Europe, to be in the midst of "a mighty revival of her energy . . . a putting forth of her spiritual and moral force in new forms of action appropriate to the conditions of the times." This was not for Williams a retreat from the action of the world. His image of Catholicism was just the opposite. His personal ideals forged in the prewar period were expanded and revitalized by a conception of the Church as "resurgent" in literature, art, and philosophy.[41]

In Williams' mind the awakening of Catholic enthusiasm during the war was decisively linked to the waning of enthusiasm among individuals and institutions who had invested the war with any sacred, social, or political mandate. Since Catholicism had made a point of opposing any promises of an earthly paradise, it felt no sting of defeat when the conflict brought more clouded vision than paradise.[42] Catholics returned from exile attempting a religious *tour de force* on the arching back of a broken world.

The distinguishing characteristic of this revival, claimed Williams and indeed many other Catholics, was its "appeal to the reason of the world steeped in mere emotion or led astray by excessive forms of Materialism and Idealism." The "appeal to reason" was really an appeal for stability and order. Reason was an instrument for the fashioning of a framework of certitudes on which man could conduct his life with some degree of assurance. This framework was the "mental platform" by which men judge and justify their actions. In proposing such a mental platform Williams believed Catholicism responded directly to all those who were rapidly losing faith in certainties of any kind and were turning to an extreme subjectivism and emotionalism in thought, art, politics, and religion.[43]

This overriding appeal to reason affected Catholic judgment with regard to a variety of cultural concerns. For Williams, the pragmatic force of reason transferred the peculiar mystical insights of an individual into community property by institutionalizing mysticism. Authentic art, like mysticism, must take on this open-air atmosphere. The virility of any form of art depended on "a quality of homeliness, of usefulness, of real utility." That is to say, true art was not found in the exotic or understood only by the solitary few, but must be "communal" and understandable to the many. Any art form must be "docile" to the needs of the community. It should brighten, interest, and console the whole. Reason, argued Williams, made art sane so that it "may safely touch the life-giving bosom of mother earth, yet keep its soul in heaven." Reason prevented art from descending into dreary intellectualism or aestheticism and turned it away from the "madness of morbidity" or defeatism. Art based on reason could "turn its eyes once again to the stars, the high mountains, and the sea, not merely for their own sakes, but because they are the symbols of divine realities."[44]

The creative energy that propelled the "new paganism" into new directions in literature, art, and politics was a spiritual effort to break out of the confinements of nineteenth-century materialism. But Williams saw the effort rapidly leading in all directions to confusion, fragmentation, and disillusionment. Rather than creating a vigorous culture, decadence and isolation seemed more evident. Both the artist and the intellectual, in seeking to liberate the self from convention, scientific materialism, and commonplace custom, were in turn building a new kind of confinement, an individual and personal imprisonment. It was a new mysticism of isolation. They no longer related confidently to nature and society but withdrew into their own unconsciousness.[45] The forces about them were either hostile or indifferently aimless. When personal resources proved insufficient or indeed more threatening than the external world, they came near to personal and social exhaustion.

Williams was one of a number of Americans on the pathway to liberation in the prewar years. But before liberation turned inward in the aftermath of World War I, he had already found an outward and seemingly impregnable vehicle to revitalize his vision and to validate a "scheme of the universe by which to move among its mysteries and its dangers." Williams heralded a new "awakening" within Catholicism during World War I precisely on the deflation of vison and confusion among the institutions and systems of thought which he thought had "bound society together in an unstable yet, on the whole, workable mode of life during the past few centuries."[46]

In 1920 George Santayana characterized the cultural passage of America from innocence, "the land of universal good will, confidence in life, inexperience of poisons," to an acceptance of tragic experience and other "hereditary plagues of mankind." A few years later Williams was calling upon American Catholics to marshal their spiritual, moral, and intellectual energy, brought into "focus" during the war, against the "strange yet powerful apprehension" spreading throughout the country, especially among its intellectuals. Catholics should cast off their defensiveness and negative thinking and lead "all men and women of good will forward in a crusade of the mind against the false ideas and ideals of the vast, yet amorphous, the violent yet at bottom weak and feverish, forces of modern nihilism, modern vanity, modern folly and despair."[47]

A significant element of Catholic resurgence, thought Williams, was the growing awareness among Catholics and non-Catholics alike that Catholicism was both a religious and a civilizing force. In this latter aspect Catholicism must stand for "integrity of thought, clarity of expression, discipline, effort, form, and the right use of reason." It seemed to Williams that all these qualities were being undermined by the moderns' loss of confidence in reason and life itself. The modern mind, in giving way to despair, skepticism, uncertainty, and a Manichean "annihilation of consciousness," retreated from Western civilization and more immediately from the traditions of American life.

It was now up to Catholics to re-establish confidence in life and reason and thus restore a sense of innocence and expectation. The Catholic ideal provided for a vigorous civilization where, said Williams,

> the arts flower, thought is powerful, free, curious, and creative; reverence and fidelity and courage and courtesy and humor and wit and jollity are among men and part of their lives, and life is indeed worth living, and ennui and boredom and despair can only exist, if at all, outside the firm, clear, bounding line of Christendom.[48]

This cultural ideal was both American and Catholic in inspiration, and for Williams the two were enthusiastically and solidly joined.

But the belated wedding occurred in a cultural milieu in which concepts like rationalism, idealism, and even civilization itself were rejected. For many it was rather a time when, as Ernest Hemingway wrote in *A Farewell to Arms:* "Abstract words such as glory, honor, courage, or hallow were obscene beside the concrete names of villages, the numbers of roads, the names of rivers, the numbers of regiments and the dates."[49] Abstractions such as these may have become increasingly "obscene" for men like Hemingway, but for Catholics like Williams the real obscenity was in no longer trusting those abstractions to provide meaning and purpose for life.

Catholic enthusiasm in America quickened during the war and throughout the ensuing decades. Catholicism forged its destiny around restoring and defending those abstractions which the "acids of modernity" seemingly made impotent. Some, like Michael Williams, were more discriminating in what they chose to defend and espouse; but the general effort, which united the entire community that otherwise was torn by ethnic and ecclesiastical rivalry, was the desire to dominate life, to make clear the contours of the cosmos, and to fashion a habitable universe stabilized by an almost rigid moral firmament. This labor of spirit was again as much American in motive as it was Catholic. It was particularly nineteenth-century American in three distinct areas. In literary criticism Catholics continued to expound the didactic idealism of conventional American literature, putting themselves at loggerheads with American writers from Dreiser to Faulkner.

In philosophy Thomism was substituted for the philosophy of Herbert Spencer which provided Catholics with an orderly universe suited to their aspirations if not their experience. Charles Péguy's warning that a hasty rejection of Henri Bergson's thought and the introduction of Thomism as the only approved form of Catholic philosophy would result, not in a victory for Thomas Aquinas, but in the reintroduction of Herbert Spencer was more applicable to Catholics in the United States than in his own country of France. One enthusiastic Catholic nun was later to suggest that the only difference between Aquinas and Spencer was "a matter of theological discussion—not of philosophical." Finally, in the social realm the mystique of institutional proliferation and organization was championed by Catholics as evidence of strength and security. As one Catholic philosopher, William Turner, predicted in 1911, the twentieth century would continue the spirit, which he thought was temperamentally Catholic, of the nineteenth: "Not only in industry, production, transportation . . . ," Turner said, "but in organization and government, in art, literature, theology and philosophy, we are centralizing, unifying, and building up." Despite Turner's optimism, the twentieth century has moved in the opposite direction of fragmentation and alienation. But for over half a century Catholics moved in a countercurrent to this trend: for them the nineteenth century had not ended, it had become Catholic.[50]

In the 1920's Michael Williams continued with unabated vigor to enlist his fellow Catholics under the twin banners of a "resurgent" Catholicism and authentic Americanism. In 1928 one of his more mature works appeared during the heat of Al Smith's campaign for the presidency. More will be said about Williams' *Catholicism and the Modern Mind* later, but two responses to it indicate the direction of American Catholic thought in the years between the wars. Granville Hicks, writing from an emerging radical position in *The Nation,* found much that was praiseworthy in Williams' witty, intelligent, and entertaining comments on politics, books, and science. His methods were "violent" but at least, Hicks felt, he did not try "to smuggle us infidels across the boundary line of a difficult dogma;" on the other hand, Williams was asking of the modern to make a rather significant leap. Hicks observed that it might be true that many of his contemporaries were more willing to make "the big jump into the Catholic fold than the little jump into the liberal Protestant camp," but this was not so much evidence of Catholic superiority as it was evidence of a general "failure of nerve" among intellectuals following the war.[51] Catholicism appeared to men like Granville Hicks a comfortable, if extravagant, preserve for frayed minds.

A different perspective was offered by William Lyon Phelps, a "custodian" of the older American culture whose "boundless enthusiasm" to find "uplift" and beauty was extended even to the once feared and hated "Whore of Babylon." For Phelps, Williams wrote with a happy combination of earnestness, humor, and "zest for life." Williams portrayed Catholicism as a "healthy" mysticism showing "how true religious faith produces happiness, liveliness and peace of mind." Phelps would have expanded the antagonism between the "modern mind" and Catholicism to the broader, more inclusive battle between the former and Christianity. Nevertheless, it appeared to Phelps that the Catholic Church fielded "the best drilled and equipped army" for combat.[52]

In Phelps's response we have a recognition by a custodian of American innocence that a fresh group had joined the battle for its survival in an America turned inward and fearful. Catholics would decry nearly everything around them, but within their own house the qualities of American innocence—enthusiasm, cheerfulness, moralism, idealism, and optimism—persisted through World War II. Some might describe this as a spectacular feat of sheer will power and faith. Others, like Hicks, would see it as a loss of nerve, abetted by a naiveté uncharacteristic of a Church that prided itself on realism. But this was a peculiarly American Church, developing in distinctively American and Catholic ways. Michael Williams' acceptance of it was ultimately a faith commitment, but he also discovered a "spirit" in Catholicism equal to his own enthusiasm.[53]

The awakening that Williams and others heralded for Catholicism in twentieth-century America proved to be more evanescent than substantial. Catholics did display an increase in moral, spiritual, and intellectual energy; but their influence within the general culture remained inconsiderable, and their rhetoric proved unconvincing, eventually, even to themselves. For a time, Catholics sought to prove Henry Adams wrong: the Virgin did not give way to the dynamo; faith controlled technological power or, at least, stood forth in defiance. Catholics succeeded for a time in this venture, but at some cost.[54] That success and that cost will be our concern in the remainder of this study.

3. World War I
The Passage into Innocence

RECENT HISTORIANS AND OBSERVERS of American Catholicism have reacted to its development in the first half of the twentieth century with views ranging from embarrassment to annoyance. Referring to the first two decades of the century, Thomas T. McAvoy, C.S.C., was distressed by the "confused silence and inaction" of the Catholic minority. This situation contrasted unfavorably with the more tumultuous 1880's and 1890's, where historians have found at least a sense of "crisis" concerning the ecclesiastical controversy of "Americanism," which brought forth a spate of biographies dealing favorably with the period's leaders. One also found, as Robert Cross chronicled, an "emergence of liberal Catholicism," which David O'Brien and Michael Gannon have interpreted as "a nascent cultural renascence." All these lines of activity, however, seemed to come to an abrupt halt with the wave of papal penmanship condemning Americanism in 1899 and Modernism in 1907.

After these crucial dates, according to historical judgment, American Catholicism went into hiding. Intellectual and cultural initiatives were "stifled" and "repressed." Isolation from the American intellectual community was almost total. What passed for Catholic thought was, in Gannon's estimation, "dull, drab and defensive." Except for brief sparks of life associated with *The Commonweal, Catholic Worker,* and liturgical and social reform movements, Catholicism was subsumed under the gloom of ghettoism until it experienced the light of day in the 1960's. According to O'Brien, while Catholic intellectual and cultural assimilation declined and retreated in this century, the case was different for "the drive of the church and its people for acceptance, power and influence," in their yearning for social status, economic success, and political power. On these levels, then, the process of assimilation and Americanization increased rapidly. On the intellectual and cultural level, Catholic historians have found little evidence from 1900 to 1960 to indicate any kind of assimilative process at work.[1]

What follows does not dispute the major contentions of the critical study done on American Catholicism in the twentieth century. Alienation, isolation, and a rather low level of intellectual and cultural expression face the observer at almost every turn. But what is not often appreciated is the extent to which Catholics were alienated because of an assimilation into American culture which transcended simply practical and material concerns and came to a level of self-consciousness during and after World War I. Observers have too often dismissed the rhetoric of Americanism as an insecure immigrant posture and have failed to look closely into the content and assumptions of Catholic rhetorical effusions.

To "assimilate" into American thought has its own difficulties. As the country itself, this thought was a volatile compound of often contradictory movements, mixing pragmatism with romanticism, the clear and distinct with the dark and shadowy, realism with idealism, classicism with impressionism, and urge toward the boundless with a pull toward contraction and tradition. As detailed in the previous chapter, there have been efforts by American intellectual historians to distill these diverse promptings into a manageable pattern of distinctive American expression. George Santayana tried to describe it in 1911 by calling it the "genteel tradition." Henry May, as we have seen, perceived three distinctive qualities of nineteenth-century American thought: first, Americans believed in progress; second, they upheld the proposition that reality was objective, and composed of inherent moral or physical laws which man was capable of perceiving either by reason, intuition, or common sense and then charged with the responsibility of following (this by way of saying that Americans believed reality to be meaningful and harmonious to their spiritual and physical aspirations). Finally, May saw culture as the expression of these beliefs in useful and artistic forms. Art and literature were judged by how well they contributed to the moral fibre of the nation. These assumptions were the products of wedding various strains of Calvinist, Enlightenment, and Romantic thought into a useful though unstable compound that even managed to subdue for a moment the materialism and skepticism of Herbert Spencer and Charles Darwin.

In the first decades of the present century, all these assumptions came under attack by Americans. What began as a fresh attempt at approaching the threads of reality in William James's pragmatism and John Dewey's instrumentalism led eventually to a perception of reality that was much more complex and contingent than previous generations of Americans had supposed. Reality began to appear, especially in the discoveries of science, as a mass of complex and indifferent forces not easily mastered by the resources of the mind nor even hospitable to human desire. The artist unleashed his imagination and began to explore these darker regions, and in the process often bitterly derided men who seemed, in W. B. Yeats's phrase, "but weasels fighting in a hole" for the audacious confidence of former plans "to bring the world under a rule." The "dragon-ridden" days of World War I deepened and widened this new awareness, climaxing for a significant segment of American society "the end of American innocence." In the 1920's fragmentation and disillusionment became "obvious," and, as John Higham has put it, American idealism still has not found a way to instill an honest enthusiasm for itself, as what was obvious in the 1920's proceeded to become blatant by the 1970's.[2]

What were American Catholics doing in the face of all this? At first, by a gradual process of osmosis, toward the end of the nineteenth century immigrant Catholicism slowly came to a hesitating articulation of those basic American assumptions with regard to culture and thought. In the writings of Bishops John Keane, Denis O'Connell and John L. Spalding, Archbishop John Ireland and Cardinal James Gibbons, one discovers the threads of those assumptions.[3] These threads lay underneath the more visible ecclesiastical and ethnic controversy which split the American Church at the time. The condemnation of Americanism in 1899 effectively put an end to the ecclesiastical controversy but it did little to stop the increasing Catholic absorption in the assumptions of American innocence. The condemnation of Modernism in 1907 and the repression which followed had a more substantial effect. It did not so much cut off Catholics from American culture as it locked them into those nineteenth-century assumptions which Modernism (not simply the theological, but the philosophical and cultural dimensions as well) proceeded to smash. Unable, then unwilling, to challenge their own assumptions, Catholics proceeded after World War I to defend them, using patterns of thought they believed were at once American and Catholic. What they were alienated from was the compound of shattered ideals, approaches to reality, and profound skepticism that twentieth-century men and women have come to recognize as the pivot of their experience and the source of their unease.

Following Catholic thought from World War I to the mid-1960's, one discovers the source of its appeal in the continuing efforts to preserve a sense of innocence in America. In the realms of philosophy and literature this appeal found its most visible shape. In these areas Catholics were mostly concerned with criticizing disillusionment and defending innocence. In later chapters these efforts will be more thoroughly examined. We have already seen how an individual Catholic, Michael Williams, managed to pass from the upheaval of the pre–World War I decade to emerge in the 1920's with a personal sense of innocence intact. Williams' personal passage is not indicative of how the majority of Catholics came to this awareness. Most did not have the immediate involvement with the "revolt from formalism" that Williams did and therefore did not "find" Catholicism as the means to protect aspiration and control reality. For most Catholics this had already become a part of their acquired heritage in

America. It was in the air they breathed, and many began to appreciate its vigors vocally during World War I.

The most conspicuous development for American Catholic life in the years 1900 to 1917 was the dramatic swelling of its numbers with the arrival of 3,500,000 immigrants of mostly Southern and Eastern European origin, bringing the Catholic body to represent nearly one-fifth of the total American population. These newcomers found themselves a part of an American Church that was largely dominated in tone and temper of life by Americans of Irish extraction, a domination which in the following decades would cause continuing interethnic squabbling. After 1917, and with the passage of immigrant restriction laws in the 1920's, the Church set out to stabilize itself and bring the heterogeneous mixture of its members into something approaching an American Catholicism.[4]

Long burdened with what seemed to be the bottom-heavy pull of caring for a mass of indigent immigrants, the Church experienced in these years the growing pains of an emerging middle class, who desired not only to make a success of life but to make Catholicism recognized in America. This middle class was composed of such laymen as George N. Shuster, F. Scott Fitzgerald, Michael Williams, Carlton J. H. Hayes, and Theodore Maynard, and priests like Virgil Michel, John J. Burke, C.S.P., James M. Gillis, C.S.P., Edward H. Pace, Fulton J. Sheen, Peter Guilday, Francis X. Talbot, S. J., and Daniel Lord, S.J. All these men were coming to a consciousness of the Church in America that was fraught with the ambivalence of an urgent desire to succeed and current reminders of destitution.

John J. Burke, editor of the *Catholic World* from 1904 to 1922, and chief organizer of the National Catholic Welfare Council (1919), dreamed of the conversion of America to Catholicism, but the realization of his dream was blunted, he felt, by the immigrant squalor of his Church. In 1924, when George Shuster moved from the Middle West to experience his first taste of urban Catholicism in New York, he felt himself in the midst of "mighty forces":

> I think that nowhere else in America could anybody feel so keenly, for instance, the meaning of the Church as a society. Here it is beloved and hated, rich and poor, squalid and fine, as I have never thought of it being before.[5]

A more intimate glimpse of the ambivalence of pre–World War I Catholicism can be found in the diary and correspondence of Peter Guilday (1884–1947), who later organized the American Catholic Historical Association (1919) and was professor of church history at the Catholic University of America. His remarkable diary, begun in 1902 while he was a student at St. Charles Borromeo Seminary, Overbrook, in Philadelphia and kept periodically to the mid-1920's, revealed both the anxieties and aspirations of American Catholicism.

In his valedictory address at the Roman Catholic High School of Philadelphia in 1901, the young Guilday was enthralled by the opportunities of the twentieth century to do away with ignorance, disease, and hunger. He recalled John Lancaster Spalding's adage that for us "ideals are real." As a way of directing his own youthful enthusiasm he chose the priesthood and undertook studies at Overbrook Seminary. But after a few years there he was disenchanted with the attitudes and demeanor fostered by the seminary, which he described in the following effusion of prose:

> Languidness of manner . . . drooping eyelids; no signs of energy; complete relaxation; a perfect Nirvana of rest in manner; shuffling philosophic walk . . . absolute repression and extinction of individuality . . . a real contempt for knowledge, originality and enthusiasm. All ye who seek entrance to these grey portals, cast behind you now and forever, love, sentiment, enthusiasm, youthfulness, brilliancy and zeal, and you will succeed in becoming an *Overbrook Priest.*

The "decimal culture" and "intellectual coma" of seminary life conflicted with his own "burning desire to stamp my individuality on the age in which I live. . . ."

Guilday had visions of being the "Newman of America," of leading the Church "to triumph throughout the land;" but his dream ran headlong into the "boogie-boo theology" which characterized the Catholic reaction to Modernism. Even at Louvain (1907–1910) his books were confiscated, his letters opened, and he was accused by fellow students of being tainted with the deadly sin of Modernism. Guilday fought to keep his enthusiasm alive amidst efforts by others and even himself to learn "self-abasement" and "self-repression." His visions of personal success and the institutional and cultural advancement of his Church were continually haunted by an ingrained pattern of guilt associated with ambition.[6] In time, such guilt and "languidness of manner" would fade as Catholics everywhere became more assertive. More revealing, however, was the content of Guilday's enthusiasm and idealism.

Guilday was never a Modernist. Though he read George Tyrrell, Adolf Harnack, and others, Cardinal Newman seemed to settle any qualms he was having about his faith.[7] Guilday did, however, desire a faith that was spirited and not withdrawn. To the broader culture of America during these prewar years he seemed to be oblivious. In his literary tastes, for example, he described Hamilton Wright Mabie's *Books and Culture* as "very pleasant reading." Mabie epitomized "genteel" criticism before the deluge. Guilday was "bewitched" by the poetry of Francis Thompson, who even managed to replace his former giants, Wordsworth and Lowell. He thought of writing a novel "with a moral background intimated throughout." He was shocked by Paul Bourget's *Le Disciple* for its extremism in depicting reality and was relieved that English literature did not "indulge" in such realism, though he was sure "we are as bad as France."[8] Throughout his early years Guilday was coming to terms with American culture in its "genteel" formulation. His passion for ideals and concern for uplift and progress were mixing, unstably at times, with his Catholicism. When World War I came along he found an outlet for his enthusiasm and an opportunity to formally wed the two.

Before describing Guilday's and the general Catholic response to the war and its aftermath more must be said about how Catholics came into and protected innocence in the prewar years. In the realm of thought they did so largely by keeping themselves in an "intellectual coma" for two decades. William James and John Dewey excited in them nothing but unease as they perceived American thought drifting in the direction of anarchy and fragmentation. The literary renascence affected them the same way, as they continued to uphold a "do-good" literature in the face of contemporary upheaval. Politically, they were universally antisocialist. In this they followed a line of thought voiced by Archbishop Ireland:

> The toiler knows that he lives in a land of opportunities where he may be rich tomorrow, and he is glad to defend his right to possible future possessions, by defending today the rights of other men to their possessions.

Though Social Gospel Protestants like Washington Gladden saw Roman Catholics "bearing their part in the promotion of thrift and order and intelligence," their violent antisocialism made them cautious toward all but the most bland elements of the progressive era. Walter Rauschenbusch stated it best when he concluded in 1912 that the Catholic Church in America "is peculiarly many-sided, a complexity of the most ancient and modern elements, a mixture of reactionary and progressive forces."[9]

The mixture of opposing forces within Catholicism led to an equally contradictory American reaction toward them. From one direction there were fears that Catholicism's increase in the nation foretold disaster for Anglo-Saxon culture. American nativism was, however, confined at this time to scattered pockets of fanaticism. Ironically, the most favorable characterization of Catholicism in America before World War I came from the pen of Edgar Lee Masters, whose *Spoon River Anthology* (1915) later symbolized for many Catholics the decline of idealism in American letters.

Masters believed, however, that to make his portrait of the midwestern village complete, the priest, Father Malloy, and his Church had to be recognized. Amid all the clutter of petty moralism, hates, and mean-spirited characters which inhabited Masters' valley, Father Malloy "kept his way in high tranquillity," helping to make their community "a wiser, happier and fairer" place to live. As described by Masters, Father Malloy was apart from those of "wavering faith, and clouded vision and drifting hope . . . ," believing in the joy of life and not ashamed of the flesh. Masters confessed to an attraction to Malloy and his Church, as he rebelled against the cramped moralism of American life.[10]

Another radical of the time evidenced some confusion with regard to Catholicism. In a 1917 essay, "The Uses of Infallibility," Randolph Bourne found a modern note to Catholicism precisely because for over a century it had refused to be modern. The significance of Newman, Bourne thought, was that "if faith is eternal, so is skepticism, and . . . even in the most pious mind may be found the healthy poison of doubt." What Catholicism had done was to give up the quest for "certitude in dogma"—the endless game of trying to reconcile science with faith—and instead had consigned dogma to the "vault" of infallibility. Protected from "idle gossip," infallible dogma freed Catholics to pursue the more practical urgencies of life. The Protestant, on the other hand, "clacked endlessly" about dogma and made a moral code infallible, which Bourne thought was the least defensible use of infallibility. "Protestantism," he felt, "has swept thousands of excellent minds into a spiritual limbo where in their vague twilight realm of modernity which has not quite sacrificed theology, they have ceased to count for intellectual or spiritual light." Bourne was pleased that Catholicism was at least able to ward off Modernism and continue its spiritual existence by guarding its treasures of mysticism.

At this point Bourne's dissatisfaction with Protestantism was complete and his fascination with Catholicism comes to an end. By sheltering dogma and not defending it the Church becomes a mere political institution and belief "loses its moral force . . . it no longer counts excitingly. . . . One only yawns over it . . . and turns aside to the genuine issues of life." The radicals' fascination with Catholicism revolved around the relationship between dogma and poetry. To Bourne there was a kind of "wild accuracy" about Christian doctrine and a poetic vigor in its dogma. Its truth, however, had no longer the binding power of faith as an intellectual attitude, and the Church was to him simply "a poetical society of mystics." Science and experimentation had pre-empted belief. The modern assented to "higher plausibility," not to truth. For Bourne, ideals replaced belief as the power which motivated modern man. Ideals were ends which have the "seeds of progress in them." While belief put truth outside of man, idealism "merges us with the growing end we wish to achieve."[11]

A short time after he wrote this essay, even Bourne's idealism was crushed by World War I. His disillusionment became total. His observations on Catholicism were affected by his aesthetic sensibility, which seemed to attract many like Bourne, but they did not have the stamp of reality about them. Whatever mystical quality the Church preserved was even then giving way to the desire to rationalize the content of faith, to certify dogma with reason, to make of neo-Thomism the guardian of belief and the protector of innocent idealism.

An observer who came nearest to putting his finger on the pulse of the Catholic community in America was George Santayana. In 1916 he found "the tone of the American Catholics to be pleasantly American." Santayana noticed that "after being long obscure and tolerated with a smile, apparently the prelates are begging to wear their robes in public and to boast that the future of religion in America is in their hands." He felt this assurance was more American than Catholic. What was happening, he perceived, was that American life acted as a

> powerful solvent . . . as it stamps the immigrant, almost before he can speak English, with an unmistakable muscular tension, cheery self-confidence, and habitual challenge in the voice and eyes, so it seems to neutralize every intellectual element, however tough and alien it may be, and to fuse it in the native good-will, complacency, thoughtlessness and optimism.

American Catholics, while managing to keep intact—but rarely referring to—the accumulation of the Church's inheritance of mystical, liturgical, and metaphysical insights, approached their religion with an acquired American spirit.

They viewed the Church, Santayana said, as a "first rate church to belong to . . . the biggest religion on earth." The priests are "fine fellows like policemen." The parish was flourishing if it was continually rebuilding itself, "founding new schools, orphan asylums, sodalities . . . raising money" and producing future cardinals. Santayana saw little danger of Catholicism being a threat to America; in fact, the opposite was true. Catholicism as both a "perfect piece of the past" and also "modern, the one complete, stable religion alive under our noses," in Santayana's view, was to proceed in the following years to champion this acquired American spirit, unaffected by the "poisons" of modernity.[12] It neutralized the "tougher" elements of Thomism and other aspects of traditional Catholicism and the result, by and large, was the survival of cheery self-confidence, challenge in its pronouncements, a certain amount of spiritual complacency, thoughtlessness, and a consuming optimism.

With this in mind American Catholics approached World War I in a sufficiently different manner to allow them to interpret its effects on their lives without the sense of disillusionment which deeply unsettled many other Americans. In brief, Catholics had their own reasons for going to war in 1917. They did not view the war as "a crusade to make the world safe for democracy," as President Wilson encouraged. They did not go to war to restore honor, decency and sacrifice in fields of blood, though many came home feeling this was the case. They did not engulf the war with the millenial expectations of Protestant America in its campaign for the "Christianization of the world." Nor were they affected by Dewey's instrumentalist belief that somehow the wild energies the war aroused in men could be channeled for the creation of a noble, just, and efficient society.[13]

The Catholic response to World War I can best be appreciated in the fact that Catholicism's polyglot makeup in America consisted of groups who still had close family and national ties with all the combatants of the war in Europe. Irish Catholics did not go to war to defend Anglo-Saxon culture. German Catholics, in the words of Frederick Kenkel, objected to the propaganda that the war was a defense of the "great and holy cause of liberty." Poles, Italians, and Central Europeans did not cross the Atlantic to evangelize their homelands. When Cardinal James Gibbons pledged to President Wilson that Catholics would "rise as one man to serve the nation," he meant exactly what he said. Catholics would do their duty as citizens and once again "prove" their loyalty, but they stopped somewhat short of joining the "Great Crusade." Their altruism had limited objectives. Peter Guilday, who worked for British propaganda agencies to stir up enthusiasm for the war among Catholics, admitted to a friend the truth of the situation when speaking of the 260 Catholic periodicals in the country: "Their spirit is American . . . but by no means pro-ally."[14]

After the war, a disaffected Protestant minister whimsically observed: "Romanist Joe, the mechanic . . . went to France not to make the world safe for Democracy, but to see Paris." Though oversimplified, there was more than a little truth to his assertion. When F. Scott Fitzgerald enlisted, he had "social reasons." Fitzgerald at the time was in a moment of Catholic enthusiasm and trying to convert John Peale Bishop. As for the war, he felt that he was too Irish to be the "I die for America type. . . . I may get killed for America—but I'm going to die for myself." George Shuster enlisted rather than accept a commission as a personal protest against the "fallacious" reasons Americans were sent to the trenches. The general Catholic response ran the gamut from defensive patriotism through "social reasons" and personal ones to simply the sheer adventure of it all, but rarely does one find the smell of a crusader.[15]

It was during and after the war that the Catholic crusading mentality took shape. In 1918 Edward Garesche, S.J., typified a developing mood among Catholics who saw at the end of the war a release of "reconstructive energy" in the world, with America taking "a part altogether glorious." While the youth of Europe were either tired or buried, Americans were "fresh, immensely moved, matured, instructed, disciplined and inspired." Having experienced the "old culture" of Europe, Americans would return, Garesche predicted, with an admiration for what was "true, lasting, beautiful, wholesome and serene." This offered a special opportunity for Catholicism; not only had Catholics proved their loyalty but they had acquired a taste for things Catholic. Joyce Kilmer writing to Garesche from Europe was "reminded in every room of every house and at every crossroad of the Faith. . . . I think that most of us are better Catholics now than when we were at home—certainly we should be."

"The thrilling opportunities of the time," Garesche concluded, "should stir us to the deeps of our soul's capacity for enthusiasm, energy and sacrifice." Michael Williams, hibernating in California in early 1919, was restless to get to the "front." For Williams, "the great war-after-the-war, the war for social reconstruction, goes on far from peaceful Carmel, and I would be there!"[16]

The front Williams soon joined was the National Catholic War Council (NCWC), which began operations in 1917 as a means of providing relief and other wartime services for Catholics during the war. After the armistice the Catholic hierarchy continued the organization and it became, with a slight change in title, the National Catholic Welfare Council, which in spirit if not in practice gave Catholics a national organization to direct their energies in areas such as education and social reform in the postwar years.[17] The most ambitious program emanating from the Council was the broadly liberal prolabor document, *Social Reconstruction: A General Review of the Problems and Survey of the Remedies* (1919).

Such activities as these, and the enthusiasm for reconstruction, mirrored other American programs in the immediate period after the armistice. Protestants, for example, began a spectacular program, the Interchurch World Movement, which envisioned the complete christianization and democratization of the world. By 1920 the movement had collapsed through varying degrees of indifference, loss of idealism, and internal dissension. Catholics viewed this "noble dream" that "vanished into unreality" with a mixture of sadness and as a spark to their own idealism. The movement, noted the editors of the *Catholic World,* lacked a "true ideal," which meant "not a union of churches but a united Church, defying the limitations of time and space, its hands on earth, its head in heaven, it moved through time and holds eternity."[18]

The growing consciousness that the war would not bring a spiritual awakening or a return to a culture based on serenity and discipline struck Catholics almost immediately. But then they had not fought the war for those purposes; some had only hoped these might result. While others were awakening to the "shock of recognition" and experiencing the dark brown taste of disillusionment, Catholics claimed victory. Peter Guilday expressed it best in an address, "American Catholics in War and Reconstruction," on June 14, 1920, in Reading Pennsylvania. Catholics, Guilday said, were "wholehearted" in their response to the war "although we knew in our inmost hearts that we were being lied to. . . ." These "half-truths," though, were only "rifts within the lute. . . . The victory is ours. . . . The fiery trial is over."[19]

The victory Catholics perceived was the "flowering" and "liberation" of Catholicism during the war. The war resulted in "a quickening of the mass-sense of the Catholic people." They had touched the ancient shrines of Catholic Europe and returned home believing America to be, in the words of Guilday, "the second consecration of all that is noblest in the old world for the uplift of humanity." There was no illusion, however, about the postwar world. Catholic idealism and reconstruction efforts were pressed into shape with a consciousness, felt the editors of the *Catholic World,* of "a crisis in our country and our civilization, the like of which this generation has not seen, looking upon a world that gives of itself no comfort, but distress and bewilderment. . . ."[20]

Catholic idealism during and after the war was forged and protected by maintaining that the "eminent reasonableness" of the Catholic outlook toward life was simply the other side of American optimism. These twin sources of confidence merged, and Catholics undertook in the 1920's the "war for Christendom," the battle against the "new paganism" with its amorphous sense of unease about life, and the new struggle to make democracy once again "safe for the world." Church leaders began to encourage a new militance and urgency for creating a "Catholic sense" toward life, which for Edward Pace meant "a disposition of the soul readied for action." Bishops like Austin Dowling of St. Paul desired that Catholics rid themselves of a former disposition of "a timid, touchy and surely negligible group of citizens who were not yet acclimated." Peter Guilday preached throughout the 1920's that Catholics were "soldiers of the new pilgrimage," "providential hosts" alone in the world. In speaking of the Knights of Columbus, Guilday quoted Herbert Hoover's words of praise for that group, "[they] are American clear through. . . . They are disciples of cheer, apostles of joy, sympathy, help, kindliness." The Knights symbolized the new American Catholic spirit as a phalanx opposed to anarchy, disorder, and uncertainty whose mission was "to create a new spirit of contentment to American ideals."[21]

Carlton J. H. Hayes preached to Catholics of their "obligations to America" made imperative by growing indifference, loss of idealism, and decline in morality unleashed after the war, and the concomitant decline in self-confidence among Protestants. The Jesuit Gerald C. Treacy concluded that in the face of "the disillusioned, bankrupt and muddled world . . . Catholic American youth should have in reality a timely optimistic outlook. . . . For Catholic youth has a heritage of Catholicism and Americanism." Paulist James Gillis assumed the editorship of the *Catholic World* in 1922 and promptly announced his optimism about America despite the tirades of Mencken and George Jean Nathan. A "curious anomaly" had occurred, thought Gillis:

> We Catholics are more hopeful for modern civilization than are they who built modern civilization. We cannot be said to be the creators of the modern system, yet we do not consider it to be altogether hopeless. We believe that the world has a future. . . . We are more modern than the moderns.

The scientists, philosophers, and artists all had lost confidence and had become "world weary" or cynical. Though they were the creators of the modern world, Gillis proclaimed, "We [Catholics] shall be its saviors." For him Americans were incapable of pessimism. They only played at it. Quoting Chesterton to those who still felt ill at ease with optimism, Gillis concluded: "Confidence in the value of existence and in the intrinsic victory of virtue is not optimism but religion." Similarly, Peter Guilday intoned that "sadness is not a Christian virtue." Men have a right to joy which is indispensable for "health, moral health and works."[22]

Following World War I the cultural and intellectual horizons of American Catholics took shape around a patchwork of images. The first was a picture of the Church unchained. Catholics took comfort in the thought that they had nothing to do with the liberal nineteenth-century's "tremendous march to breakdown and impasse." Ross Hoffman translated for Catholics this view of Catholicism, which was really European but which appeared to have enough truth in it to be accepted by Americans. This image was largely the production of converts who needed, psychologically and spiritually, to find an institution they could trust after being disillusioned with everything else. So for Hoffman, a convert from socialism, Catholicism stood apart and was "totally exonerated from all responsibility and involvement" in the breakdown that led to war and fragmentation, "for the Church had been sent into exile and the frontiers closed around it." At the point of "insolvency when doubt had reached its final term was it possible for Catholicism to return." The only fault he found with Catholicism in the previous era was that it had been too defensive; its "faith was not great enough." After the war the Church became "resurgent," in Michael

Williams' often repeated description, and to Hoffman "more manifestly alive" than anything else in the modern world.[23]

American Catholics generally accepted this image, but with different emotional corollaries. In reality, Catholics, conservative and liberal alike, were hardly "in exile" during the nineteenth century. With a few exceptions they were never participants in the extreme ultramontanist reactionary movement of the Church. They were, in fact, gradually acclimating themselves to American democratic institutions. Catholic immigrants were ingeniously using political machines in America, while their cousins in Europe were fervently praying for the restoration or continued survival of the Bourbon and Hapsburg monarchies. They were learning to approach reality as opportunity, something to be manipulated, controlled, and used to serve man's ends. Democratic strenuousness and optimism reached a level of self-consciousness in the late nineteenth century among Catholics associated with the liberal Americanist group. For the conservatives, these qualities characterized their practical concerns but had not yet surfaced in their thinking, which contributed to their hostility toward their more vocal counterparts.

American Catholic "exile" did have some meaning on the social and cultural level, where for the most part it had long been associated with impoverishment and out of touch with American middle-class gentility. However, this only acted as a further spur to their efforts to "make it" in the land of opportunity. World War I symbolized for American Catholics not so much their "return from exile" as their "arrival." It heightened their optimism while deepening their attachment to the American way and to things Catholic. To be informed that Catholicism in Europe was in the midst of an "intellectual revival" and that the Church was "resurgent" and "alive" simply confirmed their own aspirations. In the 1920's and 1930's this revival was preached and editorialized, and it became the frequent topic of discussion on the lecture circuit. Whatever the emotional and spiritual qualities of the revival meant to Europeans, Americans were more concerned with the fact than with its content.[24]

In the 1920's, with an increasingly more secure middle class, the Catholic scene, as Francis X. Talbot, S.J., editor of *Thought,* recalled in 1939, "blossomed . . . with new developments and expansions" in cultural and intellectual activity. Catholics were eager, it seemed, to build more than churches and schools. World War I had induced among them a "confidence" in their position in the country and an "awareness" of their strength. They set out to "build a Catholic culture and civilization."[25] The gravity that characterized this pursuit and that gave it an American tinge was their concern about the cultural transformation of America from the land of innocent adventure and serene confidence to one of complexity and disturbing doubt.

Thus the culture that Catholics would attempt to construct would be characterized by a confidence in man's possibilities and a view of nature and the universe that was neither threatening nor disturbing but, rather, harmonious with man's aspirations and passive to his desire for mastery. It would be a moral culture where man was assured that if he followed the laws of nature and of nature's God, individual and social success would be his reward. Using as a reference the second decade of the twentieth century, Catholics began to picture themselves, as Talbot told the public in 1938, as "the largest bloc in the dwindling number of Americans who hold fast to the constitutional and traditional Americanism that made the country what it was before 1914. . . ." As "providential hosts" in a time that gave itself no comfort, their mission, according to Joseph M. Corrigan, was to "re-Americanize America" by supernaturalizing the ways and ideas of prewar Americans. This done, the future looked bright. Writing in the midst of the Depression, Corrigan blissfully related how those early Americans "near to nature . . . responded to the impulses of nature." In so doing they managed to harmonize "individual advantage and social good." Despite his romantic visions of early America, Corrigan was venting a Catholic expression of American innocence.[26]

The trouble for Catholics, of course, was that while they sought to "re-Americanize America" they were alienating themselves from the dynamics of contemporary culture. They tended to reject ideas, art forms, educational, moral and spiritual attitudes that postdated William James. After James, it seemed to Catholics that the American pioneer relinquished his role as an agent for civilization and relapsed into the wilderness of primitive instinct, without limits, where man found himself the victim of capricious fate. In the 1920's Catholics were largely alienated from the cultural anarchy of America that was both creative and desultory. The other side of that decade, the "business of America is business" side, they complacently enjoyed—except for a few—for the material prosperity it brought them. The 1930's found them enthusiastic for the "New Deal" because its program of pragmatic meliorism seemed to be both Catholic and traditionally American. But from the passionate urgency and growing radicalism in its literature and art forms Catholics remained isolated, interpreting everything from the rather narrow perspective of anticommunism and trapping themselves in their own extremes. When a sense of urgency was felt, for example, in the Catholic Worker movement, the complexity of industrial life was shunned in favor of a return to agrarian simplicity.[27]

From one perspective, Catholic culture in America from 1920 to 1940 was an array of rear-guard actions to deny the realities and uncertainties of twentieth-century life. The reactionary mentality was not so much one of withdrawal and bitterness as it was an animated labor to survive according to their wits without doubting the cheerful optimism that was their America and the certitude that was their Catholicism. At times their sense of security was almost frightening even to themselves. Mary McGill, associate editor of *The Catholic Girl,* confided to Wilfred Parsons, S.J., editor of *America,* a sense of trembling over her own certainties. She wrote:

> But no one but a well instructed Catholic appreciates Catholicism, and no matter how *broad* our friends on the outside say they are, I find them quickly sensitive. We are so *SURE.* That characteristic would hurt me, if I didn't believe. I think I would hate people who are so certain and set apart, if I were not so favored with our *Supreme Gift*.[28]

In public discourse Catholics were more given to animation than trembling.

Theodore MacManus, a Detroit businessman, addressed a Catholic audience in 1928 and raised both Catholic certainty and alienation to the level of an honored duty. Though Catholic culture was largely "intangible," it had its consequences. "If [the Catholic] is alien," said MacManus, "if he is isolated from much of the thought and culture of his time, it is a proud and glorious isolation." He urged his audience to respond to "the strength, security and the superiority of your intellectual position":

> Think kindly and charitably of the millions of your heart-hungry and soul-hungry fellow men, the perplexed and the distraught who have none of the conviction and the certitude which you enjoy.

To give shape to this conviction he envisioned:

> a thousand agencies and activities at work in the Catholic Church of America—all fixed with zeal and holy endeavor . . . [for] the creation of a definite Catholic culture which shall penetrate into every field of research, discovering enlightenment, progress and social emancipation [coordinated by] an American Catholic Foundation underwritten for $10,000,000 and looking hopefully forward to the day when those $10,000,000 will be multiplied ten times that amount.

The Foundation was off to a fast start when MacManus immediately offered $25,000 from his own pocket. To appreciate the real intangibility of this American Catholic culture, one has to realize that this "vision" came to him while he, a midwestern Irish Catholic, was listening over the radio to the "exquisite strains" of a Gregorian chant sung by a Russian choir in New York.[29]

Proud in its isolation, firm in its conviction, Catholic culture was, nevertheless, intangible. It was so because Catholics construed its main ingredient to be ideas. It was an ideological culture, which overlaid and quite subsumed the more tangible but less bourgeois realities of life in urban villages and country towns where a multiplicity of ethnic, cultural and religious views prevailed. But by educating the individual into neo-Thomism, Americanism, and "Catholic" literary ideals, Catholics were constructing a culture which attempted to transcend the particularisms of the varied groups that composed its foundation. This culture, then, was at the very least an agency for homogenization, if not Americanization. An ideological culture was also a means for its growing middle class, whose members continually reminded themselves throughout this period that they were no longer "hewers of wood and drawers of water," to maintain a sense of identity with their roots as they strove for middle-class respectability.

Catholic culture was ideological in the sense William James, following a line of thought of G. K. Chesterton, defined philosophy: as "the dumb sense of what life honestly and deeply means . . . our individual way of just seeing and feeling the total push and pressure of the cosmos."[30] Catholics cared deeply about ideas and the effects they had on how an individual chose to live and how he related to the pressure of events or the push of reality. They saw the struggle of their time in largely ideological terms. Edward S. Dore, founder of the National Catholic Alumni Federation and Justice of the Supreme Court of New York, stated this position at a symposium in 1935:

> We of the Federation believe that the battle of this age concerning which direction the organization of society, economic, social, and governmental, shall take, is ultimately a battle of ideas, a war between these various forms of thought about life, a battle about what the thing called Man really is.[31]

Despite their passion for ideas, Catholics were wont to treat them in a rather formal fashion, betraying their own excitement. Michael Harrington has recently recalled his own education into this Catholic milieu, speaking to the ambivalence he eventually rejected:

> And yet the underlying assumption of all the sterilized categorizing was vibrant. The Jesuits were convinced that ideas have consequences, that philosophy is the record of an ongoing debate over the most important issues before mankind. It was sad that such an essentially passionate attitude toward the life of the mind was buried within stilted theses and scholia.[32]

Another aspect in the molding of Catholic culture after World War I was the educational system in which ideals were taught. Reflecting the urge for respectability without foregoing a sense of identity, Catholic college enrollment for men increased from 32,000 in 1916 to 162,000 in 1940. The "mentors" of this American middle class were the Jesuits, who have sought in their long career of educating Catholics since the Reformation to accommodate the humanistic, philosophical, and theological divisions of their *Ratio Studiorum* to the exigencies of time and place. The ideal, as summarized by John Courtney Murray, S.J., has been "to put the student in the way of developing a power of diction, a view of reality, a set of values, and a sense of style." The Jesuits toiled to mold the "whole man." Throughout the nineteenth century these educational ideals fit in remarkably well with the ideals associated with the small denominational or non-denominational colleges in the United States.[33] In a penetrating analysis of Jesuit education at Boston College toward the end of the nineteenth century, Donna Merwick has described how American and Catholic cultural ideals comfortably merged.

The ideal at Boston College was to produce the "benevolent man" from the ragtag body of immigrants entering its halls. It preached to the immigrant that to be an American was not the result of ancestry, but "fitness." It affirmed the value of culture as providing an aura of refinement and embellishment over the more day-to-day struggle to survive. It taught them that man's intellectual and moral faculties were in harmony with, and therefore could deduce, the laws of the universe as basically outlined by Newton and, to some extent Herbert Spencer. With his free will, man must also "normalize" the more passionate urgings of the "lower" regions of his nature. In sum, the immigrants were taught to imitate the college president, Robert Fulton, S.J., as an example of the true Christian gentleman: "a genius, an infatuated lover of the classics, a witty and brilliant conversationalist and yet an energetic and powerful administrator."[34]

Catholics were arriving at this "genteel" conception of culture and the type of education best suited to develop it at almost the very moment when "genteel" and the formalism associated with it became a "dirty word" for the new generation of American intellectuals. Catholic gentility passed through the "revolt against formalism" relatively unscathed. After World War I it became the emblem for their cause that Catholic culture and education were American, and confirmed their crusade to "re-Americanize America."

Boston College, however, like many other small Catholic colleges, was transformed during this time into something approaching a university. After some early ideological resistance to electivism, vocationalism, and the *summum bonum* of university training, the inductive research project,

Catholics generally accepted these oddities of the modern university as practical readjustments to the exigencies of life.[35] The goal of the "benevolent man" was still central, only now he was to be certified with a Ph.D. and imbued with a more lordly concept of a Catholic culture. Some Catholic educators would speak to the American "genteel," while others spoke primarily in "Catholic" phraseology. However, both groups, except in some extreme cases, thought they were preaching the same thing.

Within the former group, Peter Guilday believed the function of Catholic higher education, especially graduate studies, was to provide a "method of pursuit" by means of specialization in a chosen field to "push out the limits of knowledge." This, of course, followed its other two functions of accumulating acquired wisdom and transmitting it to the student. Guilday was confident, however, that research would lead ultimately to the future progress of human civilization. He also believed that graduates should consider themselves an elite, and the graduate school itself was to him "the sacred precincts." In this view the special responsibility of "elitehood" was to go out and defend deposited culture and democratic institutions; it had the task of "purifying, uplifting, and civilizing the masses to which we belong." The benevolent graduate should have none of the "corroding individualism" which divided the intellectual from the community. The elite should have "a sense of vision and the power of sacrifice." A sense of the future, which Guilday thought was "once vivid in America," had declined. As a result of the confusion about human destiny, he observed "so little joyous constructive imagination, so little poetry and art, those lovely works of free-ranging vision, at once beautiful and popular."

Looking at the contemporary condition of American universities Guilday singled out Princeton as still upholding "the sweetness and light of culture." In this state of affairs, the Catholic Church of America, he thought, should provide leadership "to the intellectual armies of the world, battered and shocked as they have been by the crash and confusion of the war. . . ." Only Catholics, owing to their freedom from state control, had escaped the "Egyptian captivity of the mind and heart. . . ." Catholic intellectuals must "set their faces courageously against the agnostic fatalism which is robbing American life of its noblest attractions."[36]

Guilday's educational ideal of the benevolent specialist spoke to the Catholic responsibility to uphold American culture. Another group attempted after the war to bring American Catholics to a more grandiose concept of Catholicism. They sought to fortify the educated Catholic in his sense of identity and responsibility. Catholicism was conceived as more than a creed; it was, in fact, a culture. William J. McGucken, S.J., of St. Louis University maintained that Catholic education did not simply train its students in religion but, more importantly, it presented them with the "whole sweep of Catholicism." Such a student acquired "a sense of ancient heritage, a pride of race, an attitude of *noblesse oblige*" which enabled him or her to know those facts that gave "meaning and coherence to the whole of life." For George Bull, S.J., of Fordham University, this culture made the Catholic's "spontaneous reaction toward life" different. To Bull, Catholic culture was at odds with contemporary culture because the former had a "totality of view" while the latter was fragmented. Like many of his fellow Catholics, Bull referred to Walter Lippmann's *Preface to Morals* (1928) to prove the departmentalization of contemporary life and its lack of an interweaving ideal. If Catholic higher education fulfilled its mission, according to Bull, there should be no Catholic graduate "who is bewildered in the grip of modern life."[37]

The concern with totalism and the advantages of coherence led, especially in the 1930's, to extremism. Though not indicative of the major trend of Catholic culture, this extremism was always an option for those who desired to breathe its air more vigorously. While George Bull inspired many Catholics to a vision of Catholic culture, that vision also led him and others into some murky waters. Besides totality, Bull thought an aspect of an educated Catholic culture was "other-worldliness." Therefore, he was proud that Catholics appeared to their fellow citizens as "inert and apathetic in certain forms of civil endeavor; callous to certain social needs; unenthusiastic about this or that 'latest movement' in sociology; reactionary, strange, foreign, even dangerous to modern life and thought." The culture Bull conceived was so radically "Catholic" that there was nothing for it to relate to except itself. As for Catholic graduate education, Bull denied that its goal was research. For him research was inimical to Catholic culture. Investigation for Catholics was not, as Guilday said, to "push out the boundaries of knowledge." It was, rather, to "penetrate into reality." Man had been given a store of wisdom about God in traditional metaphysics which no new discovery could alter. Bull was also sure that classical literature had for all time settled the issue of who man was. All that remained for the Catholic was "contemplation, penetration and enrichment."[38]

Bull's conclusions, however, represented a kind of intellectual and cultural incest which the more pragmatic Catholic mind found uncomfortable. Though Catholic education strove for a definite Catholic sensibility, its American tone and its desire for respectability prevented such wholesale withdrawal. In general, research, electivism and vocationalism found a home within Catholic education, under the guise of protecting and uplifting civilization. This acceptance was not an indication that Catholics had succumbed to subjectivism or relativism, however. Research was the method to prove or defend one's ideals. Few Catholics understood the scientific method as a means of challenging tradition or attacking dusty formalisms. Progress and research, as Thurber Smith, S.J., of St. Louis University put it in criticizing Bull, were still the "advancement of truth" into the frontiers of ignorance. The scholarly ideal presented by Guilday combined an American desire to push into the future with a Catholic emphasis on being anchored. "Only when the intellect is subject to truth, the will subject to moral law, and the passions subject to the intellect and will," said Guilday with customary caution, "can reason enlighten, direct and ennoble the scholar—the complete man—the man par excellence." In the main, Catholic education continued to serve as an avenue of social mobility as had the small ante-bellum American colleges. It provided an ordered conceptual pattern of experience which lay underneath the flux of experience and fluidity of society.[39]

The last but most active manifestation of Catholic culture was an organizational proliferation. In MacManus' "vision" a thousand agencies of holy endeavor would provide the concrete shape in which to encompass its less than tangible ideological basis. Catholics were hardly newcomers to the organizational mentality. For over a century they had been building parishes, dioceses, and archdioceses in areas where a single priest would have been sufficient. They had developed religious societies and immigrant-aid societies to meet their spiritual and social needs under the pressure of a many times hostile Protestant environment. They had also created a system of national administrative councils (the Provincial and Plenary Councils of Baltimore) which in scope and regularity were unique in the Catholic world of the nineteenth century.[40] The creation of the National Catholic Welfare Council in 1919 represented a culmination of this administrative genius. It also marked a new beginning. After 1919, organizational emphasis shifted to cultural, intellectual, and professional societies that reflected a sense of "arrival" in the United States from the social point of view and, also, the new urge to mold an ideological culture. This new burst of energy continued an old strategy of protecting the faith of Catholics from cradle to grave.[41] There was also, however, a more assertive strategy to preserve an American form of culture under Catholic auspices in the face of contemporary American discontent.

The multiple movements of Catholic culture were, as John LaFarge, S.J., called them, "communities of purpose." They were seen as signs of the flowering of Catholic life, and became agencies for the survival of innocence in America. The following partial listing indicates the scope of their purpose. In chronological order from 1900 to 1950, Catholics organized: The National Catholic Educational Association (1904), the Catholic Press Association (1911), Catholic Writers Guild of America (1919), The

American Catholic Historical Association (1919), Catholic Library Association (1921), American Catholic Philosophical Association (1926), Catholic Association for International Peace (1926), Catholic Anthropological Association (1928), Catholic Book Club (1928), Catholic Poetry Society of America (1931), Catholic Biblical Association of America (1936), Catholic Art Association (1937), the Catholic Theatre Conference (1937), American Catholic Sociological Society (1938), Catholic Renascence Society (1940), Catholic Economic Association (1941), Catholic Commission on Intellectual and Cultural Affairs (1946), and the American Catholic Psychological Association (1947). [42]

There are at least two ways of approaching such a proliferation of cultural institutions. From one angle, they were simply voluntary associations of like-minded individuals in pursuit of common goals. They demonstrated a Catholic adaptation to the American democratic genius of forging numbers into political, cultural, or professional power centers. In American society these organizations have tended to be either countervailing forces in a majority-rule environment or gap fillers where governmental agencies were silent. But from another point of view Catholic voluntary agencies have attempted to be more than a grouping of like-minded people. In the twentieth century Catholics have developed parallel organizations in history, theology, education, journalism, philosophy, anthropology, sociology, librarianship, medicine, law, psychology, poetry, art, literature, and theatre. Many of these groups found their reason for being in the belief that the Catholic spontaneous response to life was different from, if not hostile to, those of non-Catholic associations. Thus, taken as a whole they tended to form a "countersociety" which Michael Harrington has compared to the decadent Marxism of the Second International in Germany and Austria. [43]

The Catholic countersociety with its varied cultural institutions functioned to immunize its members from the dominant problems of life without. To this extent, Harrington's analogy is correct. However, Catholics were not as extremely alienated from bourgeois culture as the Marxists or the Second International. In fact, Catholic culture, as conceived by Americans, was an attempt to save middle-class culture from its own decadence. While isolating themselves from disillusionment, these agencies were busy affirming values which were either under attack, forgotten, or going through the disquieting process of transformation.

There were also degrees of alienation among and within these organizations which further eroded the possibility of a complete countersociety. For example, within the Catholic Library Association there were two groups; one which saw little difference between their objectives as Catholic librarians and the objectives of the American Library Association (1876), and another faction, led by William Kane, S.J., a disciple of George Bull, which believed that a Catholic library was run fundamentally differently from an ordinary library. Kane objected to direct reader services, an open-shelf policy, and Catholics receiving degrees from non-Catholic library schools. All of these things he felt were tainted by an "occillating emotional enthusiasm for some naturalistic utopian ideals of library work." From his Catholic realist position, Kane argued that reading was not for everyone, and that it only partially affected education anyway. In a burst of spiritual enthusiasm Kane thought "getting a man into heaven is . . . more important than getting him into a library." However, Kane, like Bull, was an apotheosis of obscurantism amidst the more general Catholic desire not to appear too obtrusive.[44]

Among associations there were also differences. The American Catholic Historical Association (ACHA) would appear to have been less disaffected than the associations of Catholic philosophers and poets. Peter Guilday, founder of the ACHA, was not so much concerned with promoting an ideology as he was intent on simply increasing Catholic interest in history. He had discovered he was one of only two priests present at the 1914 meeting of the American Historical Association (AHA). He was also interested in bringing American Catholics to an appreciation of their past in the country. By 1919 he found "a responsive chord" to his initiative, and the Association was established at the meeting of the AHA in Cleveland that year. From then on the two groups met concurrently each year, fostering at least a sense of sharing a common discipline and standards. Although Guilday edited a volume of essays *The Catholic Philosophy of History* (1936), he was not given to ideology himself. He had instead a pragmatic temper with regard to the uses of history which ranged from a defensive posture to an instrumentalist view, to practicality, to discipline, and finally to a cultural perspective where history served to ennoble man in the cause of moral goodness and social efficiency. He could identify with J. Franklin Jameson of the AHA, who delivered the opening address at the ACHA meeting in 1919; but Guilday's history was not the stuff of James Harvey Robinson or Charles A. Beard, who were more his contemporaries.[45]

There was a more extreme view of Catholic history, generally enunciated by Jesuits such as Demetrius Zema, who regularly attacked Beard's "cynical, skeptical, relativist metaphysics." To this way of thinking anyone who preferred a "wild theorizer" such as Benedetto Croce to the "prince of nineteenth century historians," Van Ranke, took a plunge into pure subjectivism and relativism. What united Guilday with his more hostile fellow Catholic historians was their firm commitment to understand history as the pursuit of objective facts which, when placed in true proportion and perspective, interpret themselves. History was the "actions of men" in society and the historian must seek to discover the "purposive acting will" behind the event.[46] The purpose of history, as Samuel Wilson, S.J., of Loyola University in Chicago said, was to train the mind to think, and to "enrich the memory" with a body of interesting incidents and the imagination with a pageant of the objectively reconstructed past.[47]

As a result, when the direction of American historical writing moved toward an appreciation of the process of economic (Beard) or intellectual (Carl Becker) forces which seemed to transcend social or individual mastery, Catholics were primarily concerned with historical biographies. Guilday's two-volume works on *The Life and Times of John Carroll, Archbishop of Baltimore, 1735–1815* (1922) and *The Life and Times of John England, First Bishop of Charleston, 1786–1842* (1927), recorded what he said of himself as a young man, how they "stamped" their individuality upon the age. Guilday's emphasis on biography was indicative of the American Catholic labor of mind to maintain a sense of control over experience while the American scene drifted into the unpredictable. The "new history" of James Harvey Robinson, Beard, and others was generally viewed by Catholics as simply "mythmaking for revolutionary ends." To Ross Hoffman it represented "a revolt against the ability of the intellect to know with any certainty." The one Catholic historian who escaped this reaction against the new history on ideological grounds was Carlton J. H. Hayes, who learned his history from Robinson and Beard at Columbia University.[48]

The attitude of mind which surrounded the origins of the Catholic Poetry Society of America provides a less cluttered view of the impulse of Catholic culture in the United States. At the prompting of Francis X. Talbot, S.J., the literary editor of *America*, the society was formed in 1931 and began publishing its journal, *Spirit*, in 1934. In 1941 the group held an anniversary symposium and reflected on its origins. In general, the society aimed toward the promotion of a richer Catholic culture in the country. Its mission was twofold, affirmation and protest; protest against the "pessimism" and "crassness" of the age and affirmation of man's dignity "as the highest in the order of creatures and partaker of the divine."[49] Thus, as Talbot said, they sought to preserve a tradition:

> During the past thirty years, the writing of poetry had been debased into experimenting with poetry. Cliques and nitwits and neurotics . . . were agonizing over a new pattern of poetry . . . A society was needed that would promote sanity among poets, that would stem the esoteric, and make way for the universal in poetry. . . .[50]

For Katherine Bregy poetry was the expression of "very certain ideals." Therefore, there was a need for Catholic art as a "corrective to the life all about us; as a defense against Egoism on the one side and Communism or totalitarianism on the other . . . as a defense against the so-called Realism of ugliness and defeat, and finally as a defense against ourselves." Though Bregy believed Catholics had room for ugliness and sensualism if approached from "the right angle of vision," the poetry of Robinson Jeffers and Edna St. Vincent Millay did not qualify. Nor could the society accept James Joyce or e. e. cummings' "torturing words and promulgating the cult of unintelligibility." The Catholic artist must be bred on "an intuition of balance, of order." In Theodore Maynard's view, the society was "an intellectual focal point . . . a firm philosophical conviction" which provided for the "extension" of a tradition and prevented a "plunge into chaos." This philosophical conviction, defined by A. M. Sullivan, was the realization "that the creation of the world" was no accident and that man was no incident in the travails of nature . . . if a man cannot save the world by his ideals, neither can he destroy them by his malice."[51]

The ideals defended by the Catholic Poetry Society and other associations were defined in a spirit of protest against the revolution in American values in art, literature, and philosophy which changed our culture in the decade which culminated in World War I. The Catholic response was to affirm a pattern of ideals twentieth-century man has found difficult to grasp in totality. Some of the ideals which Catholics vigorously proclaimed needed firm but subtle articulation. However, Catholic expression never matched its high purpose. In struggling to preserve contact with each other, with their past, and with a sense of human dignity, their convictions suffered, ironically, from the optimism and moralism in which they were rooted. The ideal of balance was defeated by a fuzzy sentimentalism about man which prevented him from wriggling, torturing words and from peering into chaos. Catholic idealism passed through the shadows of rebellion and war intact but arrived sounding hollow to a generation that was confused but not willing to return to an innocent paradise. Edgar Lee Masters was attracted to Father Malloy not because his reason dominated his passions, or because his house was a model of symmetrical design, or because he was without doubt and sadness; but rather because his hope simply appeared firm and his sins forgiven.

If there is one thread of thought which united Catholic culture in the decades following the first World War, it was the belief that its isolation from disillusionment presented Catholicism with unexpected opportunities in America. They undertook the task of grafting together the acquired sense of the promises of American life and the traditions of their Catholic heritage in the hope that Catholicism might save the country from its discontent. In "the great struggle . . . between disillusionment and hope," said George Shuster in 1921, the opportunity presented itself for Catholics to be "magnificently hopeful."[52]

4. The Repossession of Tradition
Medieval and American

"To THOUSANDS OF OUR FELLOW Americans," Leonard Feeney, S.J., wrote, "we Catholics are known merely as the people who eat fish on Friday."[1] Although Feeney became something of a celebrity himself after World War II for his extreme views concerning non-Catholics' right to salvation, (leading to his exile for some years from his fellow fish-eaters) his little quip suggested the problem Catholics had in being recognized in America in the 1920's. The question was, How would Catholic culture relate itself to the world around it? This in turn, hinged on the problem of what Catholic culture was.

The country was afforded a glimpse of what it was like in June of 1926. The occasion was the International Eucharistic Congress held in Chicago. For American Catholics, this event marked a yearning for a more significant status within the universal domain of the Church. It was also a sign of their arrival and a celebration of innocence, especially in the trappings which surrounded it. James M. Gillis editorialized in the *Catholic World* on its significance:

> At Chicago we came—so to speak—out of our holes and corners, out of our catacombs into a blinding light. We became the cynosure of the eyes of America, and of the world, and even according to the judgment of our most exacting critics, we conducted ourselves as those "to the manor born."[2]

The Chicago festival set a pattern for the less grandiose gatherings of Catholics. In the following years nearly every professional, social, intellectual, and cultural meeting of Catholics became "a ceremony of innocence" in which Catholics congratulated themselves on their certainties and propped up their optimism, while others, they thought, struggled in the darkness.

But there was another way of looking at the Eucharistic Congress, which, for a few Catholics, signalled disaster. Bernard Fay, French journalist for *Le Correspondent* of Paris, saw the event from this perspective. "The gaudy and ostentatious pomp," said Fay:

> the purple painted train, the vast public ceremonials, the display of luxury, the ornamentation surprised both Protestants and unbelievers

61

who had previously been rather favorable to Catholicism. Though the social and political prestige of Catholicism in America may have been increased by the Congress, it must be said that in certain circles its intellectual prestige suffered.

What for Gillis was the "blinding light" of those acting as "to the manor born" was seen by others as evidence that, for Catholics, the "gilded age" still lived. Its blinding effect threatened to destroy what Fay and other observers thought was the rather advantageous position Catholicism found itself in after World War I.[3]

It seemed to many the Church had not spent its "spiritual force" during the war. As one young Catholic, Cuthbert Wright, said, it "blew neither hot nor cold." By 1919 some Protestants were observing "new life and purpose" among Catholics, who seemed to know their own mind, contrary to the growing confusion among Modernists and Fundamentalists in Protestantism. To the aesthetic minded like Randolph Bourne, the mystical qualities of Catholic life compared favorably to what appeared to be the shallow moralism of Protestantism. Catholicism was not publicly identified with the last crusade of nineteenth-century Protestant America, prohibition. In the literary and intellectual attack on main street Babbittry, Catholics were rarely scrutinized and, indeed, for Edgar Lee Masters they appeared to have some saving graces. In the early 1920's H. L. Mencken's *American Mercury* was mainly silent with regard to Catholicism, except for one brief criticism of the lack of leadership and displays of power by its bishops. But this was by way of praising the "sagacious" qualities of Cardinal Gibbons. *The Nation* observed the "Bishops Program" of 1919 as "far and away the most significant social pronouncement made by any church in the United States," which "shook the assurance" of those who felt that a church that condemned Modernism could never assume effective leadership in a social democracy. The fact that fanatics like the Ku Klux Klan attacked Catholicism only rendered it more comely to those who despised fanaticism. Padraic Colum, the Irish author, summarized this trend when he said, "to certain of the intellectuals who have been thwarted by Calvinism and bored by Pragmatism, Catholicism exhibits a norm that is rich and human."[4]

Those Catholics participating in *The Commonweal* movement (1924) and, to some extent, those behind the policies of the Jesuit journal *Thought* (1926), directed their efforts to exploiting the "rich and human" qualities of their religion, taking advantage of what they considered an opportunity to contribute to American democratic and cultural discussion. Even Walter Lippman encouraged in 1928 "the expression of a point of view which has not until recently played the part in American life which as a matter of historic importance to civilization, it is entitled to play." The aim of *The Commonweal*, as Michael Williams wrote to Peter Guilday in 1922, was toward "the cultivated readers within and without the Church, but particularly at those without." A conscious elitism led *The Commonweal* group to believe that Mencken's enemies, according to Williams, were also enemies of Catholicism; "mammon worship, ugly and gross materialism, hypocritical and selfish and dishonorable statesmen and politicians; vulgarity and mediocrity in life and art. . . ." The difference between "the enlightened minority" represented by *The Commonweal*, and American intellectuals like Mencken, was, in Williams' view, the former's refusal to lose faith in the common man. The aim was to present the case for both the exceptional and the common. Williams feared the danger to national health when the elite corrupted its mysticism and severed themselves from the community.[5]

For those within *The Commonweal* orbit of influence the relationship between the intellectual and the community was of critical importance. Although the editors considered themselves independent of hierarchical control, in the larger cultural context their understanding of the role of an "enlightened minority" was not to smash idols but to create fellowship.[6] In the 1920's this was a most difficult task. The times were rife with efforts to expel the demons of American mediocrity. While *The Commonweal* began cautiously to develop Catholic self-criticism, others were less patient. The display at the International Eucharistic Congress, and the 1928 campaign of Alfred E. Smith for the presidency, tended to highlight some of what Mencken called the "weak spots" of Catholic life.

By the mid-twenties it was evident that many Catholics were ready to out-Puritan the Puritan. As James Gillis observed, it was no credit to Catholicism that many Americans thought Catholics less rigid in matters moral. The urban Irish dubbed by Heywood Broun in 1928 as "the cry-babies of the Western World" were already on their way to pick up the slack caused by a lapse in Protestant moralism. In the face of "hybrid Catholic Puritans" some felt that the "rich and human" strain of the Church was being covered by a blanket of moralism.[7] In 1926 Cuthbert Wright set out to expose the "vile sexless indecencies" of Catholicism in America, with its "vaudeville music" and neglected symbolism. To Wright it appeared that Catholicism was divided into two groups. The large majority of the faithful was in the throes of "eunuch worship" and "nervously attempting to be a department of the American Defense Society or the Purity League." The other group, the Romantics "of ritualism and the Gothic quest, of Chesterton and Belloc, of Catholic dilettantism and Catholic pragmatism . . . ," were attracted to the Church because it seemed "to work" in the social sense or because "it titillates their sentimentality." Both groups, Wright felt, were especially resentful of criticism, of new ideas, and even of old ideas that appeared novel.

Following Wright, an anonymous priest wrote in *The Atlantic Monthly* in 1928 of the Church's "formalism," loss of vitality, and excessive authoritarianism; of its school system managed by "clerical Babbitts" resulting in the commercialization of religion in the United States. The severe criticisms of this priest, of Wright, and, as we shall see, of George Shuster, were generally ignored by the majority of Catholics. These men desired to see Catholicism speak to the simpler ideals of faith, love, and hope. If such critics were not ignored they were accused of "aristocratic" pretensions by others, like Michael Williams, who, in their eagerness to show the Church "resurgent," neglected the fact that much of this resurgence needed the stimulating effect of pruning shears.[8] The rich and human element of Catholic culture was largely overgrown by the mid-twenties. It percolated in individual Catholic homes and among isolated individuals such as George Shuster. The public thrust of Catholic culture sought in a variety of ways to secure the parameters of American innocence.

There were three levels of Catholic discussion, forming a bottom-heavy pyramid. The upper point was inhabited by men like George Shuster, Robert C. Pollock, Russell Wilbur, and, to a certain extent, *The Commonweal* movement, insofar as Shuster influenced its tone of discussion. In general, this group, though within the boundaries of innocence, pierced through its cheery veneer by an approach to reality which was humble but sought fresh and expansive avenues of exploration. Occupying the base points of the pyramid were the majority of Catholics and Catholic thinkers. On one side were those who sought to recover the American pioneer mentality of conquering reality by fusing neo-Thomism, medievalism, and classicism with traditional modes of American thought. Despite this group's efforts to maintain contact with American cultural forces, both in the past and the present, there was a tendency among many of them to step to the other side and into a retreat from reality altogether. These "100 percent Catholics," as they were called, followed George Bull, S.J., and his concept of a complete Catholic ethos, which was in total opposition to life around it. They believed Catholicism to be in a "constant state of cultural conflict and contradiction" in America, which forced it to be alert even to the "fringe of evil." Salvation for this group lay not in compromise but in recapturing "the cultural spirit of pre-Reformation Catholicism."[9]

Despite the radical isolationist mentality of this last group, the unitive quality of Catholic writing was intent on expressing what Harold Gardiner, S.J., thought was the purpose of the Jesuit magazine *America:* to "show the Catholic implications of the American way of life . . . and the American implications of the Catholic way of life."[10] These implications varied according to what was understood to be the significance of Catholicism and America. A sampling of editorial opinion in *The Commonweal* through the twenties affords an indication of how one group of Catholics approached this task.[11]

The cultural horizon of Michael Williams, the founder of *The Commonweal*, was marked by two imposing realities: (1) the Church resurgent and (2) the spiritual and intellectual malaise of contemporary American culture. The American writers' revolt against New England "righteousness" and the "conventionalistic veneer" of the old idealism was applauded for its honesty and its attack on "self-complacency." But the editors were also aware that, as a result of this revolt, writing in America had lost "social faith." For the men and women behind *The Commonweal*, artistic creation must aspire to the ideal; to a "recognition of holiness" which was not surface decorum but rather "sublimation—the adventure of being lifted up over nature." The naturalistic pathos of contemporary literature, with its image of man struggling against an indifferent cosmic tide, had corrupted the mysticism of the authentic American romantic. For *The Commonweal*, and especially for George N. Shuster, who became its managing editor in 1928, the American tradition did not stand or fall with Puritanism or pragmatism. The Romantic tradition, impressed by Emerson, was the unifying element of the American past. *The Commonweal* discerned it as a "sacramental view of life. . . ."

> That man lives to expand courageously his vision of reality; that the universe is a garment of God made for his holiday, and not a snare or an illusion; that laughter is the fife of victory and not the shriek of hopelessness—these things have been held sacred in America for 300 years or more.

In the twentieth century American writing lost its grip on this vision. In the face of this malaise, *The Commonweal* was unwilling to entrust the future to the "technological civilization" offered by the group of writers who composed Charles Beard's symposium *Whither Mankind* (1928). The unifying force of technology was chimerical, as was made evident by the destruction it wrought during the war. Technology was simply harnessed energy and was dependent upon man's convictions regarding the nature of human community. It could feed millions, but it could not form an organic society. In the creative literature of the 1920's such technological optimism sounded obscene, and so it did to *The Commonweal*.

Rather than any technological umbrella, *The Commonweal* desired to house the American Romantic's quest for personal and social beatitude within the "organic reality" of Catholicism, where the vulnerable innocence of the romantic might find an "ennobling faith" and a full measure of hope. The energy behind *The Commonweal* was, as its editors described in 1926, "the secret of confidence, of wonder, of that most beautiful thing called innocence." They were involved in an "adventure in quest of a place where the beautiful sacredness of life may be housed." As they conceived it, "the Catholic implications of the American way of life" were that the Romantic's quest for holiness did not have to end in disillusion—that man, though small in the tumult of the universe, could discover in human fellowship and expansive outreach the caress of the divine.

Conversely, "the American implications for the Catholic way of life" were that Catholics must learn to expand their vision of reality beyond the limits imposed by their own rationalism and classicism, to allow man to test the boundaries of his experience, to strive for sanctity rather than settle for the comfort of a secured universe.[12] These implications for Catholic life in America were discerned by only a small number of Catholics and were not impressively evident even in the journal which fostered them. There was, however, another set of implications which many Catholics espoused with some zeal.

One of the more common traits of Catholic thought was its "nostalgic medievalism."[13] For a group which cherished the notion that it was the largest bloc of defenders of the American way of life, and which hoped to see its religion become the moral and intellectual center of American society, the mixture of medievalism with Americanism was at least capable of being misunderstood by others and was a cause of some confusion among themselves. The medieval pull operated in a number of ways. For the great majority, simple nostalgia was the key. While some were anxious to fossilize Catholic expression in Gothic stone, others were more concerned with defending the medieval heritage as one component of a general defense of western values. Underneath much of this medievalism, however, was the feeling that somehow the medieval knight and the optimistic American pioneer were spiritual cousins.

In the early part of the twentieth century Catholics were eager to dress up in something other than immigrant rags. The Middle Ages provided a memory of a golden age of Catholic influence and power and a source of pride which mitigated the ambivalence of their transition from poverty to cultural influence and wealth. In this atmosphere James J. Walsh's *The Thirteenth: Greatest of Centuries* (1907) tickled Catholic nostalgic sensibilities for half a century. Walsh (1865–1942) was a doctor by profession, but was more aptly described by Cardinal Hayes of New York as "the Catholic knight." His extravagant claim that the thirteenth century had done "more for human progress than . . . any like period in human history" rested on a desire to picture Catholicism as the inspirational element in the creation of universities, trade schools, libraries, Gothic architecture, literature, art, and the early beginnings of democratic liberties. The book was hailed by reviewers because it allowed Catholics to "lift up their heads" in a society which many times confused their religion with cultural impoverishment.[14]

The sense of nostalgia for past glory led to displays such as that of Daniel Lord, S.J. in his multimedia production of "The Battle Called Life" at the 1928 meeting of the National Catholic Alumni Federation in New York City. Lord, who worked as a religious adviser for Cecil B. DeMille's cinema spectacular *King of Kings,* specialized in producing for Catholics his own kind of pageantry. Lord had the meeting room designed as a medieval collegiate banquet hall where, through a host of actors, film, and slides, "the treasures of Catholic principles and Catholic culture were brought before the audience." The highlight of the program was the procession of men in medieval dress, bearing shields with the names of the great universities of Europe founded by the Church during the Middle Ages. If the program had ended there it would have been simply a pageant of innocent nostalgia. In the final episode, however, Lord drew a lesson. In the rejection of the faith by the modern world, he dramatized the concomitant weakening of loyalty to the country. The scene ended with the actors calling upon Catholics to fight valiantly for "cross and flag." Such patriotic nonsense was not uncommon, but the intertwining of medievalism and Americanism had definite implications for American Catholic thought and culture.[15]

Supporting their own sense of medievalism, a large group of Catholics was bowled over by the Gothic hypnotism of Ralph Adams Cram, a scion of New England genteel sophistication. Cram affirmed on various occasions that "all the Christian Art of the world is the product of Catholicism, and the greatest single work of art man has ever brought into being is a Pontifical High Mass sung in a Gothic Cathedral or church." Many Catholics, seduced by such statements, believed with Cram that the use of art forms like jazz music, impressionism in painting, cubism in sculpture, free verse in poetry, and even reinforced concrete in church construction was sacrilegious. Cram wanted the Church to stand firm "in the midst of whirling eddies of chance and change." The medieval Gothic ideal, according to one Catholic, was the Christian ideal, which had the devilish gargoyles on the outside while the saints kept vigil within. To build churches with "blocks of obscene concrete reinforced by Bessemer steel" only gave the "appearance of stability to the crumbling work of a vanishing age." Reinforced concrete symbolized the egoism and self-seeking of modern life.[16]

Only a few Catholics found Cram's efforts to fossilize Catholic expression in Gothic grey "ill-advised nonsense." It took an English writer, Donald Attwater, to point out the historical inaccuracy of speaking of Catholicism as the mother of the arts. The Church was, rather, a "giant consumer," and not always a very discriminating one. It was also Attwater who asked what would seem an unnecessary question: "How can concrete be obscene or natural stone chaste?"[17] The hypnotic suggestion of Catholic medievalism, reinforced by non-Catholic custodians of genteel culture, made such a question at once necessary and difficult for American Catholics to answer. Besides looking to the Middle Ages as a source of pride or as a manual for Church construction, many reflected on the period in an effort to find out "how to live."[18]

As Catholics observed the decline in American optimism and self-confidence in cultural expression, they offered their medieval heritage as a "guide to a world crying and struggling for intellectual, moral, and political peace." The missionary mentality of Catholic medievalism would supply for the modern world a "fullness of life," a sense of proportion, and an "unshakeable scheme of values."[19] In this view, Catholics did not desire a return to the Middle Ages but a resurrection of its spirit as a Catholic contribution to rejuvenate the pioneer optimist turned inward and bewildered. Ross Hoffman's passage from disillusioned liberalism to Catholicism expressed this mood, and his effort to reconstruct the medieval spirit for contemporary culture was an example of how Catholics hoped to use medievalism to preserve American innocence.

Hoffman's religious autobiography, *Restoration* (1934), was addressed, as he said, to the modern whose skepticism diminished his "capacity for action and decision"; to the postwar world where "basic certainties and a general optimism about the trend of things have given way to uncertainty and a vast measure of pessimism." His own impasse of mind was broken by "coming to grips with the mighty twelfth and thirteenth centuries." The medieval period represented to him a "fresh world" of "vigor . . . health . . . passion, heroism and hard thinking." It was a world of "fists and brains," where order and harmony did not preclude cultural variety and a defiance of pattern. The medieval man Hoffman discovered had a sense of being a "creative organ" with confidence in his reasoning abilities. His universe was "obedient to discernible principles of order." Hoffman's medieval world was not too far removed from the one inhabited by most Americans of the eighteenth and early nineteenth centuries.[20]

In contrast to the roaming and thirsting mind of Herman Hesse's *Steppenwolf* or the frustrated hopes of Joseph Wood Krutch, the Catholic mission was to recall for the modern his confidence "in a knowable universe, in the knowing powers of the mind." Catholic medievalism was basically modern but not contemporary. For Hoffman, the Catholic was "almost the last rationalist left in the world today . . .":

> Nowhere is rational philosophy so completely at home as in the Church, which insists that reason is man's special gift and mark from God and bids men trust it and use it freely and effectively as they can for discovering and appreciating the wonders of God's work.

The Catholic mind, according to Hoffman, bid the modern world to return "to a simple acceptance of the reality of things, to an acknowledgment that the world is real and that our intellects can know it and read its meaning." Such blatant confidence in man's rational abilities coming from a Catholic would probably have stunned Voltaire and Thomas Jefferson. For Krutch, however, the twentieth-century reassertion of this medieval spirit was the result of "a certain desperation" among men to arrange a world harmonious with their desires.[21]

Even though Hoffman believed his acceptance of Catholicism restored his sense of action and bearings in society, there was a certain despairing quality to his later political thoughts. His advocacy of an authoritarian, "monarchical" or "military" concept of the state brought him dangerously close to advocating a brand of fascism under the guise of defending the community good from "predatory and corrupting enemies of every sort." Although he praised the medieval man for his "defiance" of pattern," Hoffman would quash freedom of discussion if it veered from what he considered to be the principles of truth. Furthermore, he came to the conclusion that Catholics should disassociate themselves from medievalism because in Catholic tradition "the classical inheritance [was] prized more than the Gothic." In the concerted effort to ransack tradition for contemporary purposes, Hoffman led himself and others into some confusion. His eventual rejection of the medieval "logical point of view" in favor of the "psychological" view of Augustine, anticipated a development in Catholic thought in the 1950's, when a number of Catholics abandoned the technological-medieval approach to reality for a more personal but less secure role in the labyrinth of the universe.[22]

However, before World War II the medieval tradition was used with some success by Catholics intent on forging a link between their heritage as Catholics and as Americans. What they perceived to be the spirit of medievalism was the "pioneer" sense of facing a wilderness with the firm conviction that it could be mapped and successfully civilized. Thus, the editors of *The Commonweal* hoped to bring to the attention of America the two impulses of the Catholic mind: "the conservative and the conquering." What the country needed in its time of doubt was "a frank acceptance of the

Catholic attitude toward America." This was, as they expressed it, "a profound conviction that basic truths are young after 500 or 5,000 years; and . . . a brave trust that humanity can master new conditions and even a new self."[23] Despite efforts like Hoffman's to take the desire for mastery into some reactionary avenues, most Catholics were simply preoccupied with the assumption that the medieval peasant and the American pioneer shared a common universe of values.

The pull of the Middle Ages upon the Catholic imagination was a yearning to stay in touch with the world of innocence. That world, as Catholics imagined it, was an arena of vigorous activity where craftsmen built gracious cathedrals in anonymity, with no desire for personal recognition. Natural stone was undefiled by artificial reinforcement. Man still carved and created. With his "fists and brains" he employed his genius to conquer his physical, spiritual, and cosmic environment, circumscribing all three by natural laws, which, once discovered by his rational powers, became the instruments of his domination. The reality which he perceived was found to be good and provided meaning for both his laughter and his tears. The medieval man lived in a state of social and political happiness uncluttered by doubts. There existed what George Shuster described as the "spiritualization of democracy" if not a political realization. The medieval world of innocence was used by Catholics to reinforce their own developing sense of American innocence. After World War I, in a variety of ways, Catholics improvised the links which bound this spiritual democracy of the medieval world to its political realization in America at the end of the eighteenth century.

Leonard Feeney wrote of the evening in 1928 when it became evident that Alfred E. Smith had lost his bid for the presidency to Herbert Hoover, as "the night of sixteen million tragedies." Although later examinations of the election tend to downplay religion as the major element in Smith's defeat, Catholics in 1928 were unprepared for the anti-Catholic hysteria that surfaced. After an initial shock to their enthusiasm, it would appear that a tone of defiance settled upon Catholics. James Gillis spoke for many when he asserted: "We shall not wither up and blow away. . . ."[24] Despite the obvious setback to the confident belief that Catholics held the key to American promise, the 1928 election did not diminish their persistent pursuit of welding Catholicism to America.

Throughout the nineteenth-century Catholics responded to charges that their religion was inimical to the democratic way of life with a defensive rhetoric and an almost automatic willingness to prove their loyalty by supporting the nation's wars, even the unjust ones. World War I was no exception. However, the war and the intellectual ferment which surrounded it brought many Catholics to the realization that their former rhetoric could be replaced by philosophical and historical arguments which proved not only that Catholicism was not foreign to democracy, but that it had, in fact, helped to shape the political traditions appealed to by the founders of the Republic. This more sophisticated turn of Catholic identification with America was begun by Gaillard Hunt, a librarian of Congress, who published in 1917 an essay in the *Catholic Historical Review* which sought to trace the intellectual indebtedness of the Declaration of Independence to Robert Bellarmine, S.J., and the scholastic philosophy of the Middle Ages. Hunt's claims rested on the fact that Thomas Jefferson had in his library Robert Filmore's *Patriachia* (1680), which summarized Bellarmine's thought on popular sovereignty. To Hunt, Bellarmine's doctrine that government was the result of the consent of the people suspiciously resembled Jefferson's phraseology in the Declaration.[25]

Following Hunt, Catholic writers toiled in dusty tomes tracing references in the works of obscure British and medieval political theorists. From Alexander Hamilton, James Madison, James Wilson, and Thomas Jefferson, at least, in the Declaration of Independence, the trail of footnotes led to John Locke's *Two Treatises on Government* (1688) and to Algernon Sidney's *Discourses Concerning Government* (1698). Pursuing the trail of references beyond these English Whigs, Catholics discovered that Locke referred to Bellarmine and Thomas Aquinas and that Sidney referred to Bellarmine and Francisco Suárez, S.J. Other sources of the Whig tradition were pursued to Henry de Bracton's thirteenth-century work *De Legibus et Consuetudinibus Angliae* and John Fortescue's *De Laudibus Legum Angliae*. Besides theorists, Catholics examined medieval coronation oaths, which bound in contract both the governors and the governed, as well as the notion that the basis of English common law was medieval canon law.[26]

Initially, this labor of mind was intent on tracing the direct, even literal, borrowing of Catholic tradition by the framers of the Declaration of Independence and the Constitution. By paralleling passages from Aquinas, Bellarmine's *De Controversiis* and *De Summo Pontifice,* as well as Suárez's *Defensio Fidei Catholicae* and *De Legibus* with the Declaration of Independence, Catholics went beyond their previous assertions that their religious traditions conformed to American political doctrine. It was now asserted that the ideology of the revolution "derives directly from Catholicism." Accustomed to being accused of mixed allegiance, they took no little delight in proclaiming: "democracy, a 'popish' innovation" and Catholicism "the mother of democracy."[27] However, the case for direct relationship relied on rather slim evidence and was soon questioned and then dismissed by Catholics themselves.[28]

An individual who spent the two decades of the interwar period preaching the association of Catholic thought with the political philosophy of the

founders of the nation was the Jesuit Moorhouse F. X. Millar (1886–1956).
With his mother, he became a Catholic in 1896. After some early training
by the Jesuits in Tours, France, he entered that order in 1903 and began
teaching history at Fordham University in 1920. Millar's historical imagination was blunt-edged. He rejected all deterministic, naturalistic, and
evolutionistic theories of the past. History was the result "of the interplay
and functioning of men's intellects and wills working against a background
of fact." The historian was thus charged with the responsibility of passing
judgment on the truth or falsehood of those ideas. The historical fodder for
Millar's judgments included almost everything associated with modern
civilization since the Renaissance and Reformation. Despite his penchant
for blaming Luther, Descartes, Bacon, Rousseau, Kant, and others for the
unleashing of the ego, which led to postwar disillusionment and a sense of
futility, he retained an optimistic belief in the dynamic of human history.[29]

Millar was convinced that the institutions of the modern world, such as
democracy, were basically sound because of their dependence on principles
established during the Middle Ages. The problem he saw with contemporary civilization was its "precarious necessity" to exist on those institutions
"without being able to demand a reasonable acceptance of them." The
denial of natural law concepts, inalienable rights, free will, and equality,
which surfaced in the writings of Charles Beard, Carl Becker, and Oliver
Wendell Holmes, Jr., vitiated the vision of those Americans who formulated American democratic institutions. It further appeared to Millar that
Catholics were the "sole heirs by default, to this traditional vision . . .
embodied in our Constitution. . . ."[30]

In contrast to the contemporary discontent, Catholics were certain about
progress because it rested upon Aquinas' and the medieval Christian's
optimism concerning man's search for perfection and rational abilities.
Millar thought the Catholic view of progress best expressed in Robert
Browning's "A Death in the Desert":

. . . man knows partly but conceives beside,
Creeps ever on from fancies to the fact
And in this striving, this converting air
Into a solid he may grasp and use,
Finds progress, man's distinctive mark alone,
Not God's, and not the beasts': God is, they are,
Man partly is and wholly hopes to be.

The modern world had reversed man's role of "converting air into a solid"
by undermining the facts and rendering them as fancies. On the other hand,
the Thomistic analysis of man assured progress. In this scheme, said Millar,

man is able "to rise above and control, dominate and shape his condition and circumstances."[31]

This philosophic thrust was the essential inspiration behind the American ideal of progress. This "living tradition" was inherited by Americans and expressed in the founding documents of the country. The chief agencies for the transfer of this tradition were the Scottish Common Sense school of philosophy and English Whig political theorists of the seventeenth and eighteenth centuries. Millar was uncertain whether Hamilton, Madison, Wilson, and Jefferson depended directly on medieval sources or indirectly through the above agencies. He was quite certain, though, that they expressed "the Medieval and Christian norm of all just government."[32] Vitiating his historical control, however, was an extreme prejudice which prevented Millar from accepting the fact that Calvinist thought, Rousseau, and "the empty moonshine of the French Enlightenment" played a significant role in forming the ideology of the Constitution and Declaration of Independence. Millar idolized Alexander Hamilton and Edmund Burke and was unwilling to admit influences other than the more conservative strains of Federalist or Whig thought, which sought to proscribe the radical individualism of Calvinism and the "Epicurean atomism" of Jefferson by associating liberty with obligations and the authoritative power of the state.[33]

During the Depression, though, Millar translated this perspective into support for the New Deal. He found Herbert Croly's *Promise of American Life* (1907) in line "with our best Constitutional tradition." Despite Croly's sense that democracy rested not so much on Aristotelian forms as it did on the infusion of moral spirit into society as a response to the irrational needs of mankind, Millar was more interested in Croly's Hamiltonian bias toward an activist and even authoritarian concept of the state. The proper function of government, said Millar, agreeing with Croly, was "to provide for the common good by *maintaining* and *promoting* unity, order, stability, security, liberty, peace, and progress, and this by means of a really binding, or properly authoritative, and edifying, or duly *directive* public policy." After World War I, when Croly became disillusioned with his own thought, Millar and other Catholics responded to his *Promise* because it appealed to their developing confidence that man as well as government was still capable of controlling and directing the forces about him.[34]

The difference was that Millar viewed the Constitution in the light of what he considered to be a genuine intellectual tradition. Ideas such as inalienable rights, equality, government by consent, and separation of powers, had validity because they were fundamental to human nature. They were not, as he thought many contemporary American intellectuals maintained, merely "forces" or expressive of "emotional tendencies." To the founding fathers they were self-evident truths. For Millar and the Catholic body as a whole they remained so:

> They were not afflicted with any of our present day cosmic qualms. . . . They knew their own minds and had a well reasoned and reasonable belief in divine Providence, which very naturally relieved them from any sense of responsibility for the universe as a whole, as well as from any fear lest somewhere behind every certainty in their own minds, it might still be playing tricks . . . they knew that whatever the abuses of men might be, the universe itself remained reasonable and that man himself was reasonably made.[35]

Millar's most sustained investigation of the relationship between Catholic philosophy and the American Constitution appeared in 1922 with his three essays which comprise the greater part of the book he wrote with John A. Ryan, *The State and the Church*. When a new edition of the book was published in 1940 his essays were deleted, ostensibly because of their unsuitability for use in a college textbook. The new edition, in fact, presumed much of Millar's historical connections in its exposition of Catholic political principles.[36] However, Millar's tendency in those essays toward the literal relationship between Bellarmine and Jefferson, and his denials that French Enlightenment and Calvinist sources had anything to do with American ideology, were no longer viable tenets for many Catholics, and seemed to exhibit an extreme defensiveness. The atmosphere in which Millar began his explorations in the 1920's accounted for many of his vagaries. It was felt by most Catholics, as Wilfred Parsons noted after Al Smith's defeat in 1928, that:

> The country was founded by non-Catholics on political principles which we recognize as Catholic, but somewhere along the line the American tradition was forgotten and is now in a sort of somersault, presented to us by some as essentially Protestant, and by others as derived from French free-thinkers. In either case, we are treated as strangers in our own land.

This feeling spurred them, as another Catholic put it, to "a crusade to recapture the holy land of our Nation's birth from modern political pagans." Examples of the latter, they thought, were Beard, Becker, Robinson, and Holmes, who variously denied or were skeptical about such abstract concepts as the natural law, self-evident truths, and inalienable rights.[37] But by the late 1930's, even Millar had noticed a shift in American political thinking, especially by Beard and Becker, toward a less skeptical view of the cultural, spiritual, and intellectual traditions of American democracy, a shift noted with approval by Catholics.[38]

Furthermore, Catholics were beginning to realize that even Calvinism and the French Enlightenment could be viewed within the spirit of their own traditions. In the mid-thirties James J. Walsh's *Education of the Founding Fathers of the Republic* brought to the intellectual community in general the importance of the medieval and Scholastic framework of colonial and early nineteenth-century American education. By examining commencement broadsides and thesis sheets which students at Harvard, Yale, Princeton, Columbia, the University of Pennsylvania, and Brown College defended upon graduation, Walsh noted striking similarities not only to the thesis he had defended at graduation from St. John's College (Fordham) in 1884 but to those defended at Boston College in 1930. In addition, the commencement broadsides indicated that the principal subjects of study, the classics, and, especially, the emphasis on mental and moral philosophy during the last two years of instruction, were equally in conformity with the Catholic scholastic tradition.[39] In another book Walsh maintained that even though the Catholic Charles Carroll of Carrollton received his education in Europe from the Jesuits, for all practical purposes it was the same as that of his fellow framers of the Constitution, who had been educated in America.[40]

Such discoveries had two effects. First, they confirmed Catholics in their own highly formal rational and abstract educational theories, which were proven to be not only Catholic but American. Only by stressing the classical and rational could innocence be preserved when faced with the complexities of life. The problems attendant upon a universe of relativity and a democracy in the throes of a depression remained for Catholics solvable problems, because they were not the result of "automatic forces" but rather of "human free choices," which their Catholic education, philosophy, and literature emphasized, and which the upwardly mobile environment (which was the promise of America) seemed to require.[41] Secondly, such investigations as Walsh's indicated that Puritanism, and even to some extent the Enlightenment, were not the spiritual and religious wastelands they had previously thought them to be.

It was possible by the mid-1930's for Catholics not to deny Protestantism or even the Enlightenment their cultural role in the shaping of America. As Benjamin Masse expressed it in 1935, both were the chief sources of American culture. Though they formed an unstable compound, in Catholicism they were made integral:

> The characteristic doctrines of Calvin are truths as old as Catholic Europe. . . . Liberalism plucked some of the finest flowers of Catholic

tradition. The brotherhood of man, the Fatherhood of God, the idea of liberty, the belief in the inherent value of the individual, confidence in reason, the dream of progress and perfection, and upon them attempted to found a new and brighter order.

Catholicism was for Masse the instrument to restore "the new and brighter order" that was the American vision. Wilfred Parsons, S.J., felt a "natural affinity" toward the early Puritans:

> The modern intelligent Catholic finds himself drawing ever more closely to American cultural origins at the same time that his fellow non-Catholic Americans are disavowing those origins with almost indecent haste. A strange turn of history has brought it about that the very Catholics who were hated and persecuted by the old Puritans, now find themselves looking back upon them with something approaching affection, or, at least, with a sort of nostalgic and sympathetic understanding.

The Reformation was not a complete break with Catholicism, Parsons argued; therefore, it was possible to accept the Protestant origins of America. In a variety of attitudes the Puritans continued to be Catholic. Contemporary disillusionment with, and the disintegration of, American culture was the result, according to Parsons, of overlaying a newly acquired "social, literary, educational and philosophical culture which is essentially naturalistic and positivistic . . . on juridical and poetical forms and institutions that are essentially Christian and metaphysical in their origin."[42]

The new understanding did much to further Catholic ecumenism as it expanded Catholics' historical and political horizons. All the footnote tracing and ransacking of medieval, Whig, and Scottish sources brought many Catholics and even other Americans by the 1940's to the awareness that the ideology of the American Revolution was an inheritance of many centuries of European thought, of which the Scholastic and medieval was one component, but that it included others, such as the French Enlightenment, John Locke, Calvinism, and even Jean Jacques Rousseau. It also dawned on more than a few that the ideology of the Declaration of Independence was more than a defense of rational certitude; it was a primary source of American reform—from the abolition of slavery to universal education, trade unions, women's rights, child labor laws, and social security, to name a few.[43]

The trail of footnotes culminated in the thought of John Courtney Murray, S.J. Operating on the foundations built by Millar and others, Murray raised the conjunction of Catholic tradition and American polity to a level of sophistication unmatched by his predecessors. Many of his ideas were developed in the context of the 1940's and 1950's, and, eventually published in *We Hold These Truths* (1960), earned him a *Time* magazine cover story. In the post-World War II intellectual atmosphere of "consensus" history and the "end of ideology," Murray's assertion that the American political tradition was based on a broad consensus of ideas and a pragmatic manipulation of them to fit the American experience sounded neither queer nor defensive.[44] As he explained the American system, it was "an ensemble of substantive truths, a structure of basic knowledge, an order of elementary affirmations that reflect realities in the order of existence." If his concept of consensus resonated for others in the milieu of the 1950's, Murray's thought was definitely shaped in the post–World War I context of the Catholic survival of innocence.

For Murray, the path of twentieth-century American thought was largely a defection from the consensus that had created in America "a climate of doubt and bewilderment in which clarity about the larger aims of life is dimmed and the self-confidence of the people is destroyed." At the same time, Murray believed, "the guardianship of the original American consensus" was passed to the Catholic community. He was convinced that Catholic participation in the American proposition "has been full and free, unreserved and unembarrassed, because the contents of this consensus—the ethical and political principles drawn from the traditions of the natural law—approve themselves to the Catholic intelligence and conscience."[45] To this point Murray's contentions were to a great extent simply a more sophisticated rendering of the Catholic thought which preceded him.

But Murray also discovered that the implications of the American consensus enabled Catholicism to accept the doctrines of separation of church and state and religious freedom in principle: not, as Ryan and Millar had previously argued, from expediency. According to Murray, the American consensus, resting on the foundation of classic western political thought, limited and divided governmental powers, allowing religion to pursue its own ends without threat of interference. Murray's justification of religious liberty, as David O'Brien has pointed out, was built not on "traditional theological or ecclesiological perspectives but from the viewpoint of political theory" which enabled him to solve a universal Catholic problem with American resources.[46] Murray successfully brought to bear these "American implications for the Catholic way of life" not only in this country, but also at Vatican Council II, where much of his thought was incorporated into the Declaration on Religious Liberty.

Though there was some dissent before the 1960's on Murray's conclusions concerning the principle of religious freedom, Catholics were nearly unanimous in their support of his other assertions.[47] They believed that they held the key to American self-confidence and optimistic idealism amid a world of doubt and bewilderment. For the great majority, this key was the rational sense of certitude, emphasis on logic and discipline, and reliance on a view of reality structured to the desires and intelligence of man. In their reading of history, this was the thrust of Catholic tradition and also the primary impulse behind American democracy. This mode of thought, it was felt, guaranteed their upward social striving and provided them the cultural goal of "re-Americanizing America." While this was understood to be their unique opportunity to contribute to American cultural expression, it imposed upon the Catholic community the necessity of living in "glorious isolation" from much of American thought from Emerson to John Dewey.

It was necessary to remain aloof not only from what was frankly skeptical but also from what appeared to be vulnerable to disillusionment. By stressing universals, abstract and symmetrical designs, and the rational intelligibility of the universe, Catholics saw themselves and their cultural effort to be "lantern-bearers" to American society, carrying messages of future progress and enduring optimism.[48] The optimistic tone of much of Catholic thought, however, appeared superficial because it seemed to be more concerned with immunizing itself from complexity than with entering into contemporary experience.

Just prior to World War II an individual appeared with an approach to Catholic traditions and the American experience which sought to move Catholic culture out of isolation, if not out of innocence. Robert C. Pollock, a young, adventuresome assistant professor of philosophy at Fordham University, applied himself to the familiar task of discovering the "implications" of the Catholic and American experience. Though it is difficult to draw many conclusions from only two essays, "The Challenge of Secularism to America" (1939) and "Catholic Philosophy and American Culture" (1942), Pollock's approach in these essays is sufficiently singular in its direction to warrant investigation.[49]

The first essay could be more accurately described as the challenge of America to Catholicism. For Pollock, the rise of secularism, which he defined as absolutizing rationalism, naturalism and materialism, was primarily the result of a parallel separation and dualism in the Catholic mind between "formal religious life and life in the world." This has led to "passivity and social inertia . . . to the Platonic one-sidedness characteristic of too many Catholics who loftily brush aside real technical social problems with the glittering generality that economic anarchy is 'but an exterior sign of deep internal anarchy of spirit and intellect.' " Opposed to this dualism, he thought, was the historical record of "integral Catholicism." One of the greatest historical effects of Christianity, Pollock said, was that it freed man to involve himself in nature. This process Pollock called the "institutionalization of the intelligence." Recalling the Middle Ages, which seemed to be a prerequisite to holding an audience, Pollock took a different tack. In his perspective, the cathedrals were "engineering feats" which expressed the desire to institutionalize both ideas and nature by cramming the structure with natural artifacts. This craving was philosophically expressed in Thomism, which taught man to love things in themselves and not as means to an end, even the end of loving God. The "autonomy of the natural" in the Renaissance and modern worlds was a further development of this Christian insight of affirming the natural order.

Since the Middle Ages, though, Catholics have tended to retreat from the natural order altogether. Pollock used as an example the Catholic response to Gerard Manley Hopkins, who sought to integrate the two orders by combining a passion for the particular and the material with a religious view of life. As Pollock pointed out, Catholic critics nevertheless "viewed the twofold aspect in Hopkins as a sign of internal conflict between Hopkins the Catholic and Hopkins the man."

America represented for Pollock the political and institutional embodiment of Christian ideals which remained unrealized until the end of the eighteenth century. Aware that American secularism had its ugly and dehumanized corruptions, Pollock still found its democratic tradition, as expressed for example in its literary history, to be "an articulation of human freedom and human dignity," and more recently "an implacable war upon everything which obscures the many-sidedness of human personality. . . ."

"In America," Pollock continued:

> society is constantly being leavened from the bottom up. . . . That is why . . . despite the terrible corruptions of American life, the dream of the people's commonwealth which will serve human and not material ends has never lost its force. . . . For somehow the democratic ideal makes it impossible for the people to know rest until it receives its richest expression and fullest embodiment. Our people are restless with a restlessness which is extraordinarily meaningful. They have been described as a capturable people; as a people who are open to all the possibilities and, therefore, as a people who can only be captured high.

Viewed from America the secular impulse lost many of its terrifying aspects. Concluding the first essay, Pollock urged Catholics to begin affirming values they had neglected in the past.

The note struck by Pollock was a distinctly different approach to the problem of secularization from that which other Catholic intellectuals had taken. This can best be appreciated by comparing his essay to the companion contributions to the National Catholic Alumni Federation's symposium *Man and Modern Secularism: Essays on the Conflict of Two Cultures* (1940). While Pollock emphasized the Catholic retreat from the natural, others (for example, Ross Hoffman, Louis J. A. Mercier, Wilfred Parsons, and Robert I. Gannon) were intent on blaming everything from the Protestant Reformation to the "naive impertinence" of John Dewey for the breakup of the two orders of reality. Again, while Pollock urged the affirmation of nature and the embodiment of ideas, Mercier spoke of the supernatural "at war" with the natural and Wilfred Parsons called for the "subjugation" of nature by the supernatural through man. "The whole point," said Parsons, "about the Christian revolution is this: that man dominates the forces of nature by that simultaneous raising up of the human and the natural, and at the same moment placing it under subjection to something else."[50] The most apparent contrast between Pollock and the others is his critical approach and the note of self-complacency characteristic of the rest of the symposium.

Pollock saw America as symbolizing the restless urge of man to extend himself into nature and embody his ideals in institutions. There was a certain amount of danger and risk involved in this venture because the very restlessness which motivated the extension was vulnerable to corruption and disillusionment. Contrary to his fellow Catholics who sought to preclude the possibility of corruption by defining America with "glittering generalities," Pollock was more attuned to its restless possibilities. These ideas were expanded on in his second essay, in which he sought to re-express Catholic traditions for Americans and redefine America for Catholics.

The distinctive qualities of American culture, it seemed to Pollock, were its restless energy, need of action, power of practical observation, hunger for the novel, keen inventiveness, and a "certain irrepressible ideality in regard to human possibilities, individual and social." The general desire to achieve a continuity between thought and experience had led to a "distrust of speculative reason," which, to some extent, blinded the American mind "to the nature of man taken in his plenitude and to the rich deliverances of human consciousness." Unlike others before him, Pollock was intent on facing the effort to link thought and action squarely and seeing it as a "positive and real" thing, not to be lightly dismissed. Examples of the American mind at its best were Emerson and William James, especially the latter. Both men express the desire to seize the singular and concrete rather than the abstract. Experience was a preparation for thought leading to visions of truth and beauty.

Emerson anticipated James in what Pollock described as his "feeling for the profundity of things, a never failing appreciation of the infinite significance of the moment, which like eternity itself is unfathomable, and a deep sense of the miraculous character of phenomena that reveals itself in sudden flashes." In men like Emerson, Pollock saw "the impulse toward embodiment" and the "drive towards the reconstruction of life and the creation of a new world, which is the spring and source of the American quest for concreteness, even in philosophy." Thus, William James personified the American mind past and present, spanning Calvinism, evangelistic millenialism, and transcendentalism. James combined a spontaneous impulsiveness with a "compassionate and religious nature." According to Pollock, he was "full of the marvel of existence. Reality is richer than essence, and existence has priority over knowledge." His pluralistic approach to reality included the logical but distrusted general ideas and fought against an "arid rationalism." He desired a creative relationship with the world designed to realize the good. To him the world was "incomplete and full of endless possibilities." Pollock responded to accusations that James simply made success and relevance the criterion of truth as "muddling thought."

Rather than simply brushing aside this thrust of the American mind, as other Catholics were wont to do, Pollock saw a continuity between aspects of the Catholic tradition and American pragmatism. In a surprising twist he attempted a comparison between James and Chesterton. Both, he felt, had a passionate "sensitivity to existence" and an abhorrence of "intellectuality detached from life," which was merely "light without heat." The essence of Chesterton's vision of the Christian life was symbolized by the "irregular equilibrium" and "asymmetrical balance" of Gothic architecture. For most Catholics the essence of the medieval spirit was its geometric orderliness; but for Pollock, symmetrical balance was really classical and Greek, not medieval. In fact, there was little balance at all, but rather a design "wherein the most apparently antithetical elements can co-exist, faith and reason, love and logic, contemplation and action, theory and practice, understanding and willing, a passionate love of the abstract and just as passionate a love of the concrete."[51]

In a digression Pollock pointed to the interesting paradox of Henry Adams, who despaired of a world of blind and wild power but who was fascinated by medieval Catholic life for its "quest for novelty," "appetite for living," and belief that love was above logic. To Pollock these were the very traits active in the American culture on which Adams had turned his back. Pollock recalled Adams writing of the " 'peril of the heavy tower, of the restless vault, of the vagrant buttress' " and was reminded of "the distinctive American traits, the love of risk and adventure, an incurable restlessness and a liking for going off at tangents." Pollock's imaginative use of Catholic sources was striking in a group that generally thought the highlight of the medieval aspiration was to make tangents impossible and life placid and untroubled.

Pursuing the relationship between Catholicism and America further, Pollock quoted Whitehead's description of western intelligence as the "deliberate formation of institutions." Western man's "incarnational mentality," said Pollock, was the desire to see "the idea embodied and the ideal concretized." Rejecting Dewey's assertion that traditional thought led to a " 'morality of acquiescence,' " he claimed that those traditions were in fact the very impetus behind Dewey's own instrumentalist philosophy:

> Christianity from its first moment proved itself to be a force for building up and determining history, for deep within the Christian spirit was an obligation to bring things to perfection, to complete the universe, to accelerate the world's movement to its end, and to release and summon into action its latent forces. . . . It brought men to see that it is not enough to gather the universe together in concept for things must also be brought together in reality, wholeness must be realized in fact as well as in idea.

James's pragmatism, Dewey's and Whitehead's instrumentalism, were the most recent embodiments of Christian incarnationalism, and America as the "people's commonwealth" symbolized it in terms of national objectives.

For Pollock, American Catholics occupied an advantageous position in relation to this genius. It was necessary, however, in order for Catholics to recognize their relationship to American concretism, to have a "total repossession of our tradition." A total repossession would require Catholics to accept their tradition as something more than the scholastic, systematic, logical, and metaphysical point of view. It in fact also contained the Augustinian "profound awareness of historical and psychological realities," with its view of man as an actual and concrete being situated in history. In possession of both forces, Catholics might then respond more openly and creatively to the "rareness" of James even while they provided the "philosophical penetration into the nature of things" necessary, he felt, to rescue both James's pragmatism and Dewey's instrumentalism from being "left hanging in the air."

In the context of Catholic thought in America, from Junipero Serra in the California missions to Archbishop John Carroll, its first national bishop, to the mid-nineteenth-century converts Orestes Brownson and Isaac Hecker, to the Americanists Archbishop John Ireland and Cardinal James Gibbons, and even to John Courtney Murray, Pollock's essays mark a significant *tour de force* in the use of Catholic traditions and a veritable *bouleversement* in their approach to America. If, as Murray claimed in 1960, Catholic participation in America was full, free, and unembarrassed, this was carefully circumscribed to the "glittering generalities" expressed in the Declaration of

Independence and the Constitution, which coincided remarkably with their own intellectual habit of universalizing whatever they touched. To the America represented by Emerson and James, Catholics had registered varying degrees of shock and simplistic rejection, preferring to see the democratic tradition these men expressed as an aberration from the norm. Pollock was one of the first Catholics to use this tradition creatively and to find in it something more than anarchy of thought.

On the other hand, Pollock remained within the general atmosphere of American Catholic thought between 1920 and 1940. His attention to medieval sources was characteristic of nearly every Catholic who wrote during the period. Even though he used those sources in a more imaginative and refreshing way, the urge to repossess tradition was universal among Catholics and had a specific purpose. Also characteristic was the return to pre–World War I American sources. Here again, Pollock did not limit himself as most Catholic writers did to the pre-1840's. However, the recovering of American cultural materials before World War I, as well as the recovery of medieval materials, was fundamental to the Catholic effort to recapture and preserve American innocence in the context of post–World War I disillusionment.

Regardless of the distortions and evident romanticizing of the medieval and American past, the cultural impulse of Catholic thought was rooted in the desire to hold on to American optimism and confidence from the threat of corruption in whatever way it could. The emotional interplay between the medieval image of a vigorous world of "fists and brains", and the Whig sense of order and decorum, and the harmonious Enlightenment universe of clear and distinct natural laws, and the romantic version of the universe as "a garment of God made for man's holiday" and, finally, the pragmatists' world of "endless possibilities," all helped in varying degrees to preserve for Catholics the optimistic promise of America.[52] Millar's and Murray's concept of America as resting on common assent to self-evident truths or Pollock's more concrete but no less ideal vision of the "people's commonwealth," though dissimilar in approach, relied on a common assumption (which after World War I was no longer taken for granted by a significant number of Americans) that such an ideal could be rationally, experientially, or emotionally realized "this side of paradise."

The major thrust of Catholic culture moved in the direction of rationally certifying or sentimentally assuming optimism and confidence and thereby gaining its cultural opportunity to reconstruct America after the war. Before Pollock, another ripple in this ocean of rationalism and sentimentalism was George N. Shuster, a born and bred Catholic intellectual who managed to be both troubled and hopeful.

5. George N. Shuster
A Romantic in a Pasture of Logicians

It is at the end of both necessity and passion that the life of
reason is permissible.

George N. Shuster[1]

FRANK SHEED, A TIRELESS ADVOCATE of Catholicism and culture, once
caustically observed: "From the Catholic life and the Catholic vision, it is
something of a shock to come to the Catholic."[2] In considering George
Shuster's efforts to interpret Catholics for Americans and America for
Catholics one's sense of shock is appreciably diminished. His genius rested
upon a graceful power for discrimination which, more than any other
quality of thought, was sorely missing among Catholics of his generation.
Toiling for a group which, at times, sounded to him "like a blend of
D.A.R., Bruce Barton, and a random devotee of Torquemada," Shuster's
path was often one of lonely isolation. His distinctiveness was acknowledged in a quip at a ceremony honoring him at Fordham University
following World War II when a friend, Father Lawrence McGinley, remarked that "there had been times when there seemed to be two kinds of
Catholics in America—George Shuster and all the others."[3]

The most celebrated instance where Shuster took a view at variance with
the flow of Catholic opinion was his neutral position on the Spanish Civil
War. With the majority of Catholics loudly pro-Franco, Shuster opened
himself to a torrent of criticism and cries of betrayal of the "corporate
influence of Catholicism" in the United States. When Michael Williams
shifted *The Commonweal's* position from neutrality to pro-Franco, Shuster
resigned from the journal, ending his career as a Catholic journalist and
beginning a new one—in education—first as president of Hunter
College—which was interrupted by a military governorship in Germany
following World War II. In 1961, he became assistant to the president at
the University of Notre Dame.[4] His public break with Catholic "corporate
influence" in 1936 was a culmination of an intellectual process begun in the

84

1920's in which Shuster managed to appropriate for himself a distinctive approach to reality, American culture, and Catholic witness. Shuster was not so much concerned with the survival of innocence as he was with the survival of hope, beauty, and human fellowship.

Shuster was born on August 27, 1894, of German parents in Lancaster, Wisconsin. He was educated in Catholic parochial schools, where he learned to appreciate German and Greek literature. His classical bent was eventually employed in what he considered his best book, his doctoral dissertation at Columbia University in 1939, *The English Ode from Milton to Keats*. He had entered Notre Dame in 1912. While reading widely in modern psychology he decided instead on a career in journalism, which, according to his instructors, was the "rainbow's end" of liberal education. Although he refused an officer's commission in World War I, an act of personal defiance toward the "fallacious" reasons Americans entered the war, he nevertheless enlisted, because he could not "reconcile . . . not sharing the burden with others my age." After service in military intelligence he returned to Notre Dame as an English professor in 1919. In 1924 he joined the editorial staff of *The Commonweal*. This venture, though admittedly elitist in patterning itself after the *New Republic*, focused for Shuster his life's goal: "to help Catholics feel intellectually at home in America."[5]

In the early twenties many Catholics shared Shuster's concern but few related to the content of his passion. Politically, Shuster was early attracted to the midwestern populism of Robert LaFollette of Wisconsin and then to the progressivism of Herbert Croly's *Promise of American Life*, which, while a student in college, he had considered to be "God's best gift to America." His liberal political views were balanced, however, by a personal religious problem which he described as a "profound yet pragmatic skepticism." Man, Shuster pondered, "had aspirations to a higher form of being. Why, then, was religion so powerless to transform even its most meticulous practitioners?" Such skepticism made him leery of other techniques to change human nature.[6]

In terms of religious philosophy, he confessed to being "more influenced by Newman, Von Hügel, and Augustine than by St. Thomas." Shuster stood nearly alone in his cool approach to the neo-Thomistic revival that enthralled Catholics after World War I. The principal value Thomism offered to contemporary culture, according to Shuster, was "its deep passion for reality . . . a new love for the things that are and a new understanding of man as a concrete object." This view was counterposed to the more prevalent inclination of American Thomists toward abstraction, order, universality, and an unearthly formalism. Even as Jacques Maritain began to captivate American audiences with his "pure Thomism," Shuster was disposed to question whether Maritain's "map" for the movement of modern Catholicism might not "suffer from too drastic curtailments." Shuster, though sympathetic to Maritain's efforts to restate the "core of the Christian tradition," was concerned that in doing so Maritain sacrificed (except where he was most modern—in his books on the arts) the romantic in favor of the classical. Shuster was convinced that it was only through "modern experience and conjecture" that "flesh and blood" would be added to this core.[7]

Shuster became passionately involved with the direction of modern Catholicism in the midst of World War I. His experiences in Europe during the war affected both his personal and cultural perspective. As he has related, before the war his Catholicism was one of "rules"; afterwards, "I was personally religious, deeply so, but no longer a subservient soul. . . . I found God across all the suffering I had seen." Although he found an element of meaning in the tragedy and suffering of war, he knew of many others who "had lost all vestige of belief, and one could not blame them." In France he also witnessed Catholicism as part of the cultural fabric of Europe, which compensated, he confessed, "for years of living as a member of a cramped minority," in his own country. Impressed by so many ancient "shrines of matchless loveliness," he began to investigate anew the faith which generations before him had felt so deeply.[8]

If for many Americans World War I had the disturbing effect of disrupting patterns of thought, traditional ideals, and one generation from another, for Shuster the experience pressed him to seek in Christianity renewed sources for holding men together. While in Europe he was attracted to the philosophy of Max Scheler, especially the latter's *On the Eternal in Man* (1921). Scheler, thought Shuster, was as radical as the Modernists, but rather than fostering atomism Scheler emphasized "reviving among Christians the sense of immediate contact which is the very definition of social life."[9] Shuster rediscovered Catholicism as "an ancient unifying tradition" bringing together the antinomies of life: the beautiful and the sad, good and evil, the spirit and the flesh, soul and body, and the ideal and the material, while ever proclaiming the "freedom and dignity of man . . . in the interests of heaven." Catholicism endowed life with a "significant order" that was not at all rational or aesthetic but rather liturgical, symbolized in the yearly calendar with its cycle of "penitence and thanksgiving, human restraint and the frenzy . . . of the Divine affection for the created soul."[10]

Shuster's freshly awakened interest in Catholicism was reconfirmed upon his return to the United States from Europe in 1919. On February 12 of that year there appeared a pamphlet, *Social Reconstruction: A General Review of the Problem and Survey of Remedies,* issued by the bishops of the Administrative Committee of the National Catholic War Council. This document set the official position of the Church on a decidedly liberal path toward social reform. Despite protests in some Catholic quarters, where it was judged "socialistic propaganda," and the fact that the bishops program languished throughout the twenties from Catholic apathy, for some it was a blast of fresh air.[11] Shuster was one who judged it "a startlingly magnificent thing" as it marked a critical turning point in the history of American Catholicism. With this document, American Catholics had finally broken their "fast of silence. . . . We have discovered our existence and the times in which we exist." In Shuster's eyes World War I was the vehicle by which American Catholics emerged from their "remoteness" to a deeper "understanding of the continuity of Christian tradition," while the bishops program awakened them to the significance of their own time. In the wake of a war that caused more problems than it solved and unsettled for many the structure of civilization, Shuster saw an ensuing "war for Christendom." Many Catholics were caught up in this battle for civilization but few shared Shuster's sense of discrimination. While the young writer saw many fronts to this combat in the social, political, philosophical, and historical realms, for him literature and art, though "trifles," were "mighty trifles, like grenades."[12]

In examining the body of criticism of literature and art offered by George Shuster from 1917 to the mid-1930's two things should be kept in mind. First, he does not equal the literary depth and range of Edmund Wilson or Van Wyck Brooks. Shuster's varied careers as teacher, journalist, editor, and educator prevented any sustained development as a literary critic. Second, in writing primarily for a Catholic audience he was forced to be more of an "exhorter" for Catholic excellence than a well-seasoned critic. However, what is evident in his writing is a passionate concern for American culture and for Catholic life within it. This concern rose above simple enthusiasm and sought a level of intelligent insight. Alfred Kazin has written that the function of criticism in America established since Robert Walsh and Ralph Waldo Emerson had been "the great American lay philosophy . . . a study of literature inherently concerned with ideals of citizenship, and often less a study of literary texts, than a search for some new and imperative moral order with which American writing could live and grow."[13] Following this tradition, Shuster was intent on bringing a Catholic "moral order" within which American literature might flourish.

As a young man in college in the years before World War I Shuster associated himself with the literary generation that Van Wyck Brooks' *America's Coming of Age* (1915) spurred to a crusade. Shuster perceived the crusade as "the construction of an American community through personality":

> The personality was really that which decided to live, partly through
> poetry and partly through action, into the concrete world of the time,
> reforming that according to the standards constructed by the wedding
> of the ethical and artistic power latent in civilization.

The crusaders attacked conventionalism and brought to America "real"
poetry and literature with "visions of a new social order." Shuster, like
Michael Williams, was fascinated by the new currents of thought swirling
around them at the time; though, unlike Williams, he was not given to fits
of depression or high egoism. Like other young men graduating from
college on the eve of America's entry into the war, he found himself
attracted to the beautiful, impatient with the formal and wooden, and
enjoying a "riotous imagination." He "mooned" over Sherwood Anderson,
"sighed" over Yeats, and "sat up nights" with *Jean-Christophe*.[14]

Shuster's first forays into the literary maelstrom, however, show him to
be a little hesitant about what to make of American "modernity." In three
articles published in the *Catholic World* for the year 1917, Shuster confronted Mark Twain's *Mysterious Stranger*, contemporary poetry, and the
novel. The "utterly pessimistic and depressing" outlook of Twain struck
Shuster as strange in a country whose professed philosophy was practical
optimism. On second glance, though, it was not so strange after all.
Twain's evolution as a writer mirrored the evolution of America in the
nineteenth century: from the simple to the complex; from nature to society
to a cosmos "without horizons, an endless cycle of infinities which we do
not even boast of mastering or being able to master." The imprint of a
century "which built up a supposedly impregnable philosophy and tore it
down again" had marked Twain's writing, eventuating in the *Mysterious
Stranger*, which represented the final "slashing and crumbling of the
Spencerian and Positivist solace." For Shuster, the world appeared in 1917
"at the parting of the ways." On the one side was the "caustic desert" of the
Mysterious Stranger and on the other "the land of the Last Supper."[15]

Shuster found in American poetry of this period evidence of a movement
out of Twain's desert. He found free verse sane and capable of expressing
"the gyrations of contemporary society," but also that it was being used as
an excuse for unutterable "inanity." Edgar Lee Masters' *Spoon River Anthology*, though a powerful story, presented the American village as "an Inferno
of mean, stinted and overfed American rustics" and preached the "most
obvious of platitudes, the existence of the ugly and wicked." Others,
however, like Vachel Lindsay and Robert Frost, were moving beyond the
barren and hungering for the sublime. Shuster characterized Lindsay as a
"spiritual searcher" having "the fervor and ecstasy of Whitman, together
with a boyish enthusiasm, that spent itself in brotherhood." Despite the

oppressive burden of the "tyranny of matter" and the fact that "cynicism walks the streets," Shuster concluded that in a "crowd of buoyant spirits" cynicism was quite alone.[16]

This was not the case with the contemporary novel. Evidence of a "philosophic retreat" disturbed him. Although the contemporary novel had exhibited a new "seriousness," it had become "the laboratory wherein the muscles of human desuetude" were analyzed. Life in the modern novel was asked to be both "enigma and solution," and, consequently, Shuster noted:

> The quest for happiness is in danger. . . . Human nature is not an answer now but a question. Love was a dream so long as fulfillment was expected; it became a problem when there seemed no destiny. In the form of a prologue, labor can appear quite comic, but seen as the denouement, it is sombre, stark and abysmal. . . . We have fallen and it is not quite certain where we are. There is a harrowing eagerness for straws.

To those who took "an optimistic credence in the war" as the arena where blind faith will transform "fields of blood" into a nobler future, Shuster responded: "Is it not rather a presumption? Armed conflict is eradically beastly and vile, and faith that has never been born out of spears is not likely to blossom out of cannon."[17]

By 1918 Shuster had concluded that the "demand of the world is for faith . . . something to live for," and he began his own construction of a response. This response was to combine elements of American cultural tradition and the more ancient traditions of Catholicism. In his mind they were both aspects of the same thing. The young critic-crusader turned to Emerson as an embodiment of what was best in both traditions. Emerson, not surprisingly, was then suffering through an eclipse in his critical reputation, and he was not rescued from the fuzz of sentimentalism which had come to surround him until Van Wyck Brooks' *The Life of Emerson* appeared in 1932. Writers of the thirties began to warm to an appreciation of Emerson in a search for "some new affirmation;" Shuster had looked to him as early as 1918. The message Emerson proclaimed was the "essential beauty and usefulness of life." Modern thought had surrendered both the individual and the beautiful into a "vacuity" and cosmic materialism. While vitality had gradually succumbed to doubt and "smudgy self-complaisance," Shuster pleaded for "the optimism of that man [Emerson]." "We must get back his faith in life, his joy in nature, his smile at the promise of night."[18]

In advancing "optimism" as an antidote for a generation that was "doomed" and "swallowed up" in fatalism, materialism, obscenity, bitterness, and "intellectual and social sloth" Shuster was not advocating a retreat from reality but a continuation of prewar vitality. What concerned him in the postwar twenties was the "downfall of the national moral creed." America, the "new land," had changed its character and become "old." Democratic derision and conflicting opinions had created uncertainty about the "aims of our national existence." This, he said, was cause for alarm: "lest a nation whose search for ideals is so evident, so eager, and so unsatisfactory, should rise in anger and break the shrines while cleansing the stables."[19]

Shuster contrasted Emerson's call to the young of America to be the "nobility of the land," to the present generation of "uprooted intelligence, homeless in its own land." Throughout the twenties Shuster mourned the passing into the "shades" of the "virile" criticism, fiction, and poetry unleashed by *The Smart Set*, *Dial*, and *New Freeman* before the war. The attack on Rotarian shallowness and commercialism associated with H. L. Mencken led to some good results in the discovery of good books and men "under a pile of literary drapery." But for Shuster the problem with the Mencken revolt was that it had "no vast social uprising" to follow it. The continual pillorying of rural stupidities sapped the movement of its strength, causing a death by "inanition on its own mountain." The Mencken mania for exploding popular myths was an example of an elitist "class consciousness . . . the spiritual state of Protestants who have discarded Protestantism; of Puritans who are nauseated with their Puritanism; of Americans who have arrived at the tragic knowledge that they are better than America."[20]

Theodore Dreiser's talents degenerated into crudity for passion's sake, while Sinclair Lewis' "obsession of routine" in America attested to the "nihilistic belief that the source of ecstasy has dried up in the world." As the modernists succeeded in dominating the public they scorned, the public itself reacted by taking on a tone of "confident disillusionment" that was the self-conscious badge of "Mrs. Countryclub" in the twenties. The Rotarian impulse had come full circle. The first-rate literature of the decade, Shuster thought, was losing its "revealing" character and "giving way to the appalling senescence of many a younger man who joined the firm hopefully. It is the cramp of mind which has settled upon the critical promise of Joseph Wood Krutch; in the paralysis of Scott Fitzgerald; and in the cheap soap-box sociology of Sinclair Lewis."[21]

To counteract this "standardization" of American intelligence after the war, Schuster called upon Americans to recover Emerson's freshness in the face of reality. Emerson, however, was only an individual embodiment of a much larger force. This Shuster called the "Catholic spirit." Shuster divined "a Catholic way of living and looking upon life" in art, literature, philosophy, which, taken together, formed the basis of a Catholic culture. The Catholic spirit demanded an understanding of the Christian traditions of European civilization and an acceptance of the principles that developed from them. To be within the purview of this spirit, one did not have to accept the Pope or all the theological formulations of Roman Catholicism. What was necessary was a feeling of connection and fellowship with the Christian heritage of the western culture, if only in a humanistic sense.[22]

For Catholics in the twenties this heritage meant the Middle Ages. There was a certain fanaticism about the Catholic approach to those times from which even Shuster was not immune. Although he recognized "a danger in too strong an affection for medievalism" which rendered the romantic spirit anemic, the circumstances of contemporary life forced him to use the Middle Ages as "a standard of comparison . . . a pattern upon which our national renaissance can be worked out. . . ." For Shuster, the creative impulse of the Catholic spirit was always the spirit seeking expression in matter. During the medieval period romanticism and realism were joined. An artist "could grow dark with the darkness of hell" yet was saved from pessimism "by remembering the connection between laughter and love." The earth was deemed good and life had meaning. That life was often treated with recklessness, and individual rights were violated; nevertheless, the motive power of Christendom was based upon a belief in the freedom of the will, individual responsibility, and personal immortality.

Art and literature were "inspired utility." There was very little egoism and philistinism because art belonged to everybody. The Middle Ages had achieved what Shuster called "the spiritualization of democracy." Similar thoughts were being expressed, as we have seen, by Michael Williams, but, whereas Williams emphasized the role of reason in sanitizing individual passion, Shuster stressed the interplay between concrete realism and romantic fancy. Even though Shuster recognized the Catholic spirit as taking visible shape in the Middle Ages, he was not prepared to uproot himself from contemporary experience. The spirit was always an ideal to be realized. Therefore, Christian art was not forever encased in the "perpendicular Gothic." The cathedral was not the "spiritual home" of contemporary man, and the "everlasting reproduction of gargoyles" was for Shuster "nothing less than a denial of everlasting life."

What the Catholic spirit forced contemporary man to accept was the radical bond that united the present with the past. In terms of creative literature this meant a balancing of perspective when focusing on man. An artist, to be accepted by humanity and to be true to the collective experience of the race, must uncover "the mixture of aspiration and perverse instinct that constitutes an individual," never forgetting the soul or the body—"the reality or the symbol." For Shuster, the "pessimistic individualism" of contemporary literature was no more honest than the "hypersentimentalism" it had replaced.[23]

Shuster came to a personal awareness of the Catholic spirit as a result of his wartime experiences in Europe. As the war shattered the "great dream of modern society," the spirit was "liberated" and a "Catholic conception of the world returned to Catholics."[24] In Europe, especially in France, Shuster came in contact with a generation described by a contemporary as driven by "a restlessness which sought a set position, aspired to find a dogma, a certainty, in order to know how to make use of their lives." For many young Frenchmen, this "need of affirmation" found embodiment in the thought of Henri Bergson, who became the spiritual and intellectual door through which many repossessed their Catholicism, this despite papal disapproval of Bergson's thought in 1914. Following Bergson, young Frenchmen began to break from the limiting mechanics of scientific materialism. They placed their confidence in free will, experimentation, self-affirmation, and an openness to the irrational which provided for them the freedom to believe again.[25]

As we have seen, a similar experience was transpiring in America, where literary and intellectual ferment led to a crusade to restore concrete experience in art, literature, and philosophy. George Shuster was in touch with both ferments and alive to the restlessness of the time. However, Shuster saw the vitality of prewar intellectuals in America being drained off after the war in a welter of conflicting affirmations which resulted in a distressing lack of vision and a pervasive disillusionment. The French Catholic revival, on the other hand, split during the war. One group, led by Charles Péguy, continued to mix Bergson with Catholic spirituality. The other group followed the path of Jacques Maritain, who rejected Bergson, or what was made of him by his followers, for the intellectualist airs of Thomistic philosophy. It stressed the rational over against the more vulnerable and less tidy aspects of intuition and feeling, the irrational and experimental. Shuster was spiritually and intellectually inclined to identify with the former group, putting himself at arm's length from the general rationalist and intellectualist trend of Catholic thought following World War I.

The unexpected liberation of the Catholic spirit during the war, made possible by modern confusion, posed a serious problem for Catholics who began to champion its cause. This problem was expressed by Shuster in the form of a question: "Shall we venture to dream of beauty and peace, of holiness and ecstasy, while the cauldron seethes?"[26] Shuster answered the question in the affirmative, with the provision that any vision of holiness and beauty must be born in, and gain intensity from, the seething cauldron of contemporary life. This response differed from the far more general reaction of Catholics whose dream of beauty was characterized by a vigorous refusal to enter the cauldron.

Also, many Catholics were of the mind that, since they had been in some sort of spiritual and intellectual "exile" during the preceding century, Catholicism was immune from some of the deadening materialistic and formalistic patterns of the century's life and thought. Shuster rejected this assumption and pointed to a legacy of "a routine materialistic attitude" and a mid-Victorian sentimentalism which continued to render the poetic significance of Catholic symbols lifeless. The novels offered to the public as "Catholic" were, in Shuster's judgment, "invariably trite, juvenile and uninspired. Our authors have begotten a limited vision. For them the world is not yet alive nor seething with the terrible fires that have been kindled." In the struggle from economic serfdom and civil prejudice to a slowly dawning social recognition, American Catholics had managed to preserve the faith. But the passage itself was largely construed in material terms, and thus an "artistic appreciation" of the struggle was negligible. Although the Bishops' Program of 1919 was an instance of Catholics speaking concretely to modern man, the cohesive and valuable aspects of the Catholic tradition were still only groping toward self-consciousness.[27]

Shuster confronted the faltering steps of this movement toward consciousness while he was a professor of literature at Notre Dame from 1919 to 1923. As the syllabus prepared for his freshman literature class indicated, he introduced his students to a wide range of contemporary literature and poetry: Sinclair Lewis, H. G. Wells, Jack London, William Dean Howells, Amy Lowell, G. K. Chesterton, Willa Cather, and others. In the course of a year Shuster felt it necessary to discuss D. H. Lawrence as well. Recognizing that this might cause a stir at the university, he chose *The Rainbow* as the most "innocuous" book of Lawrence's he could find. He placed a red star on it, which prevented others not in his class from taking it out of the library. Despite all these precautions the Prefect of Religion, John F. O'Hara, C.S.C., noticed the book on the library shelf and proceeded to tear it up. O'Hara viewed most contemporary literature as nothing less than occasions of sin. Shuster left Notre Dame as a result of the incident and was not to return until 1961.[28]

Experiences like this one forced him to the conclusion that Catholics in the United States had a problem which was largely a matter of cultural identity and confusion with regard to the vital concerns of the "Catholic Spirit." After World War I, Catholics in the country had come alive, but, in Shuster's words, this vitality found "no artistic outlet. We are enchained in our own formalism and inveterate habits. Our books are dull and asleep; our young men follow other gods." In the post-war era Shuster discerned that the task confronting everyone concerned with culture was "to civilize;

to restore the equilibrium between man and the world . . . to extricate man." It seemed, however, that Catholics had decided to preach or retreat from the action behind "unreasoned tirades" and manifestos of "towering rage."[29]

The basis for this limited response in the twenties, Shuster believed, was not entirely to be blamed on the depressed state of immigrant Catholic culture. The fact that most Catholics had been engaged in the battle for bread rather than for culture did not excuse the real harm done by an "authoritarian apologetics" which had led in the cultural sphere to the identification of art with didacticism. In the last quarter of the nineteenth century Catholics had acclimated their own apologetical bent of mind to the sentimental moralism characteristic of the standard American literature of the time. They arrived in the twenties unaffected by the literary turmoil of the first twenty-five years of the present century, preaching a literary gospel American and Catholic in its innocent moralism but made unintelligible by the fires of contemporary experience. To compound the difficulty, the "intellectualist" premises of Catholic thought after World War I further tended to rob Catholic literature of influence, producing, in Shuster's view, an avalanche of "apologetic literature in the form of tales or treatises, which are as dead as so many feet of lumber when it is carted from the press. . . ."[30]

The Catholic proclivity to view the novel as a moral tale made Catholic authors' own efforts at creative writing lifeless and heightened their insensitivity to contemporary fiction. One of the major errors of Catholic criticism, thought Shuster, occurred when it "clinches its fist against beauty and mystical insight" because of a disagreement with the view of life presented. When such criticism allied itself to a feeling of numerical strength, as Shuster saw happening among Catholics in the twenties, especially as fiction was translated into the art of moviemaking, the results were disastrous. For Shuster, numerical power was the weakest of all forms of cultural influence: "It can be organized in defense of only a few shibboleths," he said,

> none of which permit of discriminating statement. It antagonizes groups that are numerically weak, just as it annoys those who possess individuality of mind. Catholics in this country can kill a motion-picture which is offensive to their religious (or racial) convictions—but they cannot and do not accomplish anything to render the art of the cinema less stupidly sentimental and more worthy of citizens come to the age of reason.

The combination of numbers, moralism, and apologetics had taken a heavy toll on Catholic sensitivity. In Shuster's judgment it produced: "A kind of terrible contempt for thought and loveliness . . . upon American Catholicism." He saw no hope for the immediate future, even if Catholics were rushing to schools of higher learning. The same influence was present there in the form of "an ominous leveling of minds and talents . . . virtually imposed by opinion."[31]

In contrast to this bleak picture, Shuster attempted to construct a path by which American Catholics might repossess their heritage and contribute to the task of extricating man. In terms of literature, he described two avenues open to the Catholic artist. The first was "the path of terrible honesty." Here the artist would paint the face of his generation with its sores, both physical and spiritual, with its yearning for "passionate expression" and "incessant satiety," ending with "a universal outcry for the grace of God." This was the route followed by François Mauriac and Georges Bernanos in France.[32]

There was, for Shuster, however, "a more attractive possibility"—one that did not plunge the artist too deeply into the "somber drama" of contemporary man. It was instead more alive with the "absolute confidence" of the disciples of Christ. Such confidence was attained by communal existence and liturgical life, where "isolation is sacrificed more and more completely to a unity in glory and joy." "If, on the one hand," continued Shuster, "Catholic art needs the pessimism which the spectacle of a world inconsecrate engenders, we need even more the din of grateful optimism." This optimism was not one of bland innocence. It was, rather, enriched by the "wheels of time" and imbued with the "miraculous irony" of the triumph of love over death, which was not simply a question of faith but one of historical record.[33]

The vitality of Catholic literature must discover its greatest source of power in liturgical models which seemed to express for Shuster the natural rhythms of living: restraint and frenzy, confidence and vulnerability, dogma and mystical insight. Liturgy and art were both intimately involved with community: liturgy being "community religion"; art being "community intuition." Both sought to balance the interplay between the individual and his world. In the face of twentieth-century discontent, both art and religion must seek to restore contact between the two. For America, a vital Catholic literature might respond to "an unsatisfied thirst for permanence in hope, for the reliable in faith, for the unchangeable in charity, [which] has taken possession of many whose fathers were blandly optimistic about the progress of science, or the perfectibility of the race."[34]

In searching for an example of such a literature Shuster discovered the work of Sigrid Undset, which presented the varied experiences of humanity by piecing together separate images into a rhythmic whole. Undset's works combined both the charms of idealism and the realism of bitter experience. In such a context darkness and fog drift, if imperceptibly at times, toward the light. The more general Catholic reaction to Undset, however, was to recoil from her open expression of sexual emotions and to rise in horror at her mingling of reverence for God and the faith with "salacious" descriptions of the "frailties" of human nature. For Shuster, this only proved his observation correct; that is, that neither liturgy nor art nor literature could flourish in cramped quarters, and Catholics had erected something like an "armed camp." By placing man in an ethereal wonderland, Catholics forgot "that man really and truly wriggles."[35]

Living in an armed camp for so long and absorbing successive waves of immigrant recruits, Catholicism had had little opportunity and, in some respects, little desire to forge close bonds with the cultural and intellectual resources of America. Catholics opted for a kind of supranational universalism which Shuster at one time pointed out in describing the education of an average priest who "studied medieval philosophy, French pietistic literature, German church history, British apologetics and Irish poetry."[36] Consequently, Catholic writing lacked an American reference and, indeed, had little by way of a distinguishing identity.

In the late 1920's the buzz emanating from many of the country's highbrow journals concerned the attack on literary modernity and "anarchy" by the New Humanists. Irving Babbitt and Paul Elmer Moore achieved momentary fame as many toward the end of the decade rushed to separate themselves from jazz-age sloth and cynicism. Catholics in search of an intellectual and cultural foothold in the country grasped at the New Humanist movement with some enthusiasm—much as a tired swimmer reaches for a dock. Many sought to ally Catholicism with Babbitt's classicism, rationalism, and concern for order, discipline, and standards. These emphases vibrated for Catholics who understood neoscholasticism to be urging the same qualities of thought, but, of course, from a level which transcended Babbitt's Aristotelian naturalism. Many Catholics consequently looked upon the New Humanism as a "challenge" to wake up to their own heritage.[37]

Here again Shuster followed a different beat. He criticized the humanist movement from what he considered to be the Christian point of view. From this premise, he maintained, "the most astonishing part of the cosmos is not design but being." Christ was less concerned with discipline and more concerned with life. Again, Shuster understood neo-Thomism to be a movement away from reducing the universe to laws and abstract designs, symbolizing, instead, a "humility in the face of reality", an attempt to restore freshness to the earth and confidence in experiential intuition. But the humanist like Babbitt, thought Shuster, saw intuition as unrestrained instinct, the enjoyment of nature apart from reason as dangerous, and mysticism as surrender. So much emphasis on self-control, Shuster concluded, would only lead to boredom. Art was not the pursuit of safety but rather of ecstasy. "I should feel very sorry," Shuster declared in 1934, "for a young Catholic who elected to make Babbitt rather than Brooks the patron of his humanism." As it turned out, he was to do much weeping.[38]

Before the "challenge of humanism" had side-tracked Catholic aesthetics Shuster was at work attempting to forge his own link between the American experience and Catholicism. This was the brunt of his message in *The Catholic Spirit in America* (1927). Surprisingly for a Catholic at this time, he found this contact in the American Romantic movement, especially in the thought of Emerson. In the 1920's many Catholics were roaming through American history trying to find a hook to grab. Some found it in Puritanism, others in the Enlightenment or in the scholastic bent of mind characteristic of early nineteenth-century Protestant America, and still others looked to the late nineteenth-century idealism. Most blinked at Emerson and Whitman. Shuster, however, saw in American romanticism the first real attempt to speak of America as an "intellectual concept" rather than as geography. In the process, romanticism also dipped into the wells of the Catholic spirit. The movement sought new avenues of the spirit as it rejected the "straight-jacket asceticism" which previously cramped American writing. In Emerson, Shuster construed the joining of Americanism and Catholicism in a spiritual rather than in a social or political sense.

Shuster observed in Emerson everything acting and moving. He (Emerson) was opposed to fossilization in religion, literature, grammar, and philosophy. His rejection of any kind of spiritual determinism reminded Shuster of the Catholic insistence that man must choose and "entrust himself to the spirit of the world." Man developed self-reliance through surrender. Shuster also felt that Emerson's reliance upon nature as guidance for man corresponded to Catholic natural law philosophy. Finally, both Emerson and Catholicism believed in man's capacity for transcending his culture rather than being enslaved to it.[39] Shuster's approach to American romanticism was neither fully developed by him nor precise enough for one to make serious criticism of it. Nevertheless, the approach itself was singular among Catholics at the time, and it represented an effort to come to terms with American culture in an area that was not suggestive of either the rational or the formal.

In the twenties, when it appeared to him that American vitality was threatened by cynicism and indifference and that his fellow Catholics offered little but a rigid moralism and sentimental idealism, Shuster found resources for preserving a sense of innocence that were both American and Catholic and did not suffer from naivete. It was rather an innocence matured by the complexity and concreteness of life which recogized that rain "falls on just and unjust alike," and no philosophy could promise "to keep the universe at a temperature of 70 degrees." Yet, Shuster was hopeful about man's continuing struggle to make sense of life, to survive decently, and, in moments, even to flourish. He resolved for himself, at least, "that democracy shall be more than even 'normalcy'; that it must be not a signpost, but a maker of signs." In response to Santayana's counsel to be indifferent to the "indifference of the universe," he desired rather to be, with Emerson, "heroic" in the face of reality. For Shuster, this was "a test of the excellence . . . of Catholic life."[40]

In 1919 Shuster had high hopes that Catholics had found themselves in America. By 1928 he felt they were only "straining" toward a free visualization of their heritage. In 1938 the situation had grown darker than it had ever been before. An outbreak of "minority-itis," in Shuster's view, gripped Catholics following the bitterness of Al Smith's defeat in 1928, the Mexican Revolution, and Catholic fears of the rising influence of communism. In the 1930's Catholics were susceptible to the irrational appeals of anti-Semites, pro-Nazis, and Fascists. Catholic intellectuals "were never so much alone in the midst of [their] fellow men." Much of the Catholic press reflected "intellects which push conformism to the very verge of absurdity." All Shuster could do was ask of those who were not susceptible to the very same appeals not to identify them with American Catholicism. In 1940 he was reluctantly forced to conclude that American Catholicism had not yet "attained self-consciousness."[41]

It was in the area of literary expression that Catholics like Shuster were quick to observe the transformation of American cultural ideals. It was not surprising, then, to discover Catholics actively involved in the process of defending literary ideals suitable to the refined perspectives of William Dean Howells but alien to the raw forces and uncontrollable passions at work in Theodore Dreiser's *An American Tragedy.*

6. Literature
A Bastion of Tranquillity

Man will never continue in a mere state of innocence. . . . I think it will be found and ever found, as a matter of course, that Literature, no matter of what nation, is the science or history partly . . . of the natural man, partly of man in rebellion.

John Henry Newman
The Idea of a University

A CRUCIAL BUT NOT POPULARLY APPRECIATED dimension of the American writer has been, according to Robert Penn Warren, his role as "a bearer of bad tidings." Increasingly since the Civil War our poets have dramatized the disintegration of the "concept of the freeman, the responsible self" upon which the nation's dream was founded. Before World War I the artist, though wrenched from what was being made of the dream, was not alienated from its premises. He managed "to cling to some hope that it might be redeemed." This mood of glimmering optimism was characteristic even of the literary rebellion that occurred after 1910, which sought to reformulate the dream using the philosophical and literary materials supplied by pragmatism, realism, and naturalism. The idealism of this revolt, however, demanded a debunking of the "defenders of ideality," who located the ideal in forms, refined manners, conventions, and a conception of beauty and truth which soared above mundane realities. The open-minded idealism of the prewar period was based on a rejection of this formalism, and a short-lived optimism that the ideal could be salvaged by an intensely passionate plunge into the necessities of material life. The artistic endeavor was changing from one that pointed gloriously upward to one that brought it inward to face the darker regions of man's fate and nature's inscrutability.[1]

The closer the artist has inspected the American dream the more passionate has been the desire not to have it corrupted by commercialism or conformity. At the same time, the artist has become more vulnerable to

99

alienation and disillusionment. This latter consequence has to a great
extent informed the literary mind since World War I. The hope of redemp-
tion, for example, in Fitzgerald, Hemingway, Dreiser, Faulkner, e.e
cummings, and others, has been tacitly denied; and their task, as defined by
Irving Howe, has been the struggle to survive with "fragments of convictions" and "moral gestures" in a world of circumstance, conformity, and
confusion.[2] When literature began to explore the seamy crevices which
pockmarked the American quest for wholeness and beatitude, Catholic
literary alienation began in earnest. From World War I and continuing into
the 1950's their isolation from contemporary literary currents was a very
conspicuous element of American Catholic culture. In no other area of
American culture was innocence so severely strained while at the same time
never were Catholics so intent on defending its assumptions.

In the nineteenth century, when most Catholics were more concerned
with survival than with the embellishments of middle-class life, they were
not, when they chose to enter the literary arena, profoundly alienated from
the cultural standards of society. Robert Walsh (1785-1859), a Catholic
layman of some social standing, was in fact instrumental in shaping the
neoclassical and Scottish common sense philosophical influence in American criticism of the early national period. His *American Review of History and
Politics* (1811–1812) was one of the first American publications modelled
after "Scottish" journals. The *American Quarterly Review* (1827–1837),
which he founded, was a bastion of neoclassical criticism before romanticism eroded its influence. Finally, Walsh's collections of essays, *Didactics,
Social, Literary, and Political* (1836), not only indicated the function of his
thought but, as William Charvat has noted, were "a monument to the
influence of Scotch philosophy and aesthetics on the American mind."[3]
Following Walsh, Orestes Brownson's literary concerns were also guided by
the principles of classicism, opposing both sentimental didacticism and
"fanciful idealizations." The intellectualist and logical bent of Brownson's
mind ill-disposed him to, with Wordsworth, "merge with the landscape."
He admired Emerson for his breadth of expression but not his transcenden-
tal proclamations. For Brownson, the function of literature was to civilize
and refine, not spiritualize. So as not to interfere with truth and goodness,
literature must seek to "tranquillize the passions."[4]

Toward the end of the nineteenth century few Catholics could or cared to
imitate Brownson's stern criticism, though elements of his classicism
persisted. It merged however with a high-sounding idealism of Brother
Azarias (Patrick Francis Mullaney, 1848–1893), and with the gentility of
Maurice Francis Egan (1852–1924). In the former, art was the expression of
an ideal form; the actual was only a more or less perfect expression of the
ideal. The function of literature was both impractical (contemplation) and

practical as well, the latter by putting the reader in touch with useful ideas. While the aim of literature was eventually "to solve life's problems," it did this basically by transposing man "above humdrum life into the ideal world." Azarias had high praise for William Dean Howells because his novels had "purpose." Although Azarias was more sympathetic to romanticism, especially in its ideal formulations, his classical and scholastic frame of mind desired to have reason governing and not merging with the imagination.[5]

For Maurice Francis Egan, literature was primarily a prop to promote good morals and virtuous action. Although Egan was less a critic and more one who chatted about books, his genteel literary tastes were endemic to the Catholic literary mentality at the close of the century. While Egan admired Howells as "a sincere and pure-minded gentleman," and Henry James as the most distinguished American novelist, he disliked especially the latter's tone of doubt.[6] At the end of the nineteenth century Catholics were developing their own if "parochial" form of fiction and criticism. It was not, however, sorely alienated from what existed around them.[7] So long as the "defenders of ideality" like Richard Henry Stoddard, Edmond Clarence Stedman, Henry Van Dyke, and Hamilton Wright Mabie held the reins of literary expression in their grasp in journals like the *North American Review, Outlook,* and *Century,* Catholics felt increasingly comfortable. The intrusion of realism and naturalism into American literature by Stephen Crane, Frank Norris, and to some extent even by Howells, was denounced by "respectable" critics in many quarters, one of which was the niche inhabited by Catholics. For the Catholic, as one expressed it, "Art is ever pointing upward . . . where his ideal sets . . . where all is beautiful, where all is immeasurable by him until he beholds it with his glorified intelligence."[8]

The most respected Catholic poet at the end of the century was Louise Imogen Guiney (1861–1920), who sought more refinement in England than even Yankee Boston offered. She was known for her "cheerfulness" and opposed to "Wilful Sadness in Literature." A work which she thought left man miserable was inartistic and immoral. Man had to be the "master" even of his melancholy. Her conception of thought was, expressed in her phrase, a "philosophy of comment," by which the author rose to the "garrett tower" to observe the prospects of mundane affairs.[9] Catholic literary idealism mirrored the social and political idealism of the more outspoken Americanizers of the clergy, Ireland, Keane, and O'Connell. Bishop John Lancaster Spalding's range of thought, though more subtle than Ireland's, nevertheless was equally idealistic. Spalding encouraged Catholics to a higher idealization of their educational efforts. This same approach he brought to art, which, he felt, should quiet the passions as it "elevates, purifies, and refines." Any inclination in art toward the darker

side of life perverted its nature. Looking back in 1904 on the nineteenth
century, Spalding saw it as an "era of emancipation, of enlargement;" its
"optimism blew like a creative breath on the face of the people. . . ." One
of his aphorisms would symbolize the general Catholic movement in
literature and life in the twentieth century: "On life then seize: Doubt is
disease."[10]

By the 1890's many in the Catholic community perceived the nation's
culture to be one in which ideals mattered, vigorous action dominated
melancholy doubt, optimism and moralism characterized its best literature, and form counted for something. Pessimism, naturalism, and realism
they opposed but not in isolation—they were convinced that "true
Americanism" opposed them as well. In the next three decades Catholics
were to observe the near total collapse of idealism around them while they
fervently sought its preservation.

After World War I they would fondly recall, as did Michael Earls, S.J., a
professor of literature at Boston College, the "wholesome nineties," and
wish that its "Brahmin Caste were holding the stage of literature today
rather than the "Jack-in-the-box and Punch-and-Judy shouters of 'Main
Streets,' or the underground esthetes of 'psychoanalysts' from the Sodom
and Gomorrahs of decadent byways in Europe."[11] Thomas Woodlock,
financial editor of the *Wall Street Journal* and an active Catholic layman,
wistfully remembered in 1942, "how solid, how stable, how decorous the
1912 scene looks from the viewpoint of today." People, he recalled, read
Tarkington, Kipling, and Galsworthy and "Stevenson was still not without
honor; people . . . still talked of James and Howells and Holmes—even
Emerson."

But Woodlock also remembered some cracks in the general decorum of
life. Mencken was pounding Victorians. Ragtime was tuneful yet it was
"troubled"—it seemed to him "regressive" and to foretell a "resurgence of
the primitive." As Woodlock summarized, the cracks foretold a "flight
from standards and 'form,' worse a flight from beauty herself. It is the
general flight from beauty exemplified in the present state of 'arts' and
'manners' that seems to me the final stage of this general debacle that we call
the world crisis." In an introduction to a selection of Woodlock's articles
from the *Wall Street Journal,* James Edward Tobin remarked that reading
them "led inescapably to the conclusion that there was a man who stood
still, while the world raced by to sag into a deeper morass or to whirl wildly
in a typhoon."[12] Tobin's epitaph on Woodlock could be expanded to
describe how Catholics in general reacted to the tidings brought by the
whirl of twentieth-century literature.

World War I unloosed a generation of writers tormented by its
mechanized violence. e.e. cummings, John Dos Passos, Ernest Heming-

way probed the process of dehumanization. Their reaction to war paralleled an already blossoming attack on the commonplace conformity of "Main Street" American civilization by Sherwood Anderson, Sinclair Lewis, and Theodore Dreiser. Poets like Amy Lowell, Robert Frost, and Carl Sandburg experimented with verse and images in a conscious rejection of forms that symbolized a culture that had bankrupted itself in war. It was a time to "traffic in mockery," as Yeats wrote, as well as a time of disillusionment. [13] In a similar vein Catholic writers in Europe developed a style of fiction that seemed to thrive on the "desecrated soil" of western civilization. In reaction to bourgeois insipidity, the violence of war, and the threat of chaos, writers like G. K. Chesteron, Evelyn Waugh, Graham Greene, Georges Bernanos, and François Mauriac responded with a violence of images and prose. They also trafficked in mockery, described social and spiritual disintegration, and offered as relief only the unexpected and many times undesired impulses of divine grace. Salvation was achieved first by way of disaster, then by supernatural envelopment. [14]

American Catholics, at least until after World War II, were in turn alienated from all this alienation, both Catholic and non-Catholic. Their literary ideals were similar to their larger cultural objectives. Their sense of isolation was developed in the effort to maintain the decorum, idealism, and optimism which they believed were prewar American. In their literature and criticism they pictured themselves as apostles of light and healthiness amid general gloom. Their literary response to World War I was best indicated in Joyce Kilmer's reaction to the war.

Kilmer (1886–1918), a convert to Catholicism in 1913, died during the war and became a symbol to the Catholic literary community of the cultural death of his brand of "piety and mirth" poetry. Before America's entry into the conflict in Europe, Kilmer was opposed to the country's intervention. He thought it would be a dishonor and that "our children would be ashamed of us if we should join in this frantic mobbing of Germany." But, as was often the case, 1914 pacifists were by 1917 enlisted for war. Writing from France, Kilmer hoped that poetry back in America was "reflecting the virtues which are blossoming on the blood-soaked soil of this land—courage and self-abnegation, and love and faith. . . ." This, he thought, would cleanse the note of cynicism and pessimism, "the extravagances and decadence of the so-called renascence of poetry during the last five years—a renascence distinguished more by the celebration of the queer and the nasty instead of the beautiful. . . ." Kilmer found beauty, not dehumanization and nausea, in battle action. Writing to his wife, Aline, just before he died, he thought that she was the one suffering: "You, with no exhilaration of star-shells and tattoo of machine guns, you without the adventure. I feel very selfish, often." [15]

If World War I symbolized on a larger scale the disintegration of the old order, the death in 1920 of William Dean Howells represented the personal passing of a "rejected past." For Catholics, Howells belonged to "the great age of the giants," that is, Emerson, Hawthorne, Lowell, and the senior Holmes. His simplicity was unaffected by the present "lyrics of passion," said a writer in the *Catholic World*. He saw life "steadily and whole and clear." His characters were representative. John C. Reville, S.J., in *America,* praised his "sound Americanism," his matchless style and culture, especially "his staunch adherence to time honored canons of morality and art." To Brother Leo (Francis Meehan), Howells told the truth about human life and nature; for Howells, "the shambles of the human spirit [were] not fit subjects for literary portraiture." As late as 1930 Catholic critics like Marshall Lochbiler, S.J., would compare Howells with Dreiser, or Sandburg with Longfellow, and note an "alarming deterioration

> consisting in a crude and purposeless attitude towards life. Men and women jostle and whirl in a great spiritual void, where souls have been reduced to mere chemical and physical forces, where values, responsibilities, and obligations are measured by personal expediency; men and women deprived of objectives and spiritual destiny, without rational guidance and without intellectual discipline.

Howells represented what Catholics had come to appreciate as American culture. The literary types that followed him were, in the words of John J. Burke, C.S.P., editor of the *Catholic World,* "the evangelists of anarchy."[16]

One of the first areas where a noticeable stiffening in imagination occurred was in the Catholic reaction to "the poetic curiosities of our day," or "lyrics of passion" of Amy Lowell, Robert Frost, Edgar Lee Masters, and Carl Sandburg. By 1910, said Francis X. Talbot, S.J., literary editor of *America,* "poetry ceased to be defined and refused to be confined or even refined." Catholics were quick to interpret free verse, along with other movements of the time, as repudiating restraint and just another "*ignio fatuus* blown from the miasmic jungles of disorder." It resembled art, said Michael Earls, "as a scarecrow stands for a man."[17] Catholics rejected free verse and the evident trend toward Whitman, which Talbot thought was "reverse evolutionism" in that Whitman represented a return to the beasts and was the "first to stain the poetry of America." They were even more upset with the subject matter of the new American poets.

Accustomed to having their poetry uplifting, Catholic poets like Sister M. Eleanore, C.S.C., found it difficult to "enjoy poetry born in sewers, whether in the subterranean channels of the cities or in the channels of the subconscious mind." Sandburg's "irridescent colors of scum" excited them only to disgust. Aline Kilmer objected to the poetry of Robert Frost because of his

> primitive terror, the sense of a constant threat in nature . . . the threat comes from the trees and hedges themselves, from nature herself. The terror is not delicious; it is too real to be so lightly enjoyed. We are awfully afraid. A pioneer with Frost's imagination must promptly have gone mad.

In the new poetry nature was no longer the wonderland of high adventure or man's domination. It contained a barren and primitive terror which man no longer comfortably dominated.

Catholic rejection of the new poetry was primarily based on a refusal to accept a nature so real, terrifying, and undelicious. Although American Catholics were quick to point to Paul Claudel as evidence of the Catholic revival in literature and his concern for the absolute, his poetic imagination contained many of the forces they disliked about American poets. Therefore, Claudel's "violence of force," "vividness of action," and "intensity of atmosphere" appeared as "defects" because his "mystical effects are attempted merely by the confusion of ideas. Sometimes feeling is the only justification of certain ideas." To Thomas J. Gerrard these defects were the result of Claudel's being in the Far East and the United States too long. His return to France, Gerrard thought, should cleanse him of his intensity. This critic obviously knew little about what was happening in France.[18]

Meanwhile, Catholic poets continued to uphold what they believed were the traditional standards. J. R. N. Maxwell, S.J., reviewed Catholic poetry during the 1920's and approvingly observed Catholic poets holding fast to traditional rhythms. Poets like Theodore Maynard were inspired by "laughter, religion, and happy song." Gertrude Callaghan wrote of New York City and found "beauty everywhere." Aline Kilmer sang "with the tenderness of true maternal affection" in an atmosphere of "peace and restraint." Leonard Feeney, a "true romanticist," ached to make all life more beautiful. Sister Madeleva wrote "varied and wistful" poems full of "womanly fancy." To protect these airy souls, the Catholic Poetry Society (1931) provided a "cloister," according to Francis X. Connolly, its secretary and editor of the journal *Spirit,* so that Catholics would not have to accept "the strange bedfellowship with our contemporary Sandburgs." Without such a cloister the Catholic poet would be "yoked with the wildest opposites" and his "semi-priesthood" obscured. What his poetry needed was the quiet and peace of his own house rather than the antagonism and wilderness of a "Chicago."

The Society's "Manifesto on Poetry," issued in 1941, confirmed its

opposition to "cliques of men and women writers" in America who confused poetry with various "cults of unintelligibility," "sophistications of
language," and "infatuations with the obscure." For these Catholics the
poet "must aspire; he must set his sights up and out, not down and within."
Poetry was a public concern in the service of a "vision of reality which
excites, elevates and inspires a reader." Although T. S. Eliot was recognized
by John Duffy, C.S.S.R., as a "moral poet," he remained for Duffy and
many Catholics an irritating, incomprehensible and "unintelligible sym-
bolist." Eliot's poems were "disjointed fragments" without coherence.[19]

The starkness of Frost's poetry and the obscure symbolism of Eliot were
elements in a more general wave of pessimism shaping American literature
at the time. Catholics initially observed the gloomy note struck by Anderson, Lewis, and Dreiser as a "literary pose." It seemed incomprehensible to
them that anyone could be pessimistic in America. Sister Eleanore, who
taught literature at St. Mary's College in Indiana wrote: "One may excuse
German, Russian, Polish, Irish pessimism, but one cannot excuse American pessimism." American writers were merely mimicking the Europeans.
In America, she thought, there was "normal wholesome material
everywhere ready for use." Lewis' *Main Street* only discussed the vulgar. It
failed, she said, to point out "the honest working man, the women who
. . . bore children, the happy, contented old people, the little boys with
dreams of Napoleon, the little girls dreaming over their dollies of a home
and babies fashioned in the airy manner of rainbows." James Gillis haunted
Dreiser from *Sister Carrie* to *An American Tragedy*, suggesting that he "snap
out of it. . . . Look up at the sky, take a squint at the sun, go out on the
hillside and inhale deeply. Get out of the gutters. Come up from those
sewers. Be decent, be clean, and America will not seem so tragic."[20]

In response to the prophets of gloom one Catholic speaking for many,
offered "The Catholic Triumfeminate" of Alice Meynell, Louise Imogen
Guiney, and Agnes Repplier. Meynell's idealism was "quietly optimistic;"
Guiney was "hilariously optimistic;" and Repplier's common sense was
reasonably optimistic. Catholics were looking for a prophet "to fill up the
valleys of despondency." The decadence of the modern novel, Egan felt, was
that it lacked "a real feeling for romance." Blanche Mary Kelly, an activist
in the pursuit of clean literature, defended romance as "idealism called by a
Christian name" which recognized the ideal as true reality. What romance
did was to inspire, which was "marveling at the marvelous." Kelly was
quick to point out, however, that this was a "strictly logical process" and
not simply focusing on the unusual or extraordinary. "In our age of
so-called disillusion," she observed, Catholic romance was the antidote. As
another observer noted, there was "the need for more nonsense" as a
sanity-saving device.[21]

In prescribing nonsense, romance, idealism, and optimism Catholic critics were hopelessly swimming against the currents of contemporary literature. In the mid-1920's two developments raised the level of critical discussion one or two notches. First, the entry of Michael Williams and *The Commonweal* into the Catholic scene in 1924 afforded some Catholics the oportunity to take a less backward approach to American literature. Though Williams helped to popularize among Catholics the phrase "new paganism" as a description of the unease of modern writing, both he and his journal found some room for discrimination.

While opposed to Sinclair Lewis' lack of tolerance and warmth and considering the fact that much of his work had become a victim of the very conformity that Lewis satirized, Williams found Lewis' criticism of America "starkly sincere" and a passionate foe of the country's self-complacency. It should be noted that he was one of the first Catholics to think so. What Williams offered America was Catholicism as an integrating medium providing a richer, freer life than the repressive character of Puritanism but also one that was more disciplined than the "revolutionary voluptuaries" of the present. Catholicism, he thought, supplied what was best in both groups. By 1928 he was aware that a reaction to the pessimism of the twenties was shaping up, and he was convinced that "the future of American literature belongs to Catholicism."[22]

Such optimism betrayed an underlying ambivalence about contemporary literature which caused *The Commonweal* to be rather silent on the whole issue throughout the period. As one critic of the journal pointed out, it had failed even to examine the major writers of the time. There was a significant lack of discussion about Fitzgerald, Hemingway, Faulkner, Lawrence, and James Joyce, which, in a journal that considered itself a review of literature, could be interpreted as a general disdain for such writing. Again, although *The Commonweal* was instrumental in bringing to its American audience an awareness of European Catholic literature, it was not willing to accept, for example, Mauriac's concept of the novel. Describing human decay and then allowing for divine mercy was a tenable approach; but, said the editors, "that literature should add lustre to the wings of the spirit by trailing them through the mud, is to our minds at least, an untenable ambition." Walter Rathenau's remark to André Gide was especially applicable to American Catholics despite its patronizing tone. America, he said, "has no soul because she has not yet deigned to plunge into the abyss of suffering and sin."[23] It was not so much that Catholics thought they lived in a world without suffering and sin; it was, simply, not their ambition to write about it.

The second development was a heightened self-consciousness about their own writing and the literature which surrounded them. It was the magazine *America* and a group of Jesuit critics including Francis X. Talbot, Robert Parsons, and, later, Harold C. Gardiner who sought to find a niche for Catholic writing somewhere between pious sentimentalism and modern realism. This endeavor was inspired by the realization that a large number of Catholics had become "over-suspicious" prudes, reinforcing a tradition of "weak-dull, wishy-washy, pious" writing. It was apparent to these critics that within the Catholic community there was a large body of people they labeled "rigorists," Puritans, or Jansenists, who thought that the reading of most modern literature beyond fairy tales might result in eternal damnation. The aim of these critics was to protect from the over-suspicious a small and beleaguered group of writers who wrote what were called "Catholic" novels. Second, through their criticism of modern American literature they set out to demonstrate that Catholic literature was essentially different from everything around them, especially from the more famous writers. This realization, and Catholic attempts at developing a literary presence in America, contributed to what was called "Catholic literature's dilemma."[24]

Francis X. Talbot, S.J., was born of Irish parents in Philadelphia, in 1889. From 1922 to 1936 he was literary editor of *America,* and then chief editor of that magazine from 1936 to 1944. He retired from journalism to become president of Loyola College in Baltimore in 1947. He died in 1953. Besides his professional activities, Talbot was one of the most active Catholic culture organizers of the period. He initiated and was editor of *Thought* (1928), and in 1939 proposed what became one of the most respected Catholic theological journals, *Theological Studies.* His other accomplishments include the founding of the Catholic Book Club (1928) and the Catholic Poetry Society in 1930, and helping to establish the Catholic Library Association (1922) and the Catholic Theatre Conference (1937). As was the case with most Catholic initiatives following World War I, these organizations were begun with dual objectives: to establish a Catholic cultural presence in the country, and to build a house where their own idealism could dwell protected from the doubt and discontent without.[25]

From the beginning of his career with *America* Talbot's sense of idealism was abused by the spirit and form of contemporary prose and poetry. On the other hand, he was also one of the first to recognize the "abject book poverty" among Catholics. After 1925 Talbot was complaining of the sentimental and platitudinous character of Catholic writing; a "rigorist" body of critics who wanted literature "free from all references to sin . . . and natural processes" to contain only pure and "wholly edifying" thoughts. Finally, he pointed out the deplorable dearth of Catholic writing in general, which forced the Catholic Literary Awards Foundation in 1928 to give two of their three awards for the best Catholic books of the year to two non-Catholics. "We tell ourselves soothingly," Talbot remarked,

> that we have a religion that can remake the world, that we have a philosophy that can direct the world sanely, that we have a morality that can save the world. Evidently we have not the words to put them into a book that can tell the world what we have.

The Jesuit, nevertheless, was convinced that there were Catholics writing "decent" and "wholesome" fiction; the problem was, that even they were attacked by Catholic purists. Talbot found himself championing the writing of Catholic authors like Frank Spearman, Elizabeth Jordan, Kathleen Norris, Edith O'Shaughnessy, Katherine Tynan, and Lucille Borden. These writers, as Talbot said of Norris, whose fiction centered on Catholic family life (*Little Ships* [1925] and *Red Silence* [1928]), were "striving to lift up . . . readers to a saner, healthier, nobler attitude toward life."[26] But all of them, especially Norris, were denounced by many of their fellow Catholics for describing "ultramodern situations and details," birth scenes and "illicit" love, and for generally suggesting that Catholics were capable of divorce, sin, and other unseemly activities.[27]

In 1926 Talbot organized a symposium of Catholic writers in *America* which sought to bring to the attention of its readers Catholic writers of "wholesome" novels for modern times. This eventually appeared as *Fiction by Its Makers* (1928). The rather low state of Catholic literary endeavor was highlighted by the participating authors, who Talbot thought represented the best of contemporary Catholic literature. Agnes Repplier, a genteel essayist, wanted the novel to present neither uplift nor degradation, but to exhibit human nature in such a way as to show "light in the darkness and some reassuring traits." Elizabeth Jordan, who wrote mystery stories and was drama critic for *America*, believed the novel to be primarily a form of entertainment. If the author, she said, led the reader into the sordid and unbeautiful he betrayed his reader "as shamefully as we betray a child to whom we tell a tragic story just before he goes to sleep." She wanted normal "red-blooded, lovable" characters in her novels, concluding that "the eternal child" in everyone "demands its favorite fairy tale."

Kathleen Norris pleaded for her own brand of "realism," in which she portrayed Catholic weaknesses but weaknesses redeemed through faith. Lucille Borden thought that the Church's laws made the novelists' work "easier" by clearly defining the limits of morality. "What more logical," she asked, "than to take a disputed theme of the day, or other days, weave it into a romance, interlace through it the dictum of ecclesiastical authority?" Sister Eleanore believed the world needed "a return to sentiment—good clean wholesome sentiment" with regard to man's love for home, honor, God, and nature. Edith O'Shaughnessy wanted virtue painted white and vice "boldly" black. Sex was a legitimate subject for literature but it must be presented in an inspiring manner full of "the glory and the dream."[28]

These authors supposedly represented to Talbot the middle road between the "righteousness" of the Catholic rigorist and the "mud" of modern fiction. His own concept of literature was biased toward its role as a medium of propaganda. For him "the novelist works in an arsenal that is packed with bombs of moral significance. He cannot write vitally unless he is a teacher and a moralist, and even a propagandist."[29] With this concept of literature Talbot was not too much different from the purists he so vigorously denounced. Thus, while he was a great admirer of Sigrid Undset as "thoroughly and enthusiastically a Catholic," and sponsored and organized a lecture tour for her in 1940, he rather wished she would delete many descriptive scenes in her books. Talbot himself came in for a good deal of criticism for his support of Undset, from other Catholics who thought the European author's works were the result of a "diseased mind" and from those who sought to rescue their daughters from Undset's "dirty thoughts."[30]

Talbot's bias toward art as propaganda also affected his judgment in the 1930's when many authors and playwrights increasingly used their work as a vehicle for social reform and Marxism. During the 1930's Talbot was concerned with the "daily" penetration of communism into movies, theatre, and literature. He was nervously alert and wary of everything that hinted of a red hue. He had to reject two drama reviews of Elizabeth Jordan, who was proud of her own ability to detect "dirt and communism" because she praised *Key Largo* and *Sing Out the News*. Talbot had heard that the latter was "extremely leftist," and the former he felt had a "background that was Red." Though Jordan hadn't detected these faults, she was happy that Talbot pointed them out to her.[31] Talbot was one of the first to recognize that Catholics had a "problem" with literature, but his own middle of the road approach offered little room for creative literature and more often than not wavered toward the extremes he himself disliked.

Following Talbot a number of critics addressed themselves to the issue of what was wrong with the literary mentality of Catholics. Robert Parsons, S.J., who worked with Talbot at *America*, thought the problem lay in the fact that most Catholics thirty-five and older were "hopelessly Victorian." They stopped reading with Scott, Dickens, and Tennyson. Since the 1890's, said Parsons, "the Catholic author, out of a spirit of renunciation or otherwise, refused to write in a modern style." Younger Catholics simply refused, in turn, to read anything Catholic because they identified it with pious preachment. While Parsons believed Catholics could write a *Main*

Street or *An American Tragedy,* it would be necessary for them to show that the real reasons for America's failures involved a "lack of faith" and not simply a "lack of beauty."

Catholics were attracted to the Victorian age because, as one put it, it represented "a sane philosophy of life, its respect for the laws of God, of men, its sound idealism. . . ." Catholics had held onto Victorian idealism even while Victorians themselves were secretly doubting their own sentiments. To Camile John McCole, a professor of literature at Notre Dame, this lingering idealism prevented Catholics from living life "deeply" and taking for granted life's "profundities," thereby frustrating any attempts to create an enduring literature.[32]

As the 1930's progressed, Catholics were not only beginning to wonder, "Is there a Catholic novel?" but, more significantly, "Can a Catholic write a novel?" This last question was asked by a Catholic clergyman in the *American Mercury* under the pen name Jack English. In his view it was almost impossible because of the moral and dogmatic training a Catholic youth received. Before he was ten years of age, said English, he was taught the basic tenets of God's existence; he was convinced that life has an eternal purpose; human acts were divided for him into the good, bad, and indifferent; "he becomes acutely conscious that his every thought, word, or deed is a stroke upon the eternal canvas." If taken in isolation his training would force one to conclude that "there is not an uncertain moment in the young Catholic's acceptance of established creed. . . . There is not an elastic idea in the structure of his belief."[33]

While English may have doubted whether Catholics ever could write a novel, most Catholics were sure they could—even a realistic one. But Catholics had their own peculiar notion of what realism meant. A writer could, for example, write about evil and failure as long as he showed that "right must predominate over the wrong," said Robert Broderick, critic for *Ave Maria* magazine. Realism meant for Broderick a delicate handling of subject matter to impress upon the reader "the idea of good triumphing over evil in mind if not in actuality." Broderick's contortions carried rationalization to an art form itself. Catholic writers, according to his "realistic" ideal, were forbidden by their sense of beauty "from both the description and the glorification of what is ugly. For Blanche Mary Kelly the only possible use of anarchy and ugliness was the service they rendered to emphasize beauty, "to throw it into high and radiant relief." The great sin of modern art, said Kelly, was the creation of a "horrible universe" with no direction to it and the deformation of beauty in the modern portrayal of ugliness.[34]

John Hugo, a theology student at St. Vincent's Seminary in Latrobe, Pennsylvania, found that in fairy stories an important realism was preserved, the "realism of values." This realism, according to Hugo, preserved a purpose and a "tremendous meaning in all endeavor and the good *must* win." He allowed for the description of sin because at the very least it had "a sacramental value in the development of character." "Real realism," however, was man's ceaseless battle with evil. "This is realism," Hugo concluded:

> and the goal of infinite love; the apparently insuperable odds, the deep pitfalls, and the endless fighting are, besides, so many elements of an exciting romance. In this warfare no quarter is given to the dark defense of futility and despair; enterprise and laughter are the realities.

In developing this sense of realism one critic believed he had found the formula for the great American Catholic novel. This formula would allow the author to write of love but leave sex alone; to write of good "in all nobility" and evil "in all its baseness without offending the common sense of decency." The hero must be one in whom a "high state of Catholicism has been perfected." Besides the hero, the other characters must know who they are and where they are going. Finally, they must all be inspired with both hope and optimism in their struggles with life.[35]

The desire for characters who mastered themselves and their environment was the Catholic response to Wyndham Lewis' observation of the Hemingway hero that he belonged to "the multitudinous ranks of those to whom things happen." As Harold Gardiner pointed out, "they do not will, they make no choices." Francis X. Connolly interpreted the "decline" of poetry and fiction in his time in the light of this hesitating attitude toward man. "For many," said Connolly, "man is a problem . . . a thing acted upon rather than an actor. He is a recorder rather than a reasoner . . . man has become a creature without mystery, or meaning, without grace or splendor." According to Connolly, man's special glory was his "splendor of mind." It was the mind that brought understanding, balance, tranquillity, and freedom. It was the mind that enabled man to transcend the limits of time and place by "a timeless intuitive grasp of essential forms." The loss of the heroic sense in contemporary writing was due to ignoring "the struggle of free men against the forces of nature and evil."

In the face of the "bad tidings" portrayed by contemporary novelists, Catholics were provoked into a general retreat from American literature. As one convert, C. J. Eustace, confessed, the Catholic's "study of literature tends only to bewilder him, if not to make him embittered."[36] Failing to create a satisfying literature of their own, little remained for them but to call for a "return to tradition," offer "books of Christian classics", and continue in their isolation rather than suffer bewilderment.[37]

The peculiar dilemma and self-imposed isolation of the Catholic critic is best illustrated by the career of Francis X. Connolly. Educated at Fordham University, he came on the literary scene in 1930, objecting to "Catholic Puritans" and hopeful that the Catholic writer could find materials for his unique expression somewhere between "heaven" and the "marshes." With regard to the spirit of contemporary literature, which he observed as the struggle of the ego to find a place in the cosmos, he felt that for Catholics all this discontent and struggle were "vain histrionics" and appeared "childish" because they did not have "to waste precious spiritual energies over the first two pages of the catechism." After this initial outburst Connolly looked more deeply into the discontent of the modern artist. By 1934 he was able to perceive, as few others did, that the artist's unease was not so much a mirror of modern egoism as a critique and rebellion "against a world of shambles and fakes. . . ." Catholics, Connolly insisted, must accept the "essential honesty of intention" of the artist. It seemed to the young Fordham graduate that Catholics were illogically demanding from the artist "a calm and objective treatment of the universe when it seemed to him a monstrous gallery of mocking circumstance." The "turn inward," use of Freudian symbols, and attention to instinct were not, according to Connolly, the slippery slope to chaos but "a search for a center."[38]

Connolly interpreted the artist's rejection of the world as the same reason which prompted the monk to seek out his cell to explore the deeper realms, "venturing bodily into the hinterland of the spirit." Viewed in this light, it was not the function of the Catholic critic to "hunt heresy" but to contribute to the search for salvation. Catholics should look not to the "scholarly abstractions" of the humanists but to the profound, if blind, mysticism of the artist. This was a most unusual stance for a Catholic to be taking. To prefer D. H. Lawrence to Lord Macaulay, as Connolly suggested, was dangerous and evidenced a distinct shift in Catholic thinking. In fact, it was so dangerous that Connolly immediately retreated from this precarious position. Two things contributed to his reversal by the mid-1930's. First, he came under the spell of George Bull, S.J., and Bull's concept of a Catholic culture as "totality of view" at odds with everything around it. Second, the artist's "search for a center" led many in the 1930's into the certitude of Marxism. Once the artist shook off disillusionment and began affirming, Catholics were confronted, not with malaise, but with a system of affirmations and certainties which not only equaled but challenged their own. In reaction to this new atmosphere, according to Connolly, "the Catholic then must concern himself not with adaptation to his new environment, but with a stronger union with his own intellectual tradition. . . ."[39] For Connolly, this tradition came to mean emphasizing man's "splendor of mind," idealization of truth and beauty, and a literary moralism.

By 1940 Connolly had rejected his previous belief in the integrity of

modern literature as well as its "bodiness." American literature of the
1920's and the 1930's suffered in his view from "prolonged intellectual
clay-eating." The affirmations of Marxists in the 1930's did not change the
mood of the previous decade but rather narrowed and intensified it. The
world of John Steinbeck's *Grapes of Wrath* was a deterministic world where,
as Connolly quoted from the author, " 'There ain't no sin and there ain't no
virtue; there's just stuff folks do.' " Characterizing the moral universe as
Steinbeck did between " 'nice' " and " 'ain't so nice,' " did not satisfy
Connolly's desire for definite and certain moral judgments. The experimental and private worlds of Gertrude Stein and James Joyce symbolized the
modern mood of being "swept along in the flood of life, the victim rather
than the master of impressions." The path of fiction, Connolly concluded,
"led only to dejection and despair." It exhibited a civilization in decay, and
even as it protested against evil it failed to achieve any idea of the good.[40]

With such a severe outlook toward contemporary fiction it was not
surprising that Connolly saw a "problem" for Catholics in adapting their
writing to the modern world. Connolly observed two tendencies among
Catholics: the majority wished to preserve their heritage by creating a total
Catholic ethos; the "new school," on the other hand, sought to cooperate
with the modern ethos—accept Freudian psychology, and "baptize Dos
Passos, Wolfe, and Hemingway." They looked to the time when "the
Catholic writer will be recognized as the forward-looking thinker of his
day." The "barrenness" of Catholic literature in America was the result of
this doubt and conflict about what the Catholic way should be. There was
no doubt in Connolly's mind, however, that the problem of Catholic
literature was but one aspect of the general problem of Catholic culture,
which, as he said, had not taken root in America because the larger culture
was primarily "Protestant-agnostic, democratic, and commercial."
Catholic culture existed only in religious houses, colleges and organizations, which made more vivid the "abyss" between the Catholic way of
thinking and writing and those of their contemporaries. Catholics could
not write because they were caught up in a world of "anarchic individualism." The "new school's" attempts at adaptation would only result in
frustration.

To accept realism, naturalism, and experimentation would be accepting
the ethos of the modern world and a denial of the Catholic world. To accept
Marxist fiction would mean the acceptance of class conflict. To use a
stream-of-consciousness method involved the denial of reason and freedom
of choice. These forms implied "a way of looking at life" which was inimical
to the Catholic way. Therefore, Connolly asserted, it was "sheerest idiocy"
that Catholic culture should desire a Thomas Mann or Thomas Wolfe,
because both were "basically sensual, predominantly body-conscious. . . ."

Those Catholic writers who wanted to adopt the style of Dreiser, Faulkner, and Hemingway, and to add their own philosophical comment reminded him of those who thought James Joyce's *Ulysses* was a Catholic masterpiece "because it contains so many ecclesiastical references." In another place Connolly suggested that even European Catholic writers "cling to the manners, if not the morals, of decadence." While admiring Undset, Connolly felt her writings "occasionally induce, not approval of, but preoccupation with sheer bodiness and Graham Greene rarely allows us a thrill of joy without making us eat dirt."[41] Connolly's perception of the meaning of Catholic culture and the writing that would record it was gradually reaching the point where the only thing left to write about was air, and even this in the most genteel prose possible.

In the same movement that brought American philosophers and politicians back to a re-evaluation of American tradition just prior to World War II, literary lights were calling for a return to the American way. Rejecting nihilism, Marxism, and irresponsible disillusionment, Archibald MacLeish, *The Irresponsibles* (1940), and Van Wyck Brooks, *The Opinions of Oliver Allston* (1941), among others, sought a renewed affirmation of man's reason and ability to ascertain fundamental values. Catholics were naturally quick to notice this shift and welcome it. However, for most of them it was a return to the wrong tradition. Connolly hoped the American return would "rather sponsor a salutary awareness of the lack of a sound American tradition and the necessity of forming one." He objected to the newly forming "totemistic worship of Emerson, Whitman, Melville and others who, because they stood apart, were thought to stand higher." Such a tradition would only result in more anarchy, even if this one were more "respectable" than recent varieties. Having cut himself off from nearly everything after the 1840's, Connolly was forced to travel *To An Unknown Country* (1942) with his beleaguered concept of literature and art as "essentially entertainment or recreation." Although a sometime ally of good conduct, literature served primarily as a "magic carpet" enabling individuals to transcend the everyday world of business and "the lonely island of self-hood." Life "above the level of ordinary experience" could be conducted without difficulty and in tranquillity.[42]

Before Connolly retreated to his "unknown country" many Catholics were excited by the "magic carpet" offered by the New Humanists in the late 1920's. Not surprisingly, the call for a return to tradition, standards, hierarchies of values and restraint issued by such varied figures as Irving Babbitt, Paul Elmer Moore, Robert Maynard Hutchins, Norman Forester, John Crowe Ransom, Allan Tate, Gorham Munson and others, appealed to the secured sense of stability Catholics had managed to maintain. From their point of view this development in thought was a large stride toward the doorstep of Catholicism. The New Humanist movement appeared to many Catholic as an oasis in the desert of contemporary American culture. It momentarily excited them to think that "a fresh and more careful reasonableness has entered American letters," as a *Commonweal* editorial observed.

The futility and "hysteria of gloom" which characterized the literature of the 1920's was subsiding, according to Leo R. Ward, C.S.C., of Notre Dame, because the New Humanism "denies to Nature any necessary cruel tyranny over human life."[43] More importantly, the revival of interest in standards in America prepared the way for what William Franklin Sands predicted would be a "blossoming of intellectual Catholicism." This blossoming would come as a result of the defeat of naturalism and realism by the combined forces of humanism and neoscholasticism, the latter providing the needed philosophical and religious principles to shore up the humanists' limitations.[44]

The most outspoken and recalcitrant leader of the literary and philosophical phase of the humanist movement was Irving Babbitt, who fought from his Harvard citadel the encroachment of romanticism and naturalism into literature. For him the path of the literary mind since the neoclassicism of the eighteenth century was one long rush to darkness. He was generally regarded as a living anachronism in America until 1928, when the rush of events and a reaction to the "irresponsibility" of the 1920's brought him to the center of what Gorham Munson called the "battle of the books." Having once observed that the Catholic Church was the only institution left in the western world "which could be counted upon to uphold civilized standards," it was only natural that Catholics would be sympathetic to Babbitt's style of thinking, if they could not quite accept his naturalistic and stoic principles of ethical behavior. Babbitt's refusal to become Catholic or Christian himself left him open to the more critical, like Fulton Sheen, who charged that he and the other humanists represented merely a recrudescence of Pelagianism. Those, however, who sought to find evidence that American culture and Catholic culture were supportive of each other, lionized Babbitt as a champion of the intellect, an advocate of final causes, free will, restraint, and natural moral laws which placed man above nature and therefore not subject to nature's whimsy or terror.[45]

It was a Catholic, Louis J. A. Mercier, who was one of the first to develop the disparate characteristics of humanistic voices into a recognizable movement at the close of the 1920's. Mercier, though born in France, was educated in America, at Loyola University in Chicago, the University of Chicago, and Columbia University. Most of his life was spent teaching in the Department of Romance Languages at Harvard University, where he developed a friendship with Babbitt. In 1928 he wrote, for a French audience, his *Le Movement Humaniste aux Etats Unis*. In this book Mercier brought together the thought of Babbitt, Paul Elmer Moore, and W. C. Brownell, and sought to relate these American expressions of antiromanticism with similar thrusts in France which began with Paul Bourget and Ferdinand Brunetiere. By the time Mercier published the English edition, *The Challenge of Humanism* (1933), Babbitt's star had passed. But Mercier continued through the 1930's to defend Babbitt from critics who felt that his principles starved creative expression and from Catholics like Sheen who thought they were not firm enough. Later, in *American Humanism and the New Age* (1948), Mercier expanded the movement to include Robert Maynard Hutchins and Walter Lippmann as further examples that within American culture there was a continuing movement toward Catholicism.[46]

The primary attraction of the new humanism for Catholics was its concern for making man distinct in nature. They emphasized man's rational nature and his quality of self-direction or inner control. Art and literature were thus expressions of restraint and controlled energy, this in contrast to the more spontaneous and instinctual emphasis of recent literature. Form became the chief criterion for judging the value of literature, and textual criticism succeeded in gaining academic respectability.[47] Catholics took these classical standards both seriously and fanatically. Passion and imagination were feared because of their potential to outrun the intellect.

In a number of general attempts at constructing a theory of aesthetics, passion was practically outlawed from art. According to the view of Sister Mary Gonzaga Udell, O.P., fiction was the "assemblage of universal ideas and judgments." Such universality required the artist to show that true life "abounds in winnings of good over evil." It also required the near complete absence of any description of sex. For many Catholics, the sexual act was "by its very nature secret" and not a socially shared function. Udell's reaction to sex, however, went beyond the realm of taste. Her objection to its description in fiction was that it was not completely human, therefore not legitimately entitled to a place in art. A sense of "shame" surrounded the sexual embrace, concluded Udell, "because in it reason is utterly submerged by the intense gratification accruing to the animal appetite. In itself then it cannot be regarded as a strictly human act but a lowly concomitant, though not an essential element of conjugal affection." Sex only clouded and muddled fiction with too many details and complexities which, for Udell, destroyed the primary aim of any story—"to simplify and put into order the jumbled details of life."[48]

The humanist movement developed as a reaction to the supposedly reckless withdrawal of artistic endeavor in the 1920's. As John Chamberlain wrote in 1929, the interest in humanism was "evidence of a growing healthy attitude toward our world. We seem ready to accept our surroundings; we seem ready to build." The initial spirit was one of affirmation in contrast to the negations of the postwar period. With regard to writing, however, and especially in the preachments of Babbitt and Moore, what was primarily being affirmed was restraint. This quality readily approved itself to Catholics. Leo Ward applauded the presence of a group of Americans avoiding extremes,

> aiming at the normal, honoring great historic movements and declaring that within man is a power of guiding his own life, a negative inhibitory power, if you will, but essential to his manhood and, if used, the means of his control and the gateway . . . to insight. The normal, permanent man known from experience and from history, keeping himself in the path of balanced interests, controlling and directing himself. [49]

If, as many charged, the humanists were sometimes ruthless in their imposition of standards and emphasizing the will to refrain, many Catholics, as we have seen, tended toward fanaticism on these subjects. For them, restraint was the only path toward mastery. They approached literature with a large list of "oughts" and "don'ts" which left little room for the human spirit to roam. There were some Catholics who recognized these liabilities. George Shuster from the beginning and later Theodore Maynard came to reject the humanists' lack of enthusiasm and vitality and the deficiency of the human in their humanism. Russell Wilbur objected to Mercier's comparison of Babbitt's "inner check" with Christian grace. For Wilbur, grace was an expansive, even a romantic, power and not a barrier to experience. [50]

Since World War I Catholics had succeeded in creating a literary world-within-the-world which reflected similar efforts in philosophy and general social outlook. Theirs was a world of certainties where nature was malleable to human control, man was free and unperplexed by either exterior or interior complexes. A concept of beauty and truth reigned which was largely abstractive and located in ideal forms above the cauldron of experience. In their cloistered world Catholics thought they were, again, preserving an essential Americanism—the ideal of the self-controlled individual of responsible action who was innately confident in his ability to master both himself and his environment. The preservation of this ideal demanded their withdrawal from contemporary literary forms and creative expression. The pessimism and discontent characteristic of this literature appeared to Catholics as un-American and opposed to their religious ideals. These religious values were, in turn, largely informed by the optimism and moralism that was their image of America. The result was a distinctively American Catholic literary pose which contorted both the American and

Catholic elements to produce a literature characterized more by bland sentimentality than by vitality.

Their obsession with the survival of idealism in America reduced their reaction to contemporary literature to the sometimes uncomfortable but nevertheless required position of hostility toward anything which did not abound in the winning of good over evil, of the individual over himself and his surroundings. Catholic criticism suffered from the sad plight of defending only the optimistic and fearing everything else. This pathetic note was struck by Elizabeth Jordan who described the 1931 dramatic season led off by Eugene O'Neill as "a strange season this, in which all the good things are so bad."[51]

Cloistered within its own precincts, Catholic distaste for the outside literary world succeeded primarily in prolonging the fond dream of a long-hoped-for "revival" of Catholic literature. However, in the realm of literature's translation into the art of motion picture making Catholic influence transcended its own cloisters and afforded the group a leverage over an element of American culture it did not enjoy in any other area. Not surprisingly, their influence was largely of a negative variety, which tended to increase suspicion of a Catholic attempt to abridge American freedoms.

Catholic involvement in the cinema was a result of fortuitous circumstances and a persistent determination to exert their cultural standards by mobilizing their numbers. In 1926, when sound was added to film, Catholics were quick to recognize the "power" of motion pictures to "convey ideas." It became imperative, then, as Martin Joseph Quigley, editor of the *Motion Picture Herald* and *Motion Picture Daily,* noted, that the ideas conveyed be the right ones. Quigley, a Catholic educated at Niagara University and the Catholic University of America, traveled to Hollywood in the 1920's to seek his fortune. Opposed to state censorship, he was an advocate of self-regulation. Quigley applauded the 1927 code which the Motion Picture Producers and Distributors of America, Inc., adopted as an effort at self-regulation and put under the supervision of Will Hays. The administration of the code was commonly referred to as the Hays Office. This code, however, promptly languished for lack of attention.[52]

As a result of the stock market crash in 1929, many motion picture production companies came under the financial control of Halsey, Stuart and Company, a Chicago-based firm. As it happened, officials of this company regularly lunched with the Cardinal of Chicago, George Mundelein. At the prompting of Mundelein, the bankers brought financial pressure to bear which induced the industry to accept a new code. It was not widely known at the time, but the Motion Picture Production Code of 1930 was the handiwork of Catholics. Daniel Lord, S.J., was the primary author, with the assistance of Martin Quigley and FitzGeorge Dineen, another

Jesuit from Chicago. Lord wrote the code with the idea that it would appeal to all decent men and as an "opportunity to read morality and decency into mass recreation." He presented his work at a meeting of producers in Hollywood and to those in the Hays Office charged with the responsibility of enforcing it. This code, like the previous one, languished because those who were supposed to enforce it were the producers themselves. Lord, dissatisfied with the lack of moral improvement in films after 1930, mobilized Catholic youth to boycott movies he blacklisted in his magazine *The Queen's Work,* the national organ for the Catholic Sodality movement. Previously, Catholics had adopted the policy of praising movies they liked while refusing to list those they found objectionable. So successful was his policy of blacklisting and boycotting that in 1934 the National Catholic Welfare Conference established the National Catholic Office for Motion Pictures, popularly known as the Legion of Decency. This agency asked Catholics to pledge in church to boycott films rated objectionable.

Such tactics had their effect in Hollywood. More control passed to the Production Code Administration, which was given the authority to review preliminary and final scripts as well as the final edition of the film before a certification of approval was given. This department was placed under the direction of yet another Catholic, Joseph I. Breen. In no other area of American culture were Catholics so deeply involved or had more opportunity to exert an influence. Unfortunately, as Walter Kerr noted in 1953, the result of all their effort was the identification of American Catholicism "with the well-meaning second-rate."[53]

At the heart of the problem was the 1930 code itself. Although constructed by Daniel Lord, there was nothing about it that would lead one to suspect it was written by a servant of the Pope. Rather, the code embodied ideals that had a long tradition in America. In fact, as a form of criticism, the code was remarkably similar to what William Charvat has delineated as the basic principles of American criticism from 1810 to 1835. Allowing for the later infusion of idealism, the code would have made sense to such diverse literary minds as George Bancroft, James Lowell, Ralph Waldo Emerson and William Dean Howells. It continued to make sense to a significant number of Americans in 1930.

However, the code was hopelessly out of sympathy with the creative artistic mind of the twentieth century. It prohibited the questioning of moral and social standards. Good and evil, it maintained, should be clearly distinguished and just rewards meted out accordingly. If the happy ending was not required, the general tone of the code encouraged it. Violence and passion were to be minimized, and somber or obscure material was excluded.[54] The 1930 code, written by Daniel Lord and watched over by countless Catholics, epitomized their identification with a set of moralistic standards long held sacred by Americans. Catholics had unhesitatingly undertaken the stern duty of preserving this *depositum morum*. They relished the role of inheritors and unspoiled defenders of a psychological and moral outlook of the confident, secure American who knew the difference between right and wrong, sanity and insanity, heaven and hell. They were naturally perplexed, then, when other Americans accused them of being the pawns of a reactionary foreign potentate. They understood their defense of this deposit of moral convictions as utterly American in inspiration and Catholic only in flavor.

Following World War I, Catholics had withdrawn from the disillusion-ment of the 1920's, were excited by the counterattack of the new humanists at the close of that decade as evidence of a return to traditional standards, and then retreated even further in the 1930's as their affirmations collided with the less genteel affirmations of Marxists and other literary radicals of the depression era. Confident that they stood in the path of truth, many Catholics were growing anxious over the lack of creative expression within their group. It was not until the early 1940's that an American Catholic writer appeared who not only earned admiration from a growing element in his own religious community but achieved some critical attention from non-Catholics for his control of the technological art of storytelling. John F. Powers suddenly became "the white hope of the Catholic novel" in America, a burden he suffered until the mid-1950's, when he was able to share it with Flannery O'Connor.[55]

Powers was born on July 8, 1917, in Jacksonville, Illinois.[56] His early education was received in public schools but his collegiate training was supervised by the Franciscans at Quincy College in Illinois. During the Depression he survived on a succession of odd jobs in Chicago. Influenced by the Catholic Worker movement in that city, he became a pacifist and was one of the handful of Catholic citizens who refused military induction in World War II. The field of Powers' fiction was largely confined to the improbable life of parish priests in America, whom he described with both compassion and searing criticism, but always with a view to the ironic in their situations. He has produced only one novel, *Morte D'Urban* (1962). The greater part of his work has been in the form of short stories, which have been collected and published in *Prince of Darkness* (1947), *Presence of Grace* (1956), and *Look How the Fish Live* (1975). The impact of Powers' writing bears directly upon the literary imagination of Catholics formed before World War II and the slow dissolution of their firm structure of convictions which has followed.

The field for Powers' imagination lay between what Alfred Kazin noted were the poles of life: the "gravity" of reality and the surprising ways "grace" or beauty entered into that world. This middle ground had long been idealized by critics like George Shuster, Michael Williams, Francis X. Talbot, and Francis X. Connolly as the area where the Catholic artist could creatively explore. Unlike previous efforts by Catholics, however, Powers discovered in this middle realm conflict, disorder, resignation, irony, despair, mediocrity, and failure. The human predicament, though, was never reduced to unrelieved dreariness. There remained always the steady but unpredictable flickering movement of grace and the human spirit. In contrast to the violent hatred of the world depicted by European Catholic novelists, who found escape only in the sudden and mysterious effulgence of divine mercy, Powers plied his art in a slip of the wide stream of confidence he inherited from the Catholic experience in America.[57]

Contrary to the zealous bellowings of armchair optimists, Powers' sense of confidence in reality was of a more delicate nature. The themes of his stories read like critical commentaries on the optimistic culture from which he sprang. In one of his first stories, "Lions Hearts Leaping Does" (1943), the rational certitude and will assertion of Father Didymus crumbles beneath the priest's constant self-doubt and self-judgment, leading to resignation and a sense of Christian failure at his death. In "Prince of Darkness" Powers bares the shallow security and middle-class comfort of Father Bruner, whose quest for success continually eludes him. In a later story, "Look How the Fish Live" (1957), Powers deftly explores the disorder of nature: its indifference, its lack of compassion, and its continual infliction of pain. Not only is man unable to understand nature's significance, man himself is part of the travail.[58] Such themes were hardly new to American literature, but in Powers they were given expression by an American Catholic who is conscious of a philosophical commitment to moral laws and who is also aware that there is no assured coordination between those laws and life in this world.[59]

The significance of Powers' writing for Catholic culture in America was the impact of "the presence . . . of darkness" on a group which had struggled long to maintain its philosophical, literary, and social virginity. He represented the transition of the Catholic community from a world of embattled innocence to what George Scouffas has called "the world of complex innocence." Powers wrote of the rather large area between despair and moralism. The complexity of reality and moral obscurity inherent in man's view of it did not render his characters incapable of living hopeful, useful lives in society. Indeed, as Scouffas noted, Powers found a source of vitality even in human and natural disorder. Previously, Catholics were wont to perceive disorder as a sign of degeneration and as a confession of weakness. They preferred a view of nature as an ordered and benign composite and man as the primary instrument of design. There was considerable distance and novelty of approach between this view of reality and Powers' admission that even though winning was never assured "you can live and you can die well."[60]

The struggle to live and die well has been a constant element in mankind's passage through life. An American writer of Catholic lineage who was unsure whether he did either well was F. Scott Fitzgerald, one of a number of Catholic artists who wrote from the other side of innocence.

7. F. Scott Fitzgerald
The Other Side of Innocence,
The Far Side of Catholicism

IN 1930 GEORGE N. SHUSTER, THEN MANAGING EDITOR of *The Commonweal*, prefaced a book about Catholicism and contemporary literature with a disturbing thought: "From Anatole France to Theodore Dreiser the names of those who have given up their faith for literature are many and great enough to constitute something like a problem."[1] The problem, as Shuster defined it, was not an inherent dichotomy between religion and art; rather, it was the result of two interrelated circumstances. On the one hand, the modern literary personality had taken upon himself the role of "maker of images" rather than the more traditional literary objective of describing known generalities about man and the universe. As a maker of images the artist placed a high priority on freedom to hypothesize about the nature of man, the presence or absence of spiritual values in life, and the construction of the universe in which man dwells.[2]

American Catholics, as we have seen, denounced this artistic presumption because it tended "to distort the perspective of life" as well as art. This response, according to Shuster, led the Catholic writer and critic "to shy behind his blinkers at the very sight and smell of the universe," distorting the relationship between faith and art. Unfortunately, said Shuster, Catholics had developed the habit of seeing "nothing in the universe but middle-class primness—in order to avoid shocking some imaginary school-girl."[3]

Catholic writers in Europe seemed to have resolved these problems early in the present century, and their work bristled with both passion and violence as they described contemporary life. In the United States, however, Catholics looked forward to a "literary renaissance" which never seemed to develop. As late as 1951 critics bemoaned a yet unborn literary consciousness among American Catholics.[4] Whereas Shuster believed the departure of literary men like Dreiser, Hemingway, James T. Farrell, Eugene O'Neill, F. Scott Fitzgerald, and many other lesser lights constituted a problem for American Catholicism, a majority of Catholic critics concluded otherwise. Calvert Alexander saw no literary revival in America because, for one thing, a large number of authors of Catholic birth "were in various degrees seduced" by the "decadence" of American writing surrounding World War I and thus squandered their energy in a "sterile revolt."[5] Ten years later Thomas McDermott echoed Alexander's conclusions by pointing to the dearth of Catholic literature and blaming the Church's "great men" for deserting the ranks for "the smooth and easy way" and the "flesh pots of Egypt."[6]

If many of these literary personalities showed little inclination to stay within the Catholic household—and some like Farrell were rather violent in their denunciations of an inherited cultural experience that seemed to crush out life—most Catholics who took any interest in such matters were not at all distressed over the "seduction." In most cases Catholics were eager to be rid of the cultural and intellectual problems they posed. The reason for the mutual disavowal was a clash of ideological and moral perceptions of reality. As Catholics assumed the protectorship of American moralism, a significant number of American writers who happened to be Catholic were rejecting that very moralism. Consequently, if the writer in the postwar period was unsure about his relationship to America, those who were Catholic as well as American were doubly damaged. For example, one critic considered Hemingway's realism abhorrent because it was not "tempered by Catholic theology, Catholic culture and artistic taste. If these qualities be present, there can be no room for naturalism, for obscenity, for crudeness or for the vulgar. For these reasons alone . . . Hemingway must part company with his fellow-churchmen."[7]

Eugene O'Neill represented the rarely acknowledged underside of American Catholic Irish optimism. It was not surprising, then, to find Catholics irritated by O'Neill's fatalism. During the 1920's Catholics were universally repulsed by the playwright's theme of bewilderment expressed in *The Hairy Ape, Desire Under the Elms, Dynamo,* and *The Great God Brown.* They found O'Neill's art absorbed in the grotesque and lacking the necessary quality of "good" art: the concern for "uplift." His fascination with personal suffering led critics to reject what they considered his obsession with the abnormal and brutal. As a poet and philosopher O'Neill was a failure according to R. Danna Skinner, dramatic critic of *The Commonweal,* because his intelligence was submerged by emotion and "raw feelings." To Elizabeth Jordan, it was not life that was presented but life seen by the "jaundiced, red-rimmed, astigmatic eyes" of Eugene O'Neill. In the early 1930's, with the publication of *Ah! Wilderness* and *Days Without End,* many former adversaries believed O'Neill to be in the process of a purgation and on a "comeback to normalcy."[8]

While his former plays were judged to be "alien" to the Catholic spirit

because they languished in the "mists of hopelessness," the change in tone
in both *Ah! Wilderness* and, especially, *Days Without End* was for Catholics
an altogether unexpected development. As Joseph A. Daley, S.J., confessed, it was a "startling" surprise for him to learn that O'Neill was concerned
in his plays with the "surviving primitive religious instinct to find a
meaning for life . . . ," which was made imperative as a result of the "death
of the old God and the failure of science and materialism to give any
satisfying new one. . . ." These words of O'Neill's would probably have
been dismissed if they were not "confirmed" for some Catholics by his
message of laughter and love in the plays of the early 1930's. To those
associated with the playwright during this period it appeared that O'Neill
was on the verge of resuming his status as a Catholic. In fact, before *Days
Without End* was published in 1934 he asked Martin Quigley and Daniel
Lord, S.J., to review the manuscript. Both were pleased; Lord was "overwhelmed." O'Neill was grateful for their enthusiasm and wrote to Quigley
that he hoped there was "enough strength and conviction in the play to
overcome the pseudo-intellectual pose of New York critics . . . that
religious faith is an outmoded subject. . . ."[9]

Enthusiasm about O'Neill's return in *Days Without End* was not universal
among Catholics. The play itself was not placed on the list of approved plays
because of its "strong language" and a problem concerning divorce.
R. Danna Skinner tried to have this decision reversed but to no avail. A
most outspoken Catholic critic of the play was Brother Leo, who objected
to its lingering "fatalism." "Catholics know," said Leo, "that the individual
through the power of the will can triumph." O'Neill was still insufficiently
impressed with this view.[10] The Irish author was to continue to the end of
his days to struggle with the problem of his Catholicism never satisfactorily
resolving it one way or the other. A rather profound effort to come to terms
with it comprised the movement of his most famous dramatic effort, *Long
Day's Journey into Night*. A large element of his problem, however, involved
the Catholic community in America. While some could support him in
laughter, few traveled with him "into the night." Catholics were moving in
an opposite direction at the time, which, as it turned out, was a long night's
journey to cast reality into the promises of sunlight.

The departures, then, of Dreiser, Hemingway, Fitzgerald and the others
from Catholicism were indistinguishable from their general revolt against
American moralism and idealism. Innocence flowered within the Catholic
community after World War I as it withered around them. In this context,
an examination of F. Scott Fitzgerald's relationship to Catholicism, and his
eventual withdrawal from it, holds a contemporary as well as historical
fascination. Fitzgerald's critical reputation has gone through several rever-
sals. Judged first as a sentimental chronicle of the jazz age and then as a

victim of its and his own frivolity, his work has eventually come to be seen as a sensitive and graceful representation of the American experience caught in the anomaly of its own making: of "raw power . . . haunted by envisioned romance."[11]

Fitzgerald was alive to these contrasting forces because his own personality, as described by Arthur Mizener and others, was fraught with internal divisions.[12] Fitzgerald lived in the "meantime," trying to balance an experience of life as a romantic conquest frequently interrupted by disillusionments—between illusion and reality, dream and power, confidence and distrust, control and susceptibility. The "entire man" of paradise, "a sort of combination J. P. Morgan . . . and St. Francis of Assisi," was continually confronted by the "spoiled priest," the wanting creature whose fate it was to live "this side of paradise," lacking in a moment either the power of Morgan or the susceptibility of St. Francis.[13]

Contributing to, if not entirely determining, this duality of pose within Fitzgerald were social and religious factors operating in a generational context which he himself so well described as "dedicated more than the last to the fear of poverty and the worship of success; grown up to find all Gods dead, all wars fought, all faiths in men shaken. . . ."[14] Fitzgerald felt the weight of the "in between time," when the certainties of life, or what Walter Lippmann called its "accumulated convictions," were peeling away under the very pressure of experience itself. Besides the pervasive cultural note of uncertainty, other influences converged which tended to heighten his "divided nature." Some years ago Edmund Wilson suggested there were two things worth knowing about Fitzgerald in evaluating his work: one, he was a midwesterner, and, two, he was of Irish ancestry.[15] His Catholicism might profitably be added to the list. Fitzgerald was not only Irish but an American Irish Catholic. His life was spent attempting to balance the contradictory and confusing impulses of his youth. His Irishness, wavering between lighthearted gaiety, cynicism, and tragedy, continued as an "undertone" in all his stories.[16] His Catholicism strangely lingered in his memory.

Fitzgerald was born into an Irish Catholic family described by his bishop as "staunch, devout, generous."[17] On the social level, his family was neither ghetto-bound nor in the position where upward social striving was meaningless. The Fitzgeralds, along with many other Irish families during the first two decades of the twentieth century, lived "at the edge of two worlds of the insiders and the great unwashed."[18] They resided on Summit Avenue in St. Paul, Minnesota, amidst the wealthy, but even their location on the street, as J. F. Powers has noted, was "on the fringe . . . after running a half-mile at its best, Summit Avenue seems to pause and relax before it begins again."[19]

Occupying a more prominent section of the street was a complex of buildings which made St. Paul the "Vatican City" of the Northwest and gave the place a Catholic atmosphere over its already Christian name. The man responsible for this was Archbishop John Ireland (1838–1918), "the consecrated blizzard of the Northwest" who conceived his mission as a Catholic churchman to be to clean up the immigrants and dress them in garments of American color and texture. Ireland's vigorous Catholicism reflected an effort among Catholics at the turn of the century to place themselves socially and culturally within the American mainstream. Uplift, gentility, progress, moralism, and optimism were cultural symbols Catholics identified with, despite warnings of American heresy in the papal letter *Testem benevolentiae* (1899). Ten months after the publication of Leo XIII's condemnation of Americanism, Ireland addressed a banquet in Chicago on October 7, 1899, honoring President McKinley. The archbishop expressed confidence that there had been no deterioration of the national character in either its public or private life:

> In America the general tone and trend of social life make for honor and honesty, for truth and morality. Public opinion metes out stern condemnation to wrongdoing, and unstinted approval to righteous conduct. The typical American home is the shrine of domestic virtues. . . . It matters little to me what the difficulties are that confront us, be they political, social or industrial. I have trust in the good sense of the people. . . . Perils have arisen and perils will rise; America has overcome those of the past; she will overcome those of the future.[20]

Trying to condemn this kind of Americanism was as futile as attacking one's own shadow. These values were instilled in Catholics in their parochial schools, summer chautauquas, and especially in their literature.[21]

The Americanist condemnation had two quite unexpected results. It did little to uproot already pervasively held beliefs about "true Americanism" among Catholics, but it did cut off Catholic participation in an evolving process by which many other Americans began to question and criticize the presuppositions of their cultural myths. What Henry May has described as the "rebellion of the intellectuals," which took focus during the second decade of the twentieth century as a revolt against idealism, formalism, and moralism, had little support from middle-class Catholic intelligentsia, who found the values of gentility quite comfortable, essentially Catholic, and traditionally American.[22]

Fitzgerald, driven on by the worship of success as he proceeded from St. Paul to Princeton University, to New York, Paris, and Hollywood, was caught in its web but was able at moments to transcend the veneer of middle-class culture and complacency by allowing himself the experience of doubt and uncertainty about all values formed by finite man. This attitude placed him within the party of rebellion as it put him on the far side of Catholicism. In this process, however, one is struck by the indefinite quality of his rebellion and the lingering attraction of a certain kind of Catholicism. When Fitzgerald confessed to Edmund Wilson that his Catholicism was "scarcely more than a memory—no, that's wrong; it's more than that," he admitted a continuing confusion about a faith he never totally rejected but found difficult to accept in the concrete reality of its American setting.[23]

Muting his rebellion from the mores of American idealism was a quality his critics have described as a "sense of sin." Seeing life as "a dramatic conflict between good and evil," Arthur Mizener felt, was attributable to his Catholic training.[24] Fitzgerald's "moral vision," however, has been accused of lapsing into sentimentality and suffering from a lack of focus.[25] Moral obscurity was one characteristic Catholicism in the United States has hardly been accused of inculcating. Fitzgerald, noted Ernest Boyd in 1924, was intolerant of "the mores of bohemia" and cautious in his approach to sex. "There are still venial and mortal sins in his calendar," said Boyd, and continued

> His Catholic heaven is not so far away that he can be misled into mistaking the shoddy dream of a radical millenium as a substitute for Paradise. His confessions . . . will be permeated by the conviction of sin which is so much happier than the conviction that the way to Utopia is paved with adultery.[26]

It would appear that Fitzgerald approached his art and his life wanting—not unlike many other intellectuals in America—"to preach at people." His preachments, though, were something more than what Irving Howe described as "fragments of conviction," and something less than Catholic absolutism.[27]

Fitzgerald sought to combine discernment with a "heightened sensitivity to the promises of life." He was both Nick Carraway, the moral evaluator, in *The Great Gatsby,* who judged even while he was "inclined to reserve all judgments," and Jay Gatsby, whose "romantic readiness" for life's magical impulses made him seek a plane above moral evaluation of any kind.[28] These dual roles put him between one group prone to dismiss the moral weight of the past and another incapable of distinguishing frankness from morality and confusing convention with moral vision. His quest "to miss nothing" in the discovery of value brought personal insight as well as "emotional bankruptcy."

These insights of Fitzgerald's have continuing value because they are enlivened by his own sense of culpability. His "confessions," appearing as they did in "The Crack-Up" articles of 1936, were admissions of his failures and equally the attempt at a renewal of his hope. In the words of Andrew Turnbull, they were "the work of a lapsed Catholic for whom confession was a rhythm of the soul." But the Church itself was not, at this time, in the habit of making public confessions. Perhaps the "haunting sense of loss" prevalent in his writing concerning Catholicism was not that the Church appeared too weak but that it was too overpowering. Contrary to Turnbull's recollections, Fitzgerald's break with the Church was more emotional than intellectual.[29]

Fitzgerald backed away from "a convenient and ready-made" Catholicism "without priests, sacraments, or sacrifice."[30] At the same time, he was attracted by an "inconvenient" Church which demanded a discipline of mind and soul. He could not find in Catholicism an openness for his emotional vitality because the discipline he found attractive threatened to squeeze his emotions dry. Thus, he stood outside with only his memories.[31]

In his youth Fitzgerald shared with many other Americans (and not a few Catholics who came to maturity in the years 1910 to 1920) a zest for life, a desire to channel the forces of society and nature for the creation of a better world, a lively expression of culture in art, politics, religion, and science. Although this enthusiasm was expressed in wildly divergent fashions, it rested on an attitude of mind Fitzgerald later recalled in "The Crack-Up": "Life was something you dominated if you were any good. Life yielded easily to intelligence and effort. . . . It seemed a romantic business. . . ."[32] It was a time of restless egos, so openly exposed as to invite being bruised. As we have seen, Michael Williams shared Fitzgerald's restlessness.

Williams, who in the course of those years overcame hunger, tuberculosis, and alcoholism (and even survived an earthquake) while exploring socialism and nearly every kind of religious enthusiasm, wrote of his journeys as *The High Romance.* His desire was to be "a Voice of this new world, and a voice of the people, telling the new tales of hope, and singing the new songs of joy, and so to be one of the many builders, helping to build for the people, the crystal house of beauty."[33] Williams discovered in Catholicism in 1913 a hearth for his own ego. In the process, he transferred his own personal egoism into an institutional egoism which might dominate life on a level not susceptible to the bruises life dealt to the unprotected. After World War I Williams became editor of *The Commonweal,* where he spoke of a "resurgent" Church which conquered life in all its variety. Fitzgerald, on the other hand, wrote his impressionistic autobiography, *This Side of Paradise,* as a chronicle of egotistical extravagance and courage, but with a difference. Instead of cushioning the bruised ego within an institution where it could continue to make new conquests, Fitzgerald wanted "time and the absence of ulterior pressure."[34] Still eager to dominate, he desired, nevertheless, to give play to the uncertainty of his times.

Fitzgerald came to an awareness of the Catholic Church when there was some doubt whether the flickering sparks of life it manifested were momentary "phosphorescences" of a decaying institution (in Edmund Wilson's view), or whether there was indeed a "resurgence" in the making.[35] It is not surprising that his reaction to it was fraught with some ambiguity. It could be at one time "sporty" and at other times bourgeois. It was both "convenient" and "inconvenient," "dazzling" in ritual yet possibly empty of meaning. It exhibited a "cool" and refreshing symmetrical restraint, but was equally "gaudy" and paradoxical. He recognized its desire for domination of life through assertion of the will and intellect; but he was afraid such assertion excluded a capacity of susceptibility, and, indeed, that it might mean "a backing away from life." The very forces that attracted him made him leery.

While under the influence of Sigourney Cyril Fay, his alter-father, and Shane Leslie, the Irish writer, Fitzgerald saw the Church as a "dazzling golden thing . . . giving the succession of days upon grey days, passing under its plaintive ritual, the romantic glamour of an adolescent dream."[36] But it was this all-encompassing ritual that Fitzgerald most feared. In three short stories, "The Ordeal," "Benediction," and "Absolution," doubt arose at the very heart of the ritual itself, exposing an emptiness in the individual or in the symbol. In his early story, "The Ordeal" (1915), the young novice comes to a point of spiritual indifference during his ordination ceremony but is "saved" from despair by gripping and clinging to the "new presences" he feels from the "warm, red" glow of the stained glass windows in the Church.[37] Indifference is overcome, not within the ritual, but from its external ornaments. In "Absolution" the ritual enables Father Schwartz to function in the "twilight" of the confessional but at the expense of facing "the light, the madness of the four-o'clock day where life moves."[38] The ritual, however dazzling in its glamour, might be an escape from life. It might be an ornament itself, empty of symbolic value. Whatever it was, Fitzgerald, brought to it an essential distrust, afraid that exterior rituals of any kind would harness his quest to be a symbol himself.

Inhabiting Fitzgerald's Catholicism were two kinds of priests: the bourgeois, comfortable in their complacent security, and the "sporty," secure in their restlessness. The latter had a profound impact on his early life. Sigourney Cyril Fay (1875–1919) became Fitzgerald's spiritual mentor and surrogate father, and, along with Leslie, encouraged his literary imagination in the writing of *This Side of Paradise*. Fay, a convert from the Anglican Church in 1908, was ordained into the Catholic priesthood in 1910 by Cardinal James Gibbons, Archbishop of Baltimore. The two quickly became friends as Fay frequently spoke for the Cardinal on various occasions, while the latter made Fay his agent in Rome during World War

I. Fay also taught at the Catholic University of America in Washington, D.C.; and in 1917 he was made headmaster of Newman School in Hackensack, New Jersey, where he met the young Fitzgerald.

In his brief career as a Catholic (he died only eleven years after his conversion), Fay was able to maintain close relationships with such diverse figures as Gibbons, Fitzgerald, Shane Leslie, and Henry Adams. He was, as Leslie recalled, "a society priest in a country where they are very rare. . . . He could go straight from a party to give a convent retreat. . . . He could put Catholicism to the literary or luxurious with approved paradox." He was also an example of a man who "found the Faith" then "merrily teased the world," teaching "that the conventional sins were rather early Victorian and that it required a *fin de siecle* intelligence to appreciate the Mass."[39] With Fay's death on January 10, 1919, Leslie wrote to Fitzgerald that Fay's passing removed "the center from your solar system . . . the planet out of mine. Cardinal Gibbons has lost his only satisfactory satellite."[40]

Fay was rather portly, fair skinned, and carried a "childlike simplicity" and personal charm which endeared him to his friends.[41] His zest for life, which included "good company, good food and drink," was attuned to a religious awareness that he would describe as "not conscientiously pious."[42] In his understanding of the Church, Fay sought to incorporate Henri Bergson's concept of the *"elan vital."* The Church represented "life," both in its "indestructibility" and in its "ability to burst out into new forms and continually make new conquests for itself."[43]

Fay's own paradoxical bent of mind mirrored his conception of the Church as the "great paradox of history." She never sacrificed "one opposite to the other, but she carries both opposites to their highest point." The Church, he would write, managed to contain the flights of mysticism in her saints and to turn individual sanctity into "pragmatical value and practical power." The Church's use of authority has been "more imperious" and "more preemptory" than that of any other religious group, "yet, alone among all the religious bodies of the world, its members speak of it as their Mother."[44] In Fay's mind the Church was not always what it appeared to be, but one might have said that to Fay its varied appearances were more often confusing than sweetly paradoxical.

For the young Fitzgerald, who related to Fay as son to father, the priest was the perfect combination of romantic warmth and the disciplined coolness of the pragmatist. "He was intensely ritualist, startlingly dramatic, loved the idea of God enough to be a celibate and rather liked his neighbor."[45] Fitzgerald saw in Fay "the perfect understanding," the ability he recalled in "The Crack-Up" as "the test of a first rate intelligence . . . to hold two opposed ideas in the mind at the same time, and still retain the ability to function."[46] While Fitzgerald often recognized his own failure to live up to this aesthetic and intellectual ideal, it was one always present in his memory of Fay and the Church which Fay believed in and portrayed.

The Catholicism Fitzgerald learned from Fay was a religion "of lights and shadows, making all light and shadow aspects of God." In such a faith Fitzgerald felt secure. But this security was rooted, even in Fay, in an unceasing restlessness which betrayed a fundamental insecurity. To remain violently alive, to be "indispensable" to others, necessitated an admission that life was essentially a precarious venture. Fitzgerald witnessed in Fay these "moments of strange and horrible insecurity," but after Fay's death he lacked the ability to balance these opposites. They appeared, then, "inexplicable in a religion that explained even disbelief in terms of its own faith; if you doubted the devil, it was the devil that made you doubt him."[47] Fay's effort to balance the lights and shadows of religious belief was a rare venture in American Catholicism of the time.

More characteristic of its concerns was the reaction of Catholics like Peter Guilday, who was an associate of Fay at the Catholic University of America. Guilday was asked to review Fay's essays before they were published in a memorial tribute. Though he liked Fay, Guilday was not anxious that his sermons be published. He suspected in Fay a "restlessness" that was not truly Catholic. If anything were to be published, said Guilday, it "should certainly be an antidote, and a strong one, to *This Side of Paradise,* and the looseness of thought charged against him so subtly in the book."[48] While Guilday suspected Fay's "restlessness" and "looseness of thought," Fitzgerald appreciated it as a susceptibility to life. Catholics like Guilday were in the habit of driving an impenetrable wedge between security and insecurity, life and doubt, morality and immorality. They made judgments without reserve. They lived in a world T. S. Eliot described as "without shadows."[49] This habit of mind drove many like Fitzgerald to wander in the more complicated domain between the "lights and the shadows."

At other times, however, Fitzgerald was attracted by the supreme confidence of the Catholic world, its ability to put things into perspective by arranging values in their proper places. In *This Side of Paradise,* Amory Blaine, finding his mind in a riot after reading Joyce, Dreiser, Shaw, and Wells, seeks out Mrs. Lawrence, a friend of Monsignor Darcy and also a convert to the Church. Amory, Fitzgerald wrote, desired "cool people," and in Mrs. Lawrence's home Amory feels comfortably cool. It has an "air of symmetrical restraint" and grace which sets it apart from the more "condensed" parts of New York City, "obtrusive" Long Island, and the plainly "conservative" Union Club families of the Anglo-Protestant establishment. After their discussion, "there seemed suddenly to be much left in life," but even here Fitzgerald balked, and he qualifies Amory's optimism, "if only this revival of old interests did not mean that he was backing away from it again—backing away from life itself."[50] Fitzgerald distrusted the symmetrical restraint and cool gracefulness of Catholicism—which he found at times attractive—because he was not yet prepared to restrain his illusions.

He was also unable to reconcile that graceful and symmetrical restraint with the "gaudy, ritualistic, paradoxical Catholicism, whose prophet was Chesterton, whose claqueurs were such reformed rakes of literature as Huysmans and Bourget, whose American sponsor was Ralph Adams Cram, with his adulation of thirteenth-century cathedrals."[51] Fitzgerald's faith never clarified to the point where restraint did not mean a lack of passion for the less tidy experiences of life. On the other hand, the gaudy and obscure remoteness of Catholicism lacked an environmental freshness and the graceful style which he desired for his art and his life. He was incapable of controlling all these conflicting poses, as were most Catholics of his generation.

But the desire for control was deeply implanted in him and the Catholic community in general. It appeared in Fitzgerald in his penchant for classifying and listmaking. It was the hallmark of the American Catholic medievalism of the mind. Monsignor Darcy explains Amory Blaine's listmaking as a "passion for classifying and finding a type. . . . It's a desire to get something definite. It's the nucleus of scholastic philosophy."[52] In the 1930's, with the illness of his wife Zelda, and with himself unable to write or even care about writing, Fitzgerald insulated himself from everyone. He tried "resolutely not to think—instead I made lists—made lists and tore them up, hundreds of lists . . . and then suddenly, surprisingly, I got better."[53] Momentarily he was saved from despair by the sheer exertion of will and the intellectual satisfaction brought by definition and classification.

Fitzgerald could achieve only moments of security before he was to "crack like an old plate" when more bad news befell him. But American Catholics extended these moments into decades and almost succeeded in making a distinct culture of them. The neoscholastic sensibility was rampant among Catholics after World War I. It divided up the world like the classified section of the morning newspaper. In neat arrangement, there were realists, naturalists, socialists, Communists, idealists, pessimists, humanists, and agnostics. Catholics achieved security and confidence because the "enemies" were always somewhere else—all one had to do was look them up. The "Catholic way" was in and out, over and between all these various routes to salvation. American Catholicism had achieved a moment of clarity, but it was at the cost of some vision. Catholics were what Fitzgerald had Nick Carraway become after his "riotous excursions" with Jay Gatsby, "the most limited of all specialists, the 'well-rounded man' " who finds that "life is much more successfully looked at from a single window after all."[54] Fitzgerald continued to experiment with new windows, but the ideal of the "single window" was a Catholic one.

In *The Great Gatsby* Fitzgerald achieved clarity by tempering his vision with a reserve and sensitivity concerning man's essentially unattainable illusions. This enabled him to make judgments about "meretricious beauty," recognize "foul dust," and perceive "insincerity." In this novel he found for a moment the objectivity of the "single window," the "acceptable form" in which to couch his preachments.[55]

Catholic reaction to the publication of *The Great Gatsby* was almost nonexistent and continued to be so for quite some time. A short review in *The Commonweal* thought it a "mediocre" novel concerning a "sordid, cheap, little crook" (Jay Gatsby). The *America* review was even more unflattering, judging it "an inferior novel . . . feeble in theme, in portraiture and even in expression."[56] It would seem that Catholics had reduced their vision to a single frame of a multipaned window. These reactions, besides betraying a limited aesthetic sense among Catholics, made it impossible for a realistic artistic life to flourish within American Catholicism. Its perspective on life was so rigid that Catholics preferred not to recognize even someone like F. Scott Fitzgerald, who at times "wanted the world to be in uniform and at a sort of moral attention forever," as one of their own.[57] In making moral judgments without restraint they momentarily lost the sense of "infinite hope" in man, their vision clouded by their own optimism and moralism.

In searching for what lingered on in Fitzgerald of his "Catholic" sensibilities, one need go no further than the desire, already alluded to, for the domination of life by being able to define it and function confidently within it. The American Catholic mind was obsessed during this period of disillusionment with the assertion of the individual will over fate, circumstance, and environment. So much was this stressed that both intellect and will tended to become severed from personal experience and social reality.

In Fitzgerald, more than many other novelists of the time, this assertion of the will was active. Lionel Trilling has noted that in Fitzgerald's writing the world was truly the "condition, the field for tragedy," but it never imposed tragedy. "It is, he feels, *his* fate—and as much as to anything else in Fitzgerald, we respond to the delicate tension he maintained between his idea of personal free will and his idea of circumstance: we respond to that moral and intellectual energy."[58] Asserting the will even amidst tragedy was a characteristic habit of mind ingrained in American Catholics from their youth. Fitzgerald learned from Fay that the balancing of opposites was a necessary ingredient of a versatile intelligence. His "moral and intellectual energy," in this instance, was related to the cultural structure of his Catholic American inheritance.

Yet for the other side of the "delicate tension" Fitzgerald had to escape from these memories. He had to give up his desire for dominance by "breaking down the solid things" around him and unshackling the "luxuriance"of his emotions from the discipline of his will. In the process he became "terribly vulnerable," but, as he wrote in his notebooks, "to record one must be unwary."[59] He set out on a path his spiritual mentor thought a mistake: to be "romantic" without having "a good hold on the mystical side of religion." The latter, thought Fay, kept up the romance of life while enlarging the personality; otherwise, he said, "we shrivel."[60] Fitzgerald confessed to his own shrivelling later in life as being "an unwilling witness of . . . the disintegration of one's own personality."[61] But it was Fitzgerald's personal defenselessness and "riotous excursions" into the complexities of the human condition which enlivened his sensitivity and made possible his art.

In the end, however, it was neither total assertion nor total defenselessness but the constant struggle to balance the opposites. His desire to dominate was characteristically American and, indeed, American Catholic in its naively confident tone. His desire for balance was a Catholic ideal he recognized but infrequently realized in American Catholicism. His romantic urge to be "indispensable" and "unwary" was more intimately personal. Moreover, his pursuit of vulnerability put him on the far side of American Catholicism. Catholic prudence was more often than not prudish in the extreme and an escape from personal involvement in the shadows.

Fitzgerald, probably more than he realized, came closer to achieving balance than the many Catholics who relished the *via media* of Catholicism. His lingering religious sense kept him from succumbing permanently to the view he ascribed to the Theodore Dreisers and Joseph Conrads, "that life is too strong and remorseless for the sons of men."[62] He learned early, and never completely forgot, that life was never successfully confronted by sheer power or force but patiently, with style and tenderness. He was a "son of man," to be sure, but also a "son of God" who sought even in "the vast, vulgar, meretricious beauty" of this world symbols of grace. In developing what he described to his daughter as "a wise and tragic sense of life," Fitzgerald discovered on the far side of his American Catholic sensibilities that "life is essentially a cheat and its conditions are those of defeat and that the redeeming things are not 'happiness and pleasure' but the deeper satisfactions that come out of struggle. Having learned this . . . you can get a hell of a lot more enjoyment out of whatever bright things come your way."[63]

Like many American Catholics of his generation, Fitzgerald was born with an illusion, and, as one critic put it, "the attempt to make friends with reality was a constant, reluctant, but necessary pursuit."[64] The pursuit of making friends with reality has only recently taken hold within American Catholicism. During the mid-1960's, Catholics experienced their first real taste of cultural and intellectual disillusionment. In a peculiar similarity of roles, American Catholics now find themselves "unwilling witnesses" to their own patterns of disintegration. As Fitzgerald found himself living in the "in-between times," Catholic novelists describe the present Catholic condition as one of anguish—"between-gods."[65] Catholics no longer live in the certainty of paradise but more concretely this side of it.

Before patterns of disintegration came upon them Catholics experienced a period when doubt and hesitation seemed to be problems other people worried about. Contributing to their sense of security was the manner in which the revival of neo-Thomistic philosophy was adapted by American Catholics to support their social and spiritual aspirations. Not all Catholics spoke in syllogisms, but enough did so to enshrine Thomism as a distinctive expression of Catholic thought after World War I. As a system it was a multifaceted approach to reality. It was a philosophy, but it doubled for Catholics as a theology. It contained theories of aesthetics, ethics, and politics. It seemed to support both liberal and conservative social views. It was blessed by ecclesiastical orthodoxy but also attracted non-Catholic allegiance. Besides its pervasive presence, Thomism also provided a fortuitous combination of shape and limitation to reality in which an audacious temper of mind could confidently roam.

8. The American Reconstruction of Thomism I
The Road to Safety, Sanity, and Salvation

> Philosophy is only a matter of passionate vision rather than logic—logic only finding reasons for the vision afterwards.
>
> William James[1]

WILLIAM JAMES'S ASSOCIATION OF PHILOSOPHY and "passionate vision" irritated Catholic thinkers for more than half a century. Catholics invariably found his pragmatism abhorrent, irrational, subjective, and open to intellectual and social anarchism. Francis Augustine Walsh, a professor at the Catholic University of America, summarized in 1928 an already familiar Catholic refrain on James and the "dangers" implicit in the pragmatist movement. "America, said Walsh, had the dubious distinction of being "the first to exalt a weakness of human character into a philosophy." William James elevated the American passion for "novelty," unrest, and untried experience and made a philosophy out of them. "Pragmatism was the canonization of thrill, the scientific delineation of the age-old rejection of the customary and usual for the advanced and different. Aiming at objectivity, it was rooted in a sentiment. . . . It would not receive truth but tried practically to make it."[2]

Despite the overwhelming opposition to James, his approach to philosophy as a matter of "passionate vision" was a most opportune way of describing the American Catholic espousal of neoscholasticism and more particularly neo-Thomism as this philosophical outlook crystalized in Catholic thought in the years following World War I. Whatever strengths Thomism provided for the Catholic community can be traced to the meshing of thought and vision. Conversely, the major weaknesses of Thomistic philosophy in the United States were due in large measure to the substitution of passion and fervor for discriminating judgment.

The hegemony of Thomistic philosophy upon Catholic minds in the twentieth century was especially acute in the United States. In a 1966 questionnaire which enlisted the philosophic orientations of members in the departments of philosophy in Catholic colleges throughout the country, over half, 57.3 percent, called themselves Thomist.[3] This figure was more impressive in showing the residual strength of Thomism after four decades of dominance than in indicating any future directions. For by the mid-sixties "a massive flight from Thomism" was in full swing.[4]

Between World Wars I and II the influence of neo-Thomism as a philosophical and indeed cultural vision for American Catholics came into its own. After World War II it continued to develop, and even flowered with the presence of Jacques Maritain in this country during the 1950's. In the late fifties the first signs of disenchantment with Thomism were felt; its once powerful hegemony has spiraled downward ever since. The focus of this chapter concerns the springtime of Thomistic influence in the years between the two world wars.

Before World War I, Thomistic philosophy was a negligible reality in Catholic life. In its broad contours, Catholic thought in the United States in the nineteenth century could be called "Scholastic and largely derivative of European philosophers and their manuals.[5] This brand of Scholasticism was sufficiently eclectic to combine "elements of Cartesian, Lockean, and Wolffian principles" packaged within what James Collins has described as a "rationalistic framework in terminology, statement of principles, division and organization of materials, and mode of inference."[6] The pervasive note of rationalism found in the Scholastic manuals of the nineteenth century continued into the twentieth. The return to Thomism championed by Leo XIII after 1879 was in part an effort to limit the boundaries of individual reason, but the changing temperament of modern philosophy was largely antirational. Thomists, in turn, began to make their most effective appeal to the classical tradition of European rationalism.[7] Indeed, some Catholics in the twentieth century were not hesitant to link neo-Thomism with a "new aufklarung" for the contemporary world.[8]

Orestes Brownson, the most critical American Catholic writer of the nineteenth century, thought this brand of rationalist Scholasticism "unconvincing" to the non-Catholic world and was skeptical of Catholic efforts to adopt it for themselves.[9] The enthusiasm to upgrade the Thomistic synthesis of the thirteenth century for the modern world was not an enticing preoccupation of nineteenth-century American Catholics. Men like Brother Azarias (Patrick Francis Mullaney, 1848–1893), a Christian Brother who wrote literary and philosophical treatises, were if anything more Platonic and Idealist in thinking than Aristotelian or Scholastic.[10] John Gemeiner (1847–1913), a priest in Archbishop John Ireland's diocesan seminary in

St. Paul, Minnesota, was even more explicit in his readiness to reject whatever in Scholaticism conflicted with modern experimental science.[11]

It was true that when the School of Philosophy was established at the Catholic University of America in 1895 it was dedicated to the honor of St. Thomas Aquinas. Edward A. Pace (1861–1938) was chosen to develop this philosophy department along the lines indicated in the encyclical *Aeterni Patris*. From there he went on to become "the herald of the Thomistic revival in the United States." Pace himself was a student in Rome of Francesco Satolli (1839–1910), whom Leo XIII had brought in to teach Thomism at the Pontifical Seminary. Pace was entirely grounded in Thomistic philosophy and was to become in 1926 the first President of the American Catholic Philosophical Association (ACPA). But his most immediate impact at the University was to establish an experimental psychology laboratory, which at the time was only the second such institution in the country. Pace was influenced in this venture by his other mentor, Wilhelm Wundt, under whom he had studied for three years at Leipzig. Pace had wide-ranging interests, as evidenced by his early participation in the American Psychological Association and, in 1900, his work as one of the founders of the American Philosophical Association, which was largely dominated by Hegelian and idealist thought.[12]

Pace's activities were symptomatic of one offshoot of the Thomistic revival in its initial stages at the close of the nineteenth century. Rather than a strictly literal restatement of Thomistic philosophy, there appeared an adventuresome quality of mind among Catholics in both Europe and America. Though the appeal for this opening toward modern culture was based on papal encyclicals and orthodox authority, the results were often unexpectedly revolutionary. Josiah Royce, writing in 1903, pointed out that the really "momentous" and revolutionary quality of Leo XIII's revival of Thomism, for Catholic and modern thought in general, was not entirely expected. Royce correctly observed:

> St. Thomas' spirit is more potent than his letter, that the application of this spirit of inquiry to modern problems has indeed brought you into closer touch with the intellectual issues of the day, but there is also a tendency to modification and to the modernization of your own Catholic thinking—a tendency that goes further than you at first had anticipated.[13]

This spirit, thought Royce, if allowed to develop, would inevitably yield to change, even when the attempt was being made to defend traditional positions.

While Royce was writing, many Catholic thinkers were proving his observations to be correct. In the general rush to make Thomas modern, some, like George Tyrrell, made him a Modernist:

> He was the true modernist of his time and we are his true followers in
> . . . that exquisite sense for the adaptation of the Christian religion to
> the changing forms of philosophy and culture in general.[14]

Catholic Modernism though bitterly opposed by orthodox spokesmen, was closely associated with the whole revival of Catholic scholarship and particularly the revival of Thomism—the general motivational impulse in both being the opening up of Catholic thought to the modern world after a long series of mutual condemnations. But it soon became evident to the conservative forces within this "revival" that Modernism had revolutionary implications for Catholic thought and indeed for the Thomistic revival itself. In 1903, with the death of Leo XIII, Royce prophesied the coming reaction as Pius X assumed the papacy:

> But will Catholic officialism . . . permit the new Catholic scholar-
> ship liberty to develop on these lines. Will not the new pope . . .
> undertake to bring to a pause the evolution of these tendencies
> towards a reform of Catholic philosophy, and towards an era of good
> feeling between Catholic and non-Catholic science and scholarship? I
> confess to a good deal of doubt upon this subject. I confess also that I
> am rather disposed to anticipate a reaction against all this natural,
> but, as I fancy, unexpected growth that has taken place in the world of
> Catholic scholarship within the last two decades.[15]

In the frenzied and often bitter reaction to Modernism, Thomistic philosophy became not the symbol of openness but of the closed mind. After the encyclical *Pascendi Dominici gregis* (1907) Thomism was legislated and literally institutionalized as the only proper mode of Catholic thought. In *Doctoris Angelici* (1914) Pius X warned teachers of Catholic theology and philosophy "that if they deviated so much as a step from Aquinas, especially in metaphysics, they exposed themselves to grave risk."[16] As if to underscore the literal nature of this Thomism, as opposed to the "spirit" of Thomas, the Congregation of Studies in 1914 compiled a list of twenty-four theses deemed to be the essential and principal teachings of Aquinas. In 1917 when it was pointed out to the new Pope, Benedict XV, by Wlodimir Ledochowski, General of the Society of Jesus, that twenty-three of those theses were denied by Francesco Suárez, S.J., the revered Spanish Scholastic of the sixteenth century, the new Pope had to concede at least a modicum of diversity within the Scholastic household.[17]

But the institutionalization continued when the revised Code of Canon

Law (1917) required that all professors of philosophy and theology "shall adhere religiously to the method, doctrine and principles" of Thomas Aquinas. Papal decrees continued into the present century, the two most notable being Pius XI's encyclical *Studiorum Ducem* (1923) and Pius XII's *Humani Generis* (1950).[18] The net effect of this papal approbation of Thomism since *Aeterni Patris* (1879), and especially after Modernism, was to make it the most authoritative expression of Catholic thought and a safe intellectual route to orthodoxy. This fact has laid the revival of Thomistic studies open to attack from many non-Catholics as primarily a religious effort to sustain Catholic dogmas or as a political effort to maintain ecclesiastical influence in the world.[19] Although the suspicion of political motivation soon disappeared in the twentieth century, the former accusation continued to nag Thomists throughout the century, when even many Catholics began to suspect an "unholy" alliance between dogma and philosophy which produced both sterile theology and sterile philosophy.

The immediate impact of *Aeterni Patris* on Catholic thought in the United States was less than earthshaking. When Edward Pace was asked to prepare a report in 1895 on philosophy in the university for the Academic Senate of the Catholic University of America, he painted a rather bleak picture. There was only one instructor teaching philosophy, inadequate library facilities, and a total neglect of research. Indeed, most of the students taking philosophy were merely auditing the courses, and, as a rule, they could read neither French nor German.[20] The general situation of philosophy in Catholic colleges and seminaries was not too different from that Pace described as prevailing at Washington. There was no widespread effort to embark on Leo XIII's Thomistic crusade; rather, the situation was extremely fluid. Indeed, John Gemeiner's attitude toward Thomism was evidence of an independent position. Two priests, John B. Hogan, S.S., and John Talbot Smith, who strove to upgrade clerical education during the 1890's, were largely skeptical or indifferent. Hogan felt that Leo XIII was not arguing that Catholics should study only St. Thomas; but even if he were, said Hogan, the Pope was not speaking infallibly. Smith, on the other hand, did not even refer to *Aeterni Patris* and thought that philosophy itself was better presented historically than systematically.[21] There were Catholics involved in the revival of Thomism, Pace being the most conspicuous, but there was no general movement, clerical or lay, within American Catholicism. In 1909 J. B. Ceulemans, observing for a French audience, found that Thomism since *Aeterni Patris* had exerted little influence in the United States even among Catholics. General magazines like the *Catholic World* were "disinterested" while others treated it superficially or gave no attention to it at all.[22]

It was only after the Modernist crisis and the subsequent legislation of

Thomism as the only orthodox Catholic philosophy that the query, "How are we to make Scholasticism popular?" was even heard, let alone answered.[23] But the atmosphere prevailing in Catholic circles in the wake of the reaction against Modernism was such that an adventuresome approach to Thomism, or anything else, was nearly impossible. Edward Pace was so fearful lest he say something offensive to orthodox ears that he refused to give the funeral oration at the memorial mass for Father John A. Zahm, C.S.C., in Washington D.C., in 1921.[24] Zahm's book *Evolution and Dogma* (1896), which Pace had defended in the 1890's, was suspected by Rome of heterodox views and was withdrawn from further publication to prevent its being placed on the Index of Forbidden Books.

In the immediate post–World War I years, a quickening in the pace of Catholic life was noticeable and particularly evident among those who desired to make Catholicism culturally significant in the nation. As Gustave Weigel, S.J., recalled in 1951, "the young Catholics of those days saw something lucidly." What they saw was an opportunity for Catholicism "in the anxiety of the world to find a philosophy and a way of life different from the nineteenth century." These Catholics thought the "men of the twenties" just might listen. They appealed to those disaffected with the preceding century of bourgeois materialism, and to those like Randolph Bourne recently disillusioned with pragmatism as its difficulties in constructing a new moral vision became apparent during and after the war. In the years following the armistice of 1918, "a new moment had come to expose the Catholic scheme of things to America. . . ." Ready to take advantage of this moment was a highly self-conscious group of Catholics who believed that "the Catholicization of America was very possible" and that the best way to direct their enthusiasm was "in the intellectual field."[25]

As for neo-Thomism, by the mid-twenties it was possible to say with Anthony C. Cotter, S.J., a philosophy instructor at Woodstock College, Maryland: "To be called a Scholastic is no longer a term of contempt, nor yet a mark of distinction; it is something we almost expect from every student of Catholic philosophy and theology."[26] It was also true that something had happened to the neoscholastic revival that transformed its presence in America from the passive acceptance of it as the legislated will of the popes to an active enthusiasm for it as the "passionate vision" of Catholic America.

An indication of the robust enthusiasm with which Catholics now turned to Thomism can be seen in the first issues of *The Modern Schoolman,* which had the distinction of being the first journal exclusively dedicated to the neoscholastic cause in the United States. Its unpretentious birth in 1925 as a monthly organ of the Philosopher's Seminar at St. Louis University belied the editors' grandiose expectations. The aim of the journal, announced the

editors, was to reach the "American mass mind" with Scholastic philosophy. It was to reconcile the essential doctrines of Thomism with modern
science and devise ways and means "of proposing these doctrines in attractive guise to both the scientific and popular twentieth century mind."[27]

The general feeling expressed in the early issues was that the essential
doctrines were ready for the task; all that remained was the organization of a
good advertising campaign. This was the opportunity of "the seventh age"
which commenced with World War I. This new era was the "age of
restoration" which meant:

> The age in which the Church in America, capitalizing on what is
> lasting and universal in the methods of other times, will move
> forward to a full and scientific use of all the mind-reaching media that
> American genius has so far developed and by them reradicate the
> principles of Catholic philosophy . . . in the mass-mind of the
> country.

What made the editors so optimistic was that Catholicism was no longer on
the defensive but rather "New Englandism" was.[28] The intellectual and
popular attack on Protestantism or Puritanism provided these Catholics
with a vision of empire in which "the Scholastic philosopher may vision a
Thomistic thought—empire dominating the Mid-Western desert of
Puritanism."[29]

The young philosophers of St. Louis took a decidedly populist view of St.
Thomas and his thoughts. Thomism was nothing less than the "crystallized
common sense of the ages," but, more important, Thomism was uniquely
modern and American: "as new as the radio, as strong as Niagara, as big as
the American prairies. When America discovers him (and it ultimately
will) he will become a fixed American institution."[30]

A year later when it seemed that no one was yet contemplating the
erection of a memorial to Thomas Aquinas across the harbor from the Statue
of Liberty, a chastened note appeared in the pages of *The Modern Schoolman.*
One John J. O'Brien, S.J., could not understand how William James could
exert so much influence in the United States while Scholasticism, with a
greater number of teachers, had as yet made so little impact. To be sure, it
was not the fault of the Thomistic system, but rather a case of "removing
the bushel," which called for a greater determination and persistence from
its advocates. Despite the fact that Thomism did not conquer America
overnight, enthusiasm for its essential rightness for the times and its
eventual triumph was a persistent force in Catholic intellectual circles of the
period.[31]

One might be prone to dismiss the young members of the Philosopher's
Seminar in St. Louis with their occasional giddy bravado but for the fact

that they and their ebullience were not too far removed from the mood of a more sedate assemblage: fifty Catholic teachers of philosophy who met in Caldwell Hall on the campus of the Catholic University of America on January 5, 1926, to organize the American Catholic Philosophical Association. The object of the association, as stated in its constitution, was "to promote study and research in the field of philosophy, with special emphasis on Scholastic philosophy."[32] The "special emphasis" guiding the association quickly gave way to what one Catholic philosopher later recalled as "the somewhat totalitarian spirit of the high-riding Thomism of those days in the American Catholic Philosophical Association where conformity with Thomism was practically *de rigueur* for respectability. . . ."[33] Some forty years later a president of the association, Ernan McMullin, reviewed the addresses of the original meeting of 1926 and found to his embarrassment a "breathtaking combination of audacity and naiveté" which he felt sounded "inexcusably pretentious today."[34]

More important than the "naiveté" was the audacious confidence which the early members of the association brought to their task. Pace, in the inaugural address, struck what was at the time a more moderate view among Catholic philosophers but one that nevertheless expressed the general mood:

> We approach our task with the conviction that the basic ideas of Scholasticism are living truths—firm enough to support the whole fabric of knowledge yet flexible enough to allow for every addition of ascertained fact.[35]

Along with James Hugh Ryan, Pace led the moderate faction within the association which felt that it was impossible to "ignore American thinkers of the last quarter of a century" and desired a mutual sharing of ideas between Catholics and non-Catholics. But by the second meeting in 1927 a majority, estimated James A. McWilliams, S.J., believed that Scholasticism would win the day without bothering too much with the preconceived notions of other philosophers. At the second meeting the "vocal portion of the house," McWilliams reported without comment, "indulged in round denunciations of the non-Scholastic systems."[36] As if to lend tangible support to this spectacle of Catholic hysteria was the coincidence that the meeting was held on the University of Notre Dame campus "where the thundering feet of the Four Horsemen echo in the still air."[37] It would not be stretching the facts too far to suggest that the vision of Notre Dame trouncing its Ivy League competitors was seen by many Catholics, even the more intellectually inclined, as the inevitable foreshadowing of the triumph of neo-Thomism and in truth the Catholic way of life in the United States.

Considering the rather indifferent reception of the Thomistic revival prior to World War I, its transformation into a "passionate vision" must be more sharply defined. That Thomism became, through papal legislation and endorsement, institutionalized as *the* Catholic philosophy following the Modernist crisis, was one important factor in this transformation. But this alone was hardly sufficient to account for the passion with which Catholics in America took up the cause in the 1920's. Virgil Michel, O.S.B., addressing himself to this very question, was persuaded that "the mere voice of the pope could not have breathed life into a philosophy that in itself was dead."[38] However much Catholics were anxious to prove their loyalty and devotion to the papacy, this motive must give way to other, more impelling, considerations. The general enthusiasm for neo-Thomism is best explained by examining the intellectual, cultural, and social implications for the Catholic community at the time.

In 1926, Ralph Barton Perry characterized the current philosophical situation as a "lull" period.[39] Pragmatism's attack on idealism was successful, but the former never considered itself more than a method of philosophy and its success lay more in its criticism than in its construction. Pragmatism soon found itself competing with other critical philosophies. The new realism which Perry himself advocated was followed by its offshoot, critical realism. Besides this empirical orientation the new metaphysics of Henri Bergson and Alfred North Whitehead was beginning to make itself heard. The common note emphasized during this "lull" in philosophical debate was that no one philosophy claimed an exclusive hold on the truth. Indeed, truth itself became problematic. Predictions about the nature of truth replaced the certainty of ever attaining it. As the scientific mind absorbed the relativity theory, and as social scientists, lawyers, writers, and philosophers related relativity to their spheres of thought, a new philosophical world was being born. In this world former certainties about man, nature, and the universe were now rendered as "fictions," "phantoms," or "naive desires."[40]

Two philosophical conceptions of man seemed to predominate on the intellectual horizon, both of which affected man's approach to philosophy itself. Bertrand Russell, expressing the more somber pessimism of this generation, used the metaphor of a man trapped on a "narrow raft" surrounded by "the dark ocean; from the great night without, a chill blast breaks in upon our refuge; all the loneliness of humanity amid hostile forces is concentrated upon the individual soul, which must struggle alone . . . against the whole weight of a universe that cares nothing for its hopes and fears."[41]

Alfred North Whitehead was more hopeful but nonetheless sure that contemporary science had created a new world for man. While Russell saw man's plight largely as a desperate struggle, Whitehead preferred to see humanity as now confronted with "the necessity of wandering . . . a true migration into uncharted seas of adventure." He was also sure that this adventure would disclose many dangers but that the real excitement about the human venture was indeed the confrontation with the dangerous.[42]

While Russell's conception was creatively exploited by the literary mind, Whitehead's became the motivational springboard of philosophy and the social sciences, where the nature of truth was tied to an unending use of research and experimentation. Thus, "tolerance" for conflicting hypotheses was central if headway was to be made in the search for truth. But the quest for truth which supplied the emotional and intellectual undergirding of the philosophical and scientific apparatus of modern American thought was predicated on the assumption of the uncertainty of ever finally attaining it.

In the overthrowing of the classical and Newtonian conception of the universe with its central presupposition of an intelligible cosmos known by man, philosophy in the twentieth century, though open to "possibilities" and "novelties" in the universe as opposed to the materialistic determinism of the nineteenth century, nevertheless admitted to a fundamental uncertainty with regard to the capacity of reason, the nature of the universe, and the values and meaning of human association. As Russell concluded, the mission of philosophy in the "no man's land" between theology and science was "to teach how to live without certainty—and yet without being paralyzed by hesitation. . . ."[43] Even this was a decidedly humanistic conception of philosophy in the midst of a marked withdrawal of philosophy into specialized scientific concerns, and it resulted in considerable fragmentation of effort and the fractioning of thought.

What Perry interpreted as a "lull" Catholics described as "despair," "chaos," and bewilderment. The same year Perry wrote, James Hugh Ryan observed that specialized philosophizing blinded from the consideration of the synthetic aspects of philosophy had resulted in philosophy being lost in a "maze of new facts." This was confirmed for Ryan at the Sixth International Congress of Philosophy held at Harvard in 1926. This meeting of distinguished philosophers of the world appeared to be "a great confused mass without head or articulation, without order or reason," lacking any "golden thread of agreement."[44] The principle of "tolerance," argued John O. Riedl of Marquette University, was at most an expedient for a world that had despaired of ever attaining the truth. "Objective observation" and "experimentation," the modern hallmark of truth discovery, at best led only to tentative conclusions, and those who strove for a synthesis of knowledge were ridiculed for their presumptuousness and treated as prophets or poets rather than philosophers.[45]

It was in philosophy's reaction against rationalism and its concommitant emphasis on "the primacy of the will, sentiment, sense experience, mystical experience, 'action,' " that John Zybura saw the cause of the "poignant disillusionment" which had overcome not only philosophers but "thoughtful men in general . . . writers, artists, and poets."[46] Modern thought, concluded Ryan, had, especially since the war, entered a "dark night of intellectual anarchy."[47]

The Catholic rejection of the path of modern thought in the twentieth century was not entirely based on simple misinformation or failure at understanding, nor was it based entirely on a fanatical reactionary urge to protect dogmatic positions. It was, rather, a perception of the world that Catholics, from philosophers to ward politicians, refused to relinquish. Whatever promise pragmatism offered as a method of breaking out of the heavy determinism of the nineteenth century, it was, according to Francis Augustine Walsh, "shattered by the World War; the bayonet thrust, the bursting shell, the wave of poisoned gas were too much, even though the making of truth hinged on victory. The practical was found impractical. . . . There began, and continues, a social revolt resting on a determinism more iron than ever. . . ."[48] The new determinism was not mechanical or materialist as was the old, but, rather, intellectual and spiritual. It was the modern awareness of, and confrontation with, the heavy burden of an unintelligible world. In this confrontation Catholics refused to participate. In response to Bertrand Russell, Catholics replied by coopting Russell's own metaphor: "No metaphysics is barren which supplies us with a world view that keeps us from feeling that we are in a universe as terrifying, as uncontrolled, and as unpredictable as the waves of an ocean upon which a castaway sailor finds himself tossed about on a raft that may at any moment founder."[49]

If, as Catholics repeatedly maintained, the "root error" of modern times was the "denial of the supremacy of the intellect," then they would in their turn become the champions of the intellect.[50] Thomism to their delight offered a philosophy which secured "a structure of civilization" whose "soul is absoluteness, objectivity, wholesome common sense, and reign of intelligence."[51] This delight was compounded when it seemed that they were unique in their mission. Far from being the enemy of reason, they boasted that in reality Catholicism was its "greatest glorifier."[52] John O. Riedl, who summarized Thomism as "everyman's philosophy," advanced in 1935 the proposition that:

> Scholastic philosophers are somewhat unique among present-day philosophers. They still believe in Truth, in reality, in God, in the power of human reason to know real things, in an immortal soul, an

after life, and the power of man to guide his own destiny. Oddly enough, they base their belief in these fundamental verities on the authority of reason alone. They claim to be able to prove the truth of these fundamentals. Other modern philosophers, though they started out in the seventeenth century with an unbounded confidence in the power of reason, have ended by declaring the bankruptcy of reason and reason's inability to offer any guidance to man in the really important problems of life. Outside scholasticism there seems to be nothing but intellectual chaos and despair.[53]

Having diagnosed the world as being in a state of bewilderment, it became a commonplace assumption that, through its "philosophy," Catholicism had a golden opportunity to contribute to the reconstruction efforts following the twin disasters of world depression and "philosophical bankruptcy."[54] The neo-scholastic, offered James Ryan, "holds out for acceptance a systematic thought which like a great light penetrates the obscurities of the dungeon . . . and indicates the road to safety, sanity, and salvation."[55] Virgil Michel unconsciously contrasted the Scholastic's adventure with Whitehead's description of wandering in the presence of dangers:

[The Scholastic's] adventure may call for the exploring of dark unknown seas, but his is not the perplexity of the man who knows not whence to embark, nor by what means to attempt to explore, nor where, initially, he stands. There is no room for despair in the Scholastic's heart, and optimism is the soul's first fruit of life.[56]

The Scholastic philosophical adventure in the United States had no room for despair or even, one might add, for complexity. Optimism and confidence were its marching orders. Here was a classic case of a shared group experience significantly molding a body of thought to fit the aspirations of the group. Conversely, we also have a body of thought capable of being so fashioned.

The Catholic community which emerged from World War I was a community bursting with enthusiasm and desirous of firmly establishing itself in the social, political, and cultural life of the nation. As Edward Pace noted in his opening address at the original meeting of the American Catholic Philosophical Association:

Too long we have been regarded as a people and a clergy of great energy and zeal building and organizing and defending all sorts of institutions, yet quite out of sympathy with higher intellectual pursuits. . . . We are conscious of our ability to do the better things. We feel the need of them.[57]

The need to contribute on the intellectual and cultural level was strong, but it was also evident that this need would not undermine the already firmly established zeal for "building and organizing." In fact, the experience of carving and organizing a place for themselves in the urban wilderness provided the framework within which Catholics took up the study of St. Thomas. After confronting an at times hostile environment in America, they were now ready to confront the universe. As the Catholic community had learned in the previous century, the result of timidity was often a burned church. Philosophical reticence was not to be their style. Rather, Scholastic philosophy was to face the universe in the manner of a gutsy immigrant by "hack[ing] its way through what might appear to be an impenetrable jungle, nature, and the cosmos."[58]

Though Scholasticism had long been a dominant element on the American Catholic mind, it was only after the war that a real passion for it took place. At this juncture a "passionate vision" converged with the logic of the Schoolmen. John Zybura, who spent a decade trying to convince Catholics and non-Catholics alike of the "timeliness" of Thomism, put the vision in philosophical perspective when he alluded to the Thomistic doctrine of the intellect as satisfying man's "imperious voice" which was "to know and to know things." Zybura used a number of such "happy phrases" to express what Thomism offered to Catholics and to all who would heed the call. It was an offer "to conquer reality intellectually." A Thomist, according to Zybura, must unite a "sober sense of reality" with a "soaring idealism," for his mission was no less than the "taking hold of being."[59]

The "taking hold of being" was the philosophical urge to dominate supersensible reality as Catholics had learned to survive in their physical surroundings. Thomism thus became a metaphysical component of the "Americanization" of Catholicism. In conquering reality intellectually or physically, Catholics were expressing their "Catholic-American" belief that man was responsible for his own destiny. The massive structure of the universe, the contingent and often contradictory nature of its laws revealed by contemporary science, failed to dent the Catholic perception of the essential congruity between man and his universe. The cosmic loneliness men like Russell felt when faced with the indifference of being, Catholics like John A. O'Brien would characterize as sophisticated conceit or pessimism.[60] When Catholics peered at the universe, they saw, not flux and contingency, but harmony, order, and law. These rationalistic conceptions, which others accused the Thomistic mind of overlaying on the universe, were indeed often coldly abstract, but they also served a very experiential and personal function. They guaranteed not only "purposefulness, aim, intention, ambition in the universe" but also in everyday life.[61]

They created a structure for doing, if not for reverence or the sometimes distrubing results of meditation.

Some time ago Walter Ong, S.J., described the Scholastic mind as representing more the "scientific or even technological approach to reality and life" than the romantic, literary, or artistic. The initial impulse of the Thomistic philosophy in America was a militantly technological urge to "take hold of being" and conquer reality. It was precisely here that Thomism served the Catholic community with an apparently real connection between its own inner logic and the experience of the group who espoused it. As Charles A. Hart noted in his 1932 essay, "Neo-Scholastic Philosophy and American Catholic Culture," Thomism was "the great fountainhead of Catholic energy." More explicitly, as John Shields remarked in a letter to Virgil Michel, O.S.B., it was "Catholic Action in the Sphere of Thought."[62]

9. The American Reconstruction of Thomism II
The Intuitions of Innocence

UNFORTUNATELY, THE LINKAGE OF impertinence with Thomism had more often than not a sedative effect. The "imperious voice" was often heard from an armchair. In 1917, Daniel Lord, S.J., was struck by the "almost sacramental" quality of Thomistic philosophy. Not only was it sacramental but simple enough to be done perched on his favorite chair. "Why," asked Lord, "treat philosophy as false simply because it is simple?" His "armchair" Thomism was consistent, commonsensical, and even joyous. Its conclusions always rested on "proved premises." It boasted of "man's freedom" and secured for him the means to meet and cope with the spiritual and the material. It was, despite its critics' claims, even forward-looking. A philosophy that promised "to prove its God before it worships him" and offered "the rational assurance of immortality," seductively impelled Lord "to almost a lightness of heart."[1]

The "forward-looking" note of the Thomistic enterprise has not been sufficiently appreciated. For Lord, it provided him with what he called a "healthy optimism" about future progress, not the gloom and skepticism of contemporary philosophy. If optimism was endemic to the American soul, Catholics were without a philosophic justification for it until they decided that Thomism not only was "cautiously conservative" but provided for the future as well. As Charles Miltner, C.S.C., expressed it, Scholasticism as the *philosophia perennis* was not accurately described as an "authoritative, static, undeveloping and absolutely final interpretation of the universe. . . ." Rather, it was more important to consider

> whether Scholasticism, giving a rational working interpretation of all things at present really known, faces the future with principles so firmly established, as will in all likelihood enable it to be an intellectual solvent of all things yet to come.[2]

Catholics would be "prudently progressive' and even optimistic as long as

152

Thomism was capable of depriving the future of its potential for disaster.

After the first blush of youthful exuberance among Thomists and the discovery that Catholics "had a philosophic system of their own," there appeared two approaches to assessing the movement's strength.[3] The majority agreed with James A. McWilliams, S.J., who, in his presidential address to the American Catholic Philosophical Association in 1932, believed the neoscholastic movement in America to be "a conscious living organism pulsing with life." He foresaw a "great army" of lay men and women contributing with the accepted principles of Thomism "to the reconstruction of a bewildered world." With more optimism than President Franklin D. Roosevelt, McWilliams predicted: "Philosophy as well as business, may be about to turn the corner. World depression no less than philosophical bankruptcy may be our opportunity."[4]

In sharp contrast with this view was the minority's doubts. James Hugh Ryan, one of the co-founders of the association and Rector of the Catholic University of America, assessed the revival of Thomism in more somber tones. In Europe, Ryan felt, it definitely was not the "wave of the future." "Of America," he continued,

> I scarcely need to speak. Here and there, in the great universities of our country, there is a lone expositor; his pupils are a few antiquarians, medievalists, or students interested in the historical side of human thought. We are humbly grateful that among ourselves we are able to keep an organization alive.

In Ryan's view, Thomists had not yet "provided a structure within which to interpret thoughts men today are occupied with." Instead, they had settled for answering those questions with which science refused to deal. Ryan wanted philosophy once again to "reconquer science."

Another, more serious, problem for Thomists, Ryan indicated, was the matter of attitude. "There is a danger," he warned, "that while we have looked upon ourselves as housed in an impregnable fortress, we awake to find that we have dwelt in a leaning tower, an architectural and engineering blunder." The price of security for Catholics seemed to be inaction, while the restlessness of modern man was driving him on. But Ryan himself was dedicated to the Thomistic cause and thus it was not the program and principles of Thomism that were at fault but those who had failed to carry them out.[5]

By the mid-thirties the most stringent critique of the neoscholastic movement in the United States from a Catholic was issued by John F. McCormick, S.J. (1874–1943). Anton Pegis, a student of McCormick, characterized him as a Scholastic who "did not cut reality to the measure of our own knowledge nor did he clarify the transcendence of God out of existence. An intelligible mystery is always better than a clear illusion."[6] McCormick, in a symposium for *The Modern Schoolman* which sought to consider the impact of Thomism on the world since *Aeterni Patris*, was apologetic for even writing an article about the United States because of its past record. Despite the abundance of interest for the neoscholastic philosophy among Catholics, "the net result of the teaching," concluded McCormick, "may perhaps be expressed as an innoculation of the students against the prevailing Naturalism, and, as a consequence, a preservation of their receptiveness to the influence of Catholic thought." Other than produce textbooks which "impart a body of doctrine without developing philosophic thinking," Catholics had little influence on philosophy in the country. McCormick summarized the effect of all the interest American Catholics had shown for neoscholasticism as "pathetically earnest." What was lacking most of all was sound scholarship.[7]

Underneath the earnest endeavor of American Scholastics was a growing sense of frustration which supported McCormick's criticism. Martin J. Scott, S.J., was anxious in 1930 to propose a public debate with John Dewey. He wrote to Wilfred Parsons, the Jesuit editor of *America,* suggesting that Parsons be the one to confront Dewey. Parsons declined because, as he said, it "would require at least a reading of his books, and that I have absolutely no time to do." The situation left Scott somewhat discouraged. "If our system of philosophy is sound," he replied to Parsons, "and our course of studies so superior, why should not a champion of truth step out? It seems to be a dreadful arraignment of Catholic education if we cannot produce a man to combat what we claim to be in error." Parsons, in turn, confessed that he had been trying for two years to get some Catholic professors of philosophy "to study [Dewey] and answer him, but in vain."[8] Although Catholics continued to denounce Dewey from the safety of their own journals and internal platforms, a feeling that something was out of joint was slowly taking hold.

The question of scholarship raised one of the central problems for Scholastics during the period, and it also helps to explain the wide divergence of opinion discussed above which separated McWilliams from Ryan and McCormick. To those who shared McWilliams' view of Scholasticism as "pulsing with life" in the United States, with visions of an even greater future, neoscholasticism represented more a "way of life" than a "method of thought."[9] It was a cultural buttress rather than a vehicle of criticism or investigation.

This group saw as their main objective the selling or "popularization" of Thomism as "everyman's philosophy" or the philosophy of the "plain man." *Aeterni Patris* was not a signal for a revival "narrowly philosophical, but must embrace within its sweeping reaches the whole of humanity's life and learning."[10] McWilliams himself expressed it in his book *Philosophy for the Millions,* where he made it clear that he was not going to discuss "problems" as others did who thought such discussions "the acme of scholarship." Instead, McWilliams offered solutions and conclusions from a philosophical position which, he said, was neither explicitly Catholic nor Christian, but rather was based on "the reasonable interpretation of existence" and the common feelings of mankind. Thus, according to McWilliams: "Man has a free will and all men know it."[11]

The common-sense, common-man orientation of Thomism was widespread among Scholastics in this country, contrary to Europe where it was often considered exotic or even *avant garde* in some circles. Thomism was offered "as the embodiment of the wisdom of the race, because it is an easy and natural development of common and universal habits of thought: it is built on the justification and systematization of the spontaneous convictions of mankind; common sense is the salt that keeps it fresh and wholesome." In order to be wholesome, therefore, a leveling downward and a building upward produced what Catholics generally referred to as the "philosophy of the golden mean."[12]

The middle-of-the-road syndrome was most clearly stated by Daniel C. O'Grady, who listed sixteen areas where Scholasticism split extremities. It was "between" atheism and pantheism; immanence and transcendence; agnosticism and ontologism; anthropomorphism and symbolism; monism and singularism; atomism and dynamism; materialism and idealism; empiricism and rationalism; realism and nominalism; reason and revelation; determinism and chance; optimism and pessimism; individualism and socialism; *ad infinitum.*[13] Such a claim had its own kind of extravagance even while it boasted of moderation. All this "betweenness" left little opportunity to risk the security of the trunk for the vulnerability of the limb.

By defining Scholasticism as a way of life in between the extremes of modern thought and experience, Catholics hoped to keep certain truths out of the laboratory where uncertainty provided the impulse to move onward. The catechism was the Catholic countersymbol to the laboratory; in it truths were not tested but memorized. The Baltimore catechism, though not used in philosophy seminars, was in many ways a popularized condensation of more complex Scholastic arguments. Thus the close proximity of the intellectual, the student, and the common man kept alive an essential myth for the Catholic community that truth was the possession of all men and not of an elite. Catholic intellectuals therefore merely elucidated the more developed argumentation for beliefs all men were supposed to hold instinctively. They were remarkably successful in keeping the intellectual and the community in tune with each other at a time in American culture when intellectuals like H. L. Mencken derided the commonplace and the great "booboisie," and, in turn, the common man mistrusted the learned man. In Catholicism, the intellectual's role was defined in the more traditional pattern of spokesman for the eternal generalities which held the group together.

The golden mean approach to thought, though often a position of the tentative and murky, even the contradictive, was for Catholics the area of the clear and distinct. Anything that smacked of the obscure was generally excluded from the title Catholic or Scholastic. Since many Catholics were of the mind that "men cannot be serious about uncertainties," the mean was not the area of the elastic but of the hard and fast certain. This tendency of thought was best illustrated at the 1935 ACPA meeting. A professor at St. Mary's Seminary in Baltimore, John F. Cronin, S.S., read a paper entitled "Cardinal Newman's Theory of Knowledge." Cronin, discussing Newman's theory of "real idea" and the "illative sense," compared these ideas to James's pragmatism and Bergson's use of intuition as viable intellectual approaches to truth. In the discussion that followed a Father Brichel arose to question whether Newman was a philosopher at all, implying that Newman's *Grammar of Assent* was an "obscure" book, and that "if he were a real philosopher he would have been more clear." Brichel was also sure that the comparison of the thought of James and Bergson with that of Newman would if anything, mean "that Newman's teaching was condemned in the Syllabus of Pope Pius X, where the Modernist doctrine that a congeries of probabilities can lead to certainty is rejected."[14]

The most successful representative of everyman's Thomism in the United States during this time was Fulton J. Sheen. From the mid-twenties to the mid-fifties Sheen's reputation passed rapidly from perhaps an American Jacques Maritain to a clerical G. K. Chesterton and then finally rested as the Catholic counterpart of Norman Vincent Peale and Billy Graham. These comparisons, though never entirely accurate, do indicate a certain progression in popular estimation.

In 1925, after four years at the Superior Institute of Philosophy in Louvain, Belgium, one of the foremost centers of Thomistic studies in the Catholic world, Sheen returned to this country with his published dissertation embellished with an introduction by G. K. Chesterton; in a *Commonweal* review by Ernst Sutherland Bates it was touted as "one of the most important contributions to philosophy which has appeared in the present century."[15] Even though *God and Intelligence in Modern Philosophy* has not lived up to Bates's expectations, not even in Thomistic circles, and has long since been forgotten, at the time it did achieve some intellectual distinction. Wyndham Lewis, in his study *Time and Western Man* (1928), preferred Sheen's *God and Intelligence* in exposing the Thomist position for its "lucidity" and "exactness." Lewis found Maritain to be too "personal" and "tainted" with Bergsonianism.[16] Though Lewis desired to compliment Sheen, the latter's literal exactness was his greatest liability as his thoughts seemed to frost before reaching the page. Maritain's "personal" quality was primarily responsible for whatever living influence his thought achieved.

At Louvain, where Sheen learned his Thomism, he was certainly not fed a textbook Scholasticism. In a revealing letter to his former professor at the Catholic University of America, Edward Pace, Sheen praised Louvain for its total reliance on primary sources and continuous references to modern thought. But the greatest glory of Louvain, thought Sheen, was that it kept Scholasticism "alive and awake, ready to refute even the latest fad of thought."[17] Regretfully, even Louvain could not dispel the notion that being "alive and awake" meant more than being ready to "refute" Whitehead rather than an old nemesis like Descartes.

At the outset of *God and Intelligence* Sheen announced his own goal, which even in this, his most researched piece of writing, set the pattern for what followed in his own career and, indeed, for most of the Thomistic revival in America. Sheen saw his work as an attempt "to make St. Thomas functional, not for a school, but for a world." Such an objective, though not without some worth, had the seeming effect of desiring to bypass difficult problems, while avoiding the pitfalls of posing hard questions on one's own presuppositions. Thus Thomism functioned, not as a method, but, in Sheen's words, as a "remedy against anarchy of ideas, riot of philosophical systems and breakdown of spiritual forces."[18] Sheen then went on to analyze the new God of movement and becoming, and man as an "ever-perfecting" being who destroyed intellectualism by substituting emotionalism, experience, and intuition. Sheen's analysis was generally free of wild denunciations and loose generalizations, letting modern philosophers speak for themselves while trying to make a case for the intellectualism of St. Thomas.

In his second book, *Religion Without God* (1928), a sequel to the first, there is already an appreciable slippage in scholarly reserve. The modern God is here slickly defined as the development of Luther's "spiritual individualism" or subjectivism, Descartes's "rational individualism" or empiricism, and Kant's pragmatism. "Add to this . . . ," concluded Sheen, "a pinch of biology, psychology, and new physics, stir it up, bake in a pan well greased with evolution, and the finished product will be the modern God."[19] In exploiting a gift for clever phrasing, scholarship was decidedly becoming a secondary activity, soon to be completely forgotten. Following these works, which were largely based on his dissertation research, there came a succession of books which were popular extrapolations of the assertions and conclusions found in the first two.[20] Meanwhile, Sheen achieved popular acclaim with his successful radio and television appearances.

Behind his media appeal was a view of reality which had an appeal not only to Catholics but to a larger American public as well. Sheen's Americanized Thomism brought together pre–World War I American innocence and certain aspects of the Catholic tradition. The view of reality he expounded had as its objective the bringing of man to "prominence" or to the center of the universe without sacrificing the "dignity of God." The universe was a great pyramid at the base of which was mineral and chemical life which grew in intensity to the peak where it was crowned by the superior life of man. From this position man exercised dominion over life, especially through his intelligence. "The progress of man and, in a certain sense, the very progress of this universe consists in the gradual domination of all things by man." He continued:

> Domination consists in the unification of forces and the more man succeeds in conquering and domesticating the wild, untamed forces of nature, the more he has progressed and the more the universe has progressed with him. . . . The world is continually becoming more and more pointed, more and more centered in just the proportion man brings it under control.[21]

Over and above man, however, was God. In this system God necessitated man's own perfection. This had the effect of placing man at the center of the universe but not of making him "self-centered." Modern self-centered philosophy, according to Sheen, had either made God into man's image, thereby destroying the basis of man's own perfection, or reduced man to a mere speck in the universe, diminishing, through a process of "cosmic intimidation," man's own ability to control and master the forces around him.[22]

Sheen's appeal, then, was to the American desire for control and mastery. His Thomism was a vehicle for domination. It rejected modern processes of thought which made man only a part of a vast movement in the universe, and not, indeed, the mover of movement. It also rejected the disillusioned romantics of twentieth-century American letters who seemingly had made man the victim of the magnitude and complexity of the universe rather than the spokesman for order and unity.

In order for Sheen to maintain such a position, it was necessary to protect his system from at least two quite dangerous directions of modern thought. The first threat came from science itself. It was not that Sheen distrusted science; rather, it was the modern tendency to extend to philosophy, law, literature, and even theology, the latest conclusions of empirical science. Philosophical truth was not dependent on empirical evidence to corroborate its position. Accordingly, the quantum theory, said Sheen, had "nothing more to do with the proof of free will than a proton has to do with the wish to be moral." In like manner "sound philosophy" could admit the truth of relativity in the scientific order; but admitting this did not necessitate the assertion that all knowledge was relative, or that all moral truths were relative. The latter was the fatal modern error of being moonstruck by the "lyricism of science." Since Scholastic principles were eternal they did not shift with the latest currents of cosmological investigation.[23] By maintaining the principle of separation between philosophy and science, Catholics like Sheen did not have to come to terms with contingency, movement, and relativity, thereby preserving for themselves a universe of harmony and law where human reason was still the master of the spheres.

From another direction twentieth-century psychology had unleased a whole set of propositions which in their net effect tended to weaken the notion of man controlling his own destiny. It was not surprising, then, to find Catholics discounting, if not completely rejecting, the latest fads and fashions of modern psychology. For Sheen, the whole complex of psychological investigation into the unconscious or subconscious realm threatened man's role as a free and responsible decisionmaker. Behaviorism, Freudianism, and indeed most of contemporary psychology unloosed upon man what one Catholic, Charles Bruehl, called "the omnipotence of the unconscious." Hidden instincts, subliminal urges, and environmental stimuli reduced the mind and will into a state of helplessness. In eroding the rational component, modern psychologists seemed to suggest that man was not entirely responsible for his actions, making the belief in a free moral agent irrelevant if not imaginary.[24]

Protected from an exterior universe of radical contingency and an interior universe of irresistible urges, Sheen managed to maintain a philosophic structure of innocence recognizable to many Americans but championed under Catholic auspices. It was also evident to Sheen that intellectuals were primarily responsible for whatever loss of innocence American culture had suffered since World War I. Among the masses there still remained what Sheen called those "exquisite intuitions of innocence."[25]

Sheen's Thomism thus became the vehicle by which those lingering intuitions in American thought could survive the onslaughts of twentieth-century complexity and disillusionment. It was not surprising, then, to find Nicholas Murray Butler, president of Columbia University and one for whom the "intuitions of innocence" continued to resonate, applauding the members of the American Catholic Philosophical Association in 1937 for their persistence in finding something behind human experience "which is abounding in hope and good cheer" and supportive of man's aspirations and ideals.[26] Butler's words of praise attested to the growing success of

Catholics in their efforts to show that Thomism, far from being alien to the American spirit, was indeed the most persistent force for the survival of its ideals. In the words of William T. Dillon, president of the ACPA in 1937, Scholastics were the "trustees of life's grandeurs and lovers of its loveliness."[27] Life was not a field of uncertainty and doubt if one held on to the "healthy rationalism" offered by Sheen and others as authentic Thomism and traditional Americanism.

The Thomistic effort to use reason to sustain dogma as well as general cultural ideals and, at the same time, "to reduce doubt and quiet skepticism," was a most attractive quality to those who were dissatisfied with the growing irrationalism of contemporary thought.[28] Many Protestants, torn between Modernism and Fundamentalism, saw in Scholasticism a refreshing use of reason which bolstered faith instead of eroding its foundations.[29]

On the other hand, the majority of modern thinkers, though forced to admit the presence of neo-Thomism in the pantheon of modern philosophy, remained critical of the very quality which Scholastics thought was their greatest contribution. To men like Ralph Barton Perry and John Dewey, it was the Scholastic "rationalistic sense of certitude" that separated the Thomist from the modern and forged the building, especially in America, of two "intellectual worlds"—one for Catholics and another for non-Catholics. Also, it was irritating for one such as Dewey to observe among some Thomists the tendency "to assume that the truth is so finally and clearly stated in Scholasticism that most modern European philosophy is a kind of willful and perverse aberration." Protestant theologians like Henry Nelson Wieman expressed fear that the popularity of Thomism, coming as it did in the midst of philosophical war-weariness, was fraught with danger if it meant an "easy way to escape from the hazards and labors and perplexities of intellectual search . . . an easy way to achieve 'certainty.' It saves [us] from the emptiness and weariness of wonder."[30]

Most Catholics ignored such criticism from "intellectuals." From their perspective "the emptiness and weariness of wonder" were for those who had lost faith in the traditional ideals of western civilization. Catholics felt no such emptiness as long as neo-Thomism continued to supply them with an intelligible world secure from the acids of doubt. This was the strength behind everyman's Thomism in America. It did not hesitate to proclaim certainties in a world distrustful of the old certainties and groping to find new ones. In so doing Catholics were content to let the two intellectual worlds drift further apart. Seemingly secure in his own house, the Scholastic, as James McWilliams rather proudly put it,

> rejects as "anti-intellectual"—on the basis of his own principles—
> that greater part of modern speculation which presumes the sufficiency of chance or some other nonintelligible force as an ultimate

explanatory principle. . . . His reason is that if modern philosophers are going to reject the postulate of an intelligible reality and to maintain that the universe has not in itself the principles by which it may be understood, and that consequently whatever meaning and intelligibility seems to be found in the universe is in some way the projection of the subject seeking to understand, then there is no hope for rapprochement, no common ground at all.[31]

Not all Catholics were content to let the "two-world syndrome" shape the contours of their perspective. Mention has already been made of the criticism of American neo-Thomism expressed by James Hugh Ryan and John McCormick, S.J. Both men, however, shared the rationalistic perspective of the larger group they criticized. Their objections to naive confidence and lack of true scholarship, though much needed at the time, did not strike at the heart of the separation.

An early indication of discontent with Thomism as it was evolving in the United States appeared in a *Commonweal* editorial for February 12, 1930.[32] The author, in all probability George Shuster, suggested that the modern "return to reality" represented by Einstein's theories on the nature of the physical world was really a return to seeing the universe as "mystery" and "independent" of *a priori* maps concerning its construction. This, the author thought, was significant because classical Catholic philosophy had understood the universe in much the same terms. But present-day Catholics had decided to make of Thomistic doctrine "the pasture of a certain rationalistic faddism." The stress was placed on Thomas' "clarification" of Aristotle, and "his divinations of cosmic structure." Modern Thomists were reducing Aquinas to "something like a creator of a satisfactory metaphysical formula, a little more advanced than CHO, but essentially not very different." In other words, neo-Thomism had become a "logician's toy."

On the other hand, the editor felt, the most significant and contemporary aspect of the movement was the "essentially mystical quality of Thomism. It is not an institutionalist philosophy. . . . But precisely because it is based upon experience it repudiates no variety of experience." The editor attempted to expand the meaning of Thomism away from its present "pasture" of rationalism to include all of life which would permit the "infinite diversification" of experience. The placing of emphasis on diversity, mystery, and experience posed a serious challenge to those who saw Thomism as the occupant of the middle of the road and the trustee of universal and absolute principles. In 1930 few ventured down this Thomistic avenue.

Another kind of challenge came from Virgil Michel, O.S.B. (1890–1938). Michel's varied career as an American Catholic has been most often associated with his pioneer effort to make the liturgical celebrations of Catholicism more than bare rubrics.[33] His many interests ranged from literary criticism to philosophy, education, and social reform. The impulse directing all these activities was the desire to move the Church out of its "catacomb existence" of the previous four centuries and bring it to a position of leadership in the modern world.[34]

Michel first became interested in Scholastic philosophy in the immediate postwar years. With little formal training in Thomistic thought available at the Catholic University of America, his superiors decided to send him to Europe in 1924. At the International Benedictine College of St. Anselm in Rome, Michel studied under Joseph A. Gredt, O.S.B. (1863–1940). He soon discovered that being an "intellectual slave" to Gredt's Thomism was not his idea of philosophy. The self-complacency of this Thomism did not equal his own expectations of that philosophy which must "sally forth to make conquests."[35] At Louvain, Michel thought he found what he was looking for, what he called "positive Thomism." There he became a Thomist by "conviction" rather than by "faith." Now a convinced Thomist, Michel envisioned an "apostolate of philosophy" for himself when he returned to this country in 1925.[36]

His Scholastic "adventure," which he shared with a growing number of Catholics in the mid-twenties, soon gave way to the more consuming passion for liturgical reform. Throughout the twenties and thirties, however, Michel kept up his interest in philosophy by writing, lecturing, and teaching, particularly in the field of ethics. Near the end of his life he prepared two articles which summarized his philosophical mood. The first was directed at modern philosophy in general and was delivered before the American Philosophical Association in 1936. In "Philosophy at the End of an Era," Michel strongly criticized modern philosophy for capitulating to the natural sciences. Philosophy, rather than seeking to liberate man through wisdom, had participated in the chaos and disillusionment of the age by substituting experimentation for principles.[37]

Michel's arguments, though less caustic than other critics', nevertheless were part of the standard Catholic reaction to modern thought. The Benedictine monk was chastened by the criticism of G. Watts Cunningham, the editor of the *Philosophical Review*, when he rejected Michel's "Philosophy at the End of an Era" on the basis that it was "too general and hortatory" for publication.[38] As if a burden had been lifted by Cunningham's criticism, Michel decided to level his own critical acumen at the development of American Thomism since it became "conscious" of itself a decade earlier. What Michel found was a "dearth of provocative, challenging philosophical writing." Instead he discovered apologetics, "narrow and fruitless commentarism," "medieval research," a mechanical use of Scholastic adages, "spoon-feeding" educational methods, and an irritating "smugness of conviction." To underscore his remarks, he brought forth exhibits from the *Proceedings* of the ACPA and named names.[39]

"Towards a Vital Philosophy" represented for Michel his near exhaustion with the tone of Catholic self-confidence. What upset him most was "the lack of fathoming difficulties and problems or rather the total absence of any suspicion that problems exist. . . ." He asked his fellow Thomists to develop "a healthy and vigorous skepticism," warning that "there is more danger in facile reasoning than agnosticism."[40] Replete with specifics and without a "hortatory" adage, Michel succeeded in unearthing the problem of Catholic philosophizing: Catholics had not yet dealt with life's "poisons."

Virgil Michel's life ended in 1938 in rather ironic circumstances. He was preparing an essay, "Thomas of Aquin: Then and Now," which was to appear in a volume edited by Robert Brennan, O.P., *Essays in Thomism* (1942). In the process he was reviewing what was to be Brennan's essay for the volume, "The Mansions of Thomistic Philosophy." Michel was critical of Brennan's use of "admirational adjectives," latinized English, and the general tone of attributing to Aquinas the "last word" on everything. So insistent was the monk that he threatened to withdraw his own article if Brennan's appeared.[41] He died before this exchange reached a conclusion. Brennan, however, refashioned Michel's essay and it appeared in the volume instead of Brennan's essay. The revised version appeared under a new title, "Troubador of Truth," with "admirational adjectives" in abundance.[42] This must have caused some stirring in Michel's grave.

Considering that *Essays in Thomism* was dedicated to Michel, it must have caused some chagrin to his friends, at least, to read from another contributor to the volume, John K. Ryan of the Catholic University of America, an apparent reply to Michel's "Towards a Vital Philosophy." In sharp contrast to Michel, Ryan felt that "skepticism is essentially abnormal and unnatural . . . a disease of the mind." There was no such thing as a "healthy skepticism." Indeed, such open-mindedness had produced in modern philosophy and science "uncertainty, confusion, lack of stability and self-confidence . . . a weakened moral and intellectual fibre." What was even more peculiar was that Ryan had previously congratulated Michel for his "jarring truth" about the state of Catholic philosophy.[43] One has to assume that Ryan completely missed the point—as did most Catholics at the time. Michel himself was probably relieved to have passed from the scene.

Following Michel's stringent comments about the moribund smugness of Catholic thinking, there was an increase in Catholic self-criticism. Review articles in professional journals were more demanding in what merited praise and what deserved harsh criticism. Also, more sophisticated and specialized essays began to appear after 1940 in the major journals, with less emphasis on bravado and general philosophical expletives.[44] A gradual maturing process was taking place with a more sober and realistic sense of expectation. However, no fundamental change in the direction of Catholic thought occurred. It continued to affirm confidence in human reason to master the forces of society, nature and the universe, and the presence of an objective moral order. It strongly opposed relativism and skepticism and went on denouncing naturalism and pragmatism.

A significant development was taking place, however, among many non-Catholic intellectuals after 1939. Recoiling from the rude shock of Nazi nihilism and the more general menace of totalitarianism, intellectuals previously distrustful of abstractions like natural laws, principles, and moral absolutes, now began to seek with the intellectual historian Carl Becker, "some generalities that still glitter."[45] In the effort to defend democratic ideals from the forces of irrational collectivism, renewed attention was given to the Enlightenment ideals of reason, discipline, principles, and natural laws with or without supernatural foundation.

Of course, when Francis E. McMahon gave the presidential address at the ACPA meeting in 1940 and characterized his generation as "soft" and unprepared because of twenty or so years of "moral skepticism" which had eroded the foundations of American idealism, he was merely expressing an often repeated charge Catholics had made since World War I. It was something else again to have Walter Lippmann, a pre–World War I intellectual radical, give the annual dinner address at the 1941 meeting and to judge his own previous efforts at reform to be a part of "the sickness of western civilization." As Lippmann put it:

> The modern man is a sick man because—misconceiving the nature of man—he has allowed himself to become the kind of man who cannot be happy, who cannot operate the institutions of the Western World, who cannot find security and serenity in the universe.

The lack of a "rational measure of things" made the modern "dangerous." What contemporary man needed above all else, concluded Lippmann, was "the conviction that he is contained within the discipline of an ordered existence . . . which is rational and transcends his immediate promptings. . . ."[46]

Such remarks, coming from Lippmann and others, confirmed Catholics in their sense of rectitude. The present time was seen to be even more "propitious," as McMahon declared in 1940, for Catholics to demonstrate "that the ideals of democracy have their rational basis, not in pragmatism, not in subjective idealism, not in positivism, but historically and systematically in the philosophy of St. Thomas Aquinas."[47] The much publicized about-face of intellectuals like Lippmann bolstered Catholic convictions and took the bite out of the increasing self-criticism within their community. Now that others were joining them in the battle to defend democracy and the fight "to keep reason alive in the world," some Catholics, like Anton Pegis, found even a hopeful way of interpreting American pragmatism. From the perspective of World War II, James, Dewey, and Holmes were not without their virtues. To Pegis these men exhibited virtues corrupted by foreign influences. On the one hand, their "adventurous pioneer spirit" was judged by Pegis to be the chief virtue of America. But this quality was corrupted by "the despairing positivistic spirit which is one of the human illusions canonized by the fastidious Compte." American pragmatism had begun in adventure but was corrupted by European despair. "Since the days of Holmes," Pegis said, "American law . . . seems to be caught between an adventurous contingency and a despairing contingency; between saying as an American pioneer that the world is young and changing, and saying as a French positivist that the world is irrational." Catholic philosophy was to rescue the pioneer from his despairing nightmares. This rescue operation hinged on the Catholic conception of liberty.[48]

Yves R. Simon, a French refugee from the turmoil of Western Europe, presented the ideal of freedom from the Catholic perspective with a sophistication which helped to reinforce ideas instinctively held by American Catholics. For Simon, the ideal of liberty that had characterized the contemporary world was one that identified freedom as "a lack of determination." This ideal was most forcefully expressed in twentieth-century literature, where happiness "is conceived as a continual refusal to make decisive choices, an endless succession of experiments in which the person never engages himself fully, so as to preserve and ceaselessly increase the treasury of his possibilities." By refusing to be anything, Simon observed, modern man has sought "to become everything . . . the taste of the infinite." The result of linking liberty with "totality" had been disillusionment. To rescue the "adventurous contingency" of the American pioneer demanded a conception of freedom which, for Simon, meant "mastery," not totality. Man's decisive engagement in the world limited his possibilities, but, nevertheless, maintained his sense of control over the forces about him.[49] After World War II and into the 1950's Catholics remained convinced that Thomism supplied the needed remedies to bolster American confidence.

As late as 1955, Charles A. Hart noted that although there was a "decided lack of interest" in Thomistic philosophy in Europe, there was a "remarkable unanimity of viewpoint essentially Thomistic" which characterized Catholic philosophy in the United States. While European Catholics had in the thirties expanded Thomism into the broad spectrum of modern European philosophy, Americans sought a "pure Thomism." Rudolph Allers, professor of psychology at the Catholic University of America, observed in a review of *Geist in Welt* (1939) by the young German theologian Karl Rahner, S.J., that neo-Thomism was threatened by those who "modernized" Thomism by accepting as "legitimate problems" those questions of modern philosophy with which Rahner was dealing, specifically the questions of Martin Heidegger.[50] Though the influence of Etienne Gilson and Jacques Maritain was in many ways beneficial for the development of American Catholic Thomism, their combined impact was such as to obscure other avenues Thomists were pursuing in Europe. As Charles Hart noted in 1955, the easy availability of their books made them resident faculty members of every Catholic college in the country.[51]

The rift between Catholic and non-Catholic which George Santayana had described in 1926 as the separation of the modern "historical, political, adventurous" point of view and Scholasticism, which was "analytical of things in their static properties . . . a sort of geography of the logical and moral world, rather than a program for evolution or revolution," continued to be operative beyond World War II. This sense of separation made it difficult for many Thomists to approach modern philosophy, as Collins noted, "with genuine philosophical seriousness."[52] But with World War II and the arrival of a more conservative philosophical atmosphere in American intellectual circles, the rift narrowed somewhat, because revolutionary expectation in the latter group was giving way, or at least making room for more traditional modes of thought. In this context Thomism no longer appeared to be an isolated reactionary movement but rather an historically tested passageway to "the discipline of an ordered existence." With new-found allies on the American scene, Catholic Thomists felt little inclination to heed Virgil Michel's promptings for a more skeptical approach to the shroud of certainty and serenity which had draped the Thomistic movement since World War I. As Catholics had largely succeeded in maintaining the "intuitions of innocence" they were not about to plunge into skepticism when other Americans appeared to be scrambling to regain a foothold in the Garden of Eden. Though the new atomic world made life more precarious, the desire to maintain zones of security was even more pressing for Catholics and increasingly relevant in other sectors of American society.

The development of Thomistic philosophy in America since World War I was in large measure the story of the mobilization of thought to mold a structure of security within which a socially restless community could safely advance into the American mainstream. To achieve success, Thomism was used, some would say abused, to maintain a hold on reality where the value of stability triumphed over flux even while restlessness and movement were ever-present forces in American Catholic life. Stable values and principles guaranteed a sense of direction and purpose to the ubiquitous flow of upward social mobility. If progress was not inevitable, it could be attained through discipline, and by mastering the personal, social, economic, political, and cosmic dimensions of life. In other words, Catholics continued to assert that man's destiny rested in his own hands. Such confidence in turn relied on the assurance that reality was "intelligible at heart" and in no way irrational. The sweet reasonableness of life provided a set of objective moral laws extracted by reason and common sense which both guided and judged human activity. This provided Catholics with a sense of an ordered existence, within which they could move confidently toward social and spiritual salvation.

Thomism supplied Catholics anxious to "make it" in America with the philosophic dimensions of their structure of innocence. It was not a revolutionary program, as Santayana noted in 1926, but it did provide the philosophical support for Catholic activism. The zeal with which Catholics took up Thomistic philosophy was commensurate with the energetic manner in which they believed Thomism attacked reality. Thomism in the hands of American Catholics did not probe reality but charted it. It paved secure avenues for Catholics to confront the challenges of life. However, the strenuous effort to sanitize life forced them to blink at its complexities; to facilely construe a benign intelligibility operating in reality; to glorify reason to the neglect of imagination and feeling.

The appealing charm of Thomism, however, was its clean, efficient way of maneuvering among and dominating the pitfalls of reality. It delivered Catholics from the burden of carrying the weight of the universe on their shoulders. It was extremely adaptable to the American desire to get confidently on with life. As the catechism was an efficient device for passing on religious truths, so also was Thomism, though on a more sophisticated level. In Thomism there was no necessity to passionately plunge either into the divine or into the abyss. God was in his heaven and man was in possession of the road maps to eternity.

Reality, like divinity, was a manageable proposition. It was likened to the construction of schools, churches, and political machines. While these latter endeavors were many times born of necessity, the constructive qualities of American Thomism were magnified by a familiarity with ingrained social habits which seemed to require imposing structures. The Catholic sense of efficiency, however, lacked a certain delicate touch in its handling of ideas. Both truths and errors were packaged in concrete. With

Thomism, most Catholics preserved an orderly if not a comfortable universe, before there was any need to be delivered from a disordered one. Construction began on a foundation of optimism and certainty and proceeded to de-mystify the world and its problems before life was appreciated in its complexity and fullness. Lacking a sense of mystery, wonder, or perplexity, innocence was preserved; reality was mapped; the way to salvation was paved, if not with gold, then at least with reinforced concrete.

10. Conclusion

The Dispossession

WRITING TO ALLEN TATE in 1940, Christopher Dawson succinctly expressed the transformation of America in the twentieth century. "In the space of a generation," he wrote, "America ceased to be the New World and became part of the Old World; in fact it became simply the largest and richest of the Western Powers. It lost its sense of cultural inferiority, but at the same time lost its virginity, its sense of irresponsibility and freedom from the social guilt of the Old World."[1] The loss of virginity had wide-ranging ramifications in American politics, literature, philosophy, and religion. The institution that had always symbolized the haunting presence of the Old World within the New World was the Catholic Church.

Contrary to what might have been expected, American Catholics were busy during this time of transformation defending the assumptions upon which American virginity had been supported. Sensitive to the charge of being un-American, Catholics were in many ways the most solidified group of people holding onto the threads of American innocence during these years. Supporting their quite vocal claim to America were a set of philosophical and cultural imperatives. While admittedly alienated from contemporary currents of thought, Catholics were, nevertheless, convinced that what they offered had impeccable American credentials. Although few non-Catholics understood, Catholics had survived disillusionment. They had advanced into the twentieth century believing the promises of America to be real because they were imbedded in the structure of reality, planted by God, unearthed through human reason, and demonstrated by logic and common sense. For Catholics, American optimism had achieved a plateau of disconcerting exuberance. The process of the erosion of that plateau after World War II was at first hardly noticeable. Then, in the 1960's it was overwhelmed by an unexpected wave of confusion. This final chapter will concern itself with a brief examination of the Catholic dispossession of innocence.

On the face of it, the culture which Catholics began constructing after World War I was a baffling one. Wilfred Sheed has recently written of it as "an amalgam of quaintnesses plus an awful lot of football." The result of

169

this amalgam was to make Catholics different. Garry Wills's memories of
his boyhood Catholicism have emphasized the distinctive style of being
Catholic in America. Catholics spoke a unique language, visited places
other Americans did not go, i.e., the confessional. Life was immersed,
Wills recalls, in habits:

> prayers offered, heads ducked in unison, crossings, chants, christen-
> ings, grace at meals; beads, altar, incense, candles; nuns in the
> classroom alternately too sweet and too severe, priests garbed black on
> the street and brilliant at the altar; churches lit and darkened, clothed
> and stripped, to the rhythm of liturgical recurrences; the crib in
> winter, purple Februaries, and lilies in the spring; confession as
> intimidation and comfort . . . communion as reverie and discomfort;
> faith as a creed, and the creed as a catechism, Latin responses,
> salvation by rote, all things going to a rhythm, memorized. . . .

Draped over the "quaintnesses" of Catholic life was another amalgamation
of certainties which, Wills notes satisfied "the Catholic urge to codify
reality and capture it in rules."[2]

Catholic culture was dominated by rhythms, "objective" or "natural"
laws, and an abstractive turn of mind which neutralized individual passions. There was an absence of individual egoism. All of it was transfused
into an institutional egoism, which everyone shared but which was also
seemingly invulnerable to disruption. Everything operated to obscure
obscurity. This was true not only for those beliefs associated with Catholicism but also those associated with America. Both were intertwined in ways
which made American Catholicism different from Catholicism in Europe
and also made American Catholics different from other Americans.

World War II did not effect a fundamental change in the Catholic
community in America. The movements and thinking set in motion during
World War I, in fact, advanced more rapidly. The Catholic middle class
increased. Colleges, schools, seminaries, convents, and parishes expanded
and proliferated during the late 1940's and through the 1950's. Professional and cultural associations grew in membership and purpose; the
general mood and temper of Catholicism was sustained and even prospered
in an American climate more appreciative of stability. By 1955 non-
Catholics like Will Herberg could confidently proclaim that American
Catholicism "is now part of the American Way of Life." Of course,
Catholics already knew this but it was good to hear someone else say it.[3]

Not only were Catholics materially and socially prospering; even their
intellectual and cultural alienation from pre-World War II movements was
vindicated, or so it seemed, by the rush of many to repudiate first their
disillusionment and then their radicalism. In 1950 Francis X. Connolly

proudly observed in referring to literature that non-Catholics had discovered the "tone" and "vocabulary" of Catholic critics for several generations past. He singled out Lewis Mumford's essay, "Mirror of a Violent Half-Century," which appeared in the *New York Times Book Review* of January 15, 1950. Connolly pointed to Mumford's criticism of writers for "mirroring disintegration" rather than serving as "interpreters of possibilities." The writer, according to Mumford and quoted by Connolly, must seek to restore "reason to the irrational, purpose to the defeatists and drifters, value to the nihilist, hope to those sinking in despair." All of which, Connolly attested, Catholic critics had been preaching since 1917 without much effect.[4]

The decade of the 1950's also saw the high-water mark of Thomistic influence upon American Catholics. The American Catholic Philosophical Association enjoyed an increasing membership and, as Charles Hart boasted in 1955, over $15,000 in assets "carefully invested in AT & T." This allowed, he felt, "wisdom's lovers" to "more comfortably and effectively carry on their high vocation of contemplation of ultimate truth." He also proudly proclaimed that nowhere else in the Catholic world was there accomplished such a full response to Leo XIII's encyclical *Aeterni Patris*. All seemed to bode well for the philosophers. Indeed, Leo R. Ward suggested in 1959 that it would take a shelf of books to describe the varied activities of Catholics from Newman clubs to retreat movements, to crowded churches and lay institutes, to the ideas associated with Dorothy Day, Thomas Merton, Fulton Sheen, and John Courtney Murray. Excitedly Ward asked, "Where would it ever stop?" As it happened, within a few years Ward had an unexpected answer.[5]

In the presence of so much activity, self-confidence, and increasing acceptance by others, the assessment in 1957 by Walter Ong, S.J., of an "intellectual and spiritual crisis" within American Catholicism appeared at first glance to be a long leap into pure fancy.[6] Ong proved to be an accurate prophet, however. Below the buzz and fluff of Catholic life were quiet rumblings of discontent and the slow development of a different way of looking at things. An indication of the change can be detected in the kind of convert the Church began to attract in the early 1940's. Two of the more eloquent were Thomas Merton and Robert Lowell. The latter was a poet, the former became a Trappist monk who managed to transform silence into a forceful way of speaking and writing.

Thomas Merton's conversion was recorded in his best-selling autobiography *The Seven Storey Mountain* (1948), which was co-opted by the religious revival following World War II. Merton's conversion was neither marked by the significance of St. Augustine's, as many Catholics hoped, nor by the "ease and comfortableness" which non-Catholics like Lionel Trilling suspected of him and the "machine for living" type of religion of the postwar revival. Merton was more complex than most Catholics or others like Trilling were able to allow.[7] In his journals recorded after his conversion (1938) but before his entry into the Cistercian order (1941), his thoughts set the stage for a distinctive shift which would develop within the Catholic community for the next fifteen years. Unconsciously, Merton seemed to respond to the main outlines of Catholic culture described in this study. A problem that had plagued the Catholic community in previous years was the meaning of the religious life: Was it stained-glass windows, Gregorian chant, school buildings, imposing Gothic structures, or natural laws? Simply, Merton's answer was that it was the life of the soul:

> And there it exists not as a "good feeling" but as a constant purpose, an unending love that expresses itself now as patience, now as humility, now as courage, now as self-denial, now as justice, but always in a strong knot of faith and hope. . . .

In terms of literature, Merton observed that the confusion and hatred expressed toward contemporary writers like James Joyce was the result of Catholics sacralizing middle-class culture to the point where it became identified with the Mystical Body of Christ. Thus, everything that a writer like Joyce wrote seemed "blasphemous." As for Catholic philosophy, Merton bluntly wrote:

> It should be our greatest strength that we don't have, on the end of our tongues, a brief and pithy rationalization for the structure and purpose of the whole universe. . . . In certain things it is even more the glory of the Catholic than the skeptic to say "I don't know."

Finally, Merton's attraction toward the monastic life was not as un-American as it would first appear. In the Catholic drive for recognition in America many found themselves unconsciously aping the activist and pragmatic American temper. Bishops became a class of holy corporate executives, priests were honored for their management capabilities, nuns for their educational prowess, while the ordinary Catholic paid the bills to keep the whole enterprise moving. For Merton, the Trappist Abbey of Gethsemani in Kentucky was more than a momentary respite from activity or retreat from the world. It was, rather, "the center of America . . . in the wilderness." Like Thoreau's Walden it represented the wholeness of uncorrupted space, the symbolical attraction of America seen as the New World. Merton, a convert to both America and Catholicism, discovered both in an ancient order of monks praying in the hills of Kentucky. It is not surprising to find Merton later seeking contacts with Eastern mysticism in ways which earlier American romantics like Emerson had done.[9]

Merton's discoveries and thinking were leading to the expansion of

American Catholic possibilities as well as to making Catholicism more vulnerable to contemporary unease. For, while optimism can be sustained by romanticism, the intrusion of romanticism slowly eroded the rational confidence which previously characterized Catholic certainties. In Robert Lowell, who came upon the scene with *Lord Weary's Castle* (1946), another new element was added to the Catholic mixture. First, Lowell's poetry did not sing of beauty and light, but was instead the bitter cry of a man "poured out like water" at the convulsions of twentieth-century experience. After his conversion in 1940 Lowell would refer to himself as a "fire-breathing Catholic C[onscientious] O[bjector]."[9] Both Lowell's poetry and personal intensity were stripped of institutional protection. He brought to American Catholicism the daring but dangerous intensity of the exposed ego.

This quality and style Catholics had previously managed to control. But increasingly after 1945 personal egoism would begin to swell, while institutional egoism would slowly shrivel. Much of the conflict and confusion which exploded upon Catholics in the mid-1960's arose from the rivalry of egos desperately trying to promote their own visions in the absence and dilapidation of institutional vision. While the intrusion of egoism allowed the opportunity for some to break out of the monolithic mediocrity Catholics were prone to accept, it also tended to make them more susceptible to fragmentation and disillusionment. They were beginning to catch the disease, and are still trying to determine whether or not it was, in Eliot's sense, "healthy."

The mixture of romanticism and egoism combined with a continuing sense of optimism and self-confidence to create a highly volatile and unpredictable compound. In the late 1940's and early 1950's only a few Catholics were affected by this unholy mixture. But what happened to them would steadily affect greater numbers by the mid-1960's. Two young Catholics of the "generation of the third eye," as they dubbed themselves, were Daniel Callahan and Ned O'Gorman. Their paths through the 1950's are instructive.

Callahan entered Yale University in 1948. In his junior year he read F. Scott Fitzgerald's *This Side of Paradise* and found himself, like its hero, Amory Blaine, a "romantic Catholic, troubled by his faith and beguiled by the rich and beautiful. . . ." Callahan set out to be both "intelligent and Catholic at the same time." To be this in the 1950's meant to master Thomism. So he did, under the tutelage of John Courtney Murray, S.J. By graduation his sense of intellectual confidence was secure, but almost immediately it left him depressed. As he later confessed, he was both "overconfident and . . . in a constant state of anxiety. I was forever at the mercy of some new quandary, some new argument or evidence. Thinking itself became a threat."

What he sought now was "detachment," much as Fitzgerald had Amory

Blaine recoil from the "ulterior pressure." While recognized as a liberal and reformer in the exciting days of Vatican II, Callahan was in reality more skeptical of the transformation taking place. Reform might mean simply a "failure of nerves." In rejecting the rationalistic inclinations of the past Catholics were admitting to a "loss of confidence" and self-security. To compensate, Callahan observed, there was "a retreat from reason into mystery; from clear and distinct ideas to muddy (but rich) experience; from rational choice to commitment. . . ." The popular reform cry of "relevance" was really a confession of weakness. Throughout, Callahan was developing a sense for the complexity of things which was disturbing the innocent confidence of both "ghetto" Catholicism and the liberated reformers of the 1960's.[10]

While Callahan envied the good life of his Groton classmates at Yale, Ned O'Gorman in 1950 found himself in the hills of western Pennsylvania with three other men and a young woman who comprised "The Center for Men of Christ the Kind." The antinomian impulse that was so much a part of American religious history had, among Catholics, been tightly restrained. Most Catholics disdained an openly pious sort of religion. Religion was a matter of the head, of quiet observance and reverence. But for O'Gorman, who was educated in Catholic schools, the attractions of an individualistic piety led him to the Center, as he recounted, "to find out if the Church had selected us to begin, in the midst of the modern world we all found wanting, a new life." Rising beneath the rigid surface of Catholic life was a pool of sentimentalism which a community that took the name of "Christ the Kind" sought to satisfy.

The Center was actually a compound of conflicting currents. Its purpose, according to O'Gorman, was to achieve a "nirvana, some serene liturgical empathy." This search took place, however, in an atmosphere he described as "a madhouse of sexual, liturgical, and aesthetic bedlam. In the air [was] the lust for power and an obsession with religion that . . . was so personal, so intricate, so bound to the unfulfilled heart. . . ." O'Gorman's experiences would be multiplied many times in the 1960's by Catholics, clergy and laity alike, seeking emotional outlets of expression for an already brimming sense of optimism.[11]

Previously, Catholic optimism had been confined to hard and fast rules of the mind and to the laws of nature. In the 1960's the optimism shifted to the emotional and romantic. Retreats, conferences, and meetings of Catholics were fashioned into intimate encounters for the purpose of religious growth, producing enthusiastic expectations that eventually led to disaster. Nevertheless, in the process of testing emotional limits which sometimes strained common sense, a note of refreshing vulnerability was added to Catholic life which has resulted not only in disillusionment but in a certain amount of awkward creativity as well.

Throughout the 1950's, however, Merton's "errand into the wilderness," Lowell's egoism, Callahan's "detachment," and O'Gorman's romanticism remained relatively isolated forms of Catholic expression. The innocent Catholicism of the pre–World War II period appeared solid and growing stronger, particularly as it began to shed some of its more naive manifestations of self-confidence and defensive combativeness. A severe shock to this placidity came in 1955 when Monsignor John Tracy Ellis, a respected historian of American Catholicism, levelled what amounted to an indictment against the path of Catholic success.

In brief, Ellis' *American Catholics and the Intellectual Life* undermined Catholic self-complacency. Although Catholics had advanced in social and material prosperity, Ellis found them singularly wanting when it came to effective thinking. Phrasing his critism in carefully constructed historical arguments, Ellis succeeded, where previous critics had failed, in blowing the lid off. What came packaged as Catholic thought appeared to Ellis, who quoted Peter Viereck, as really "middle-class-Jansenist Catholicism, puritanized, Calvinized, and dehydrated. . . ." Following Ellis' analysis, a host of critics poured out of the woodwork as if some magic spell had been broken.[12]

The most analytical critic was the sociologist Thomas F. O'Dea. O'Dea recited a litany of isms as primary factors for the low state of Catholic thought: formalism, authoritarianism, clericalism, and moralism. These charges, along with defensiveness, were not unlike those which rebellious intellectuals had brought against American thought in general fifty years earlier, and which eventually resulted in the "revolt against formalism." Now, in the late 1950's, the rebellion had finally caught up with Catholics, and with similar effect. After Ellis, criticism escalated to the point that in the mid-1960's some questioned whether Catholic and intellectual were mutually exclusive descriptions.[13]

More importantly, O'Dea's analysis helped to focus Catholic discontent on Thomism. Since World War I Thomism had supplied the philosophical bulwark that had enabled Catholics to maintain an aggressive sense of control over reality even if they had to erect a hyperdefensive posture to maintain it. The philosophical confidence Catholics brought to their thinking was achieved by keeping their discussions at the level of abstraction. The rational glitter which surrounded Catholic certainties served to blind Catholics to the dust accumulating on the fragile edges. Also, for increasing numbers of Catholics anxious to move out of the ghetto, Thomistic philosophy came to symbolize all that was wrong with Catholic life in it, especially its defensiveness. If philosophic idealism was the bogeyman of formalism to American intellectuals like James, Dewey, and Holmes at the turn of the century, Thomism played this role for dissatisfied Catholics during the late 1950's and early 1960's.

From 1958 to 1968 the domination of Thomism over Catholic philosophy in America began to recede. There developed two distinct reactions. Some took a highly critical view and openly called upon Catholics to abandon the Aristotelian and Scholastic methodology and world view upon which Catholics had constructed not only their philosophy but their theological and cultural perspectives as well. The more characteristic response was simply a loss of enthusiasm for making Thomism appear forward-looking. For many, the Thomistic synthesis died from weariness. The constant struggle to adapt it to new insights and new worlds absorbed too much energy. It seemed better just to accept the new world.[14] Although many educated Catholics had grown tired of Thomism, they had not yet lost their enthusiasm, optimism, and confident manner. They were simply more daring. Like the early pragmatists, they talked happily of taking risks, of experimenting, of possibilities. Even in the newly discovered sense of uncertainty, the "new generation," Michael Novak confidently predicted in 1964, was destined to be creative.[15]

The exuberance Catholics once brought to Thomism some now transferred to Teilhard de Chardin. Chardin satisfied the already ingrained Catholic desire to grab reality whole. Chardin's grand evolutionary perspective lifted many to a lightness of heart as the Thomistic synthesis once had done to the young Jesuit Daniel Lord and others of his generation. Chardin's thought not only seemed to conquer reality intellectually, but poetically, scientifically, historically, and theologically, as well. Initially what attracted Catholics to Thomas now attracted them to Chardin, only the latter also appealed to a newly acquired sense of daring. While Thomism had cemented their optimism, the thought of Chardin left it precariously exposed. Enthusiasm for the latter depended upon the fragile necessity of things going well. The aloof quality of Thomism enabled Catholics to be optimistic, even if everything around them was disintegrating. However, in the late 1950's and early 1960's everything seemed to be going well. The social, political, and religious atmosphere of the period was one of expectation, even fulfillment.

American Catholics were not clamoring at the walls of Rome in 1958 when Pope John XXIII called for a general ecumenical council of the Church, Vatican II (1960–1965). They were rather invited just to sit in on a European discussion that had been waxing and waning since the first Vatican Council ended in 1870. Once there, however, many liked what they saw. Some returned in a glow of liberation, while others came back afraid. The seeds of the disruptions which were about to beset American Catholicism had already been planted and would have grown without the Council. Vatican II, however, did have its important consequences. Overall it served, as had World War I, as a mechanism for acceleration. It speeded up the process of change and reform, heightened expectancy, and focused energy.

Michael Novak, for instance, excited by the possibilities of the time, envisioned a church which was "one large community: full of free speech, argument, dissent, respect for diversity, and the slow search for consensus." Novak's concentrated enthusiasm soon left him "bored," however, while others, such as Daniel Callahan, simply became tired of the slowness with which the Kingdom was coming. One of the primary results of Vatican II was to leave American Catholicism fragmented like most other institutions, churches, and organizations of the modern world. This is not to say that Catholics were part of a seamless web before; the condition simply became more obvious by the mid-1960's. A sense of internal alienation had come to disrupt both liberals and conservatives.[16]

Concurrently, Catholic optimism was further bolstered by the election of President John F. Kennedy in 1960. Not only did Kennedy shatter the last political barrier obstructing America's acceptance of Catholicism, but the kind of spirit he represented seemed to fulfill Catholic aspirations in America. Kennedy, it appeared, brought to his presidency a vigorous combination of pragmatism and idealism which neither the complexities of national problems nor the weight of an ambiguous universe seemed to disturb. He relished the role of decisionmaker and manipulator of power. He sought to conquer new frontiers while others before him had given up on the old ones. Here was a Catholic out to save America and the world, exactly what Catholics had been claiming they were doing since World War I. Enlivened by Kennedy's activism and Pope John XXIII's humanism, Catholic energy—long drained by the defensive effort to keep idealism alive—now found itself exploding in a variety of social, religious, and political reform movements. As one Catholic nun expressed it while marching from civil rights rallies to the popular lectures of Martin Luther King and the German theologian Hans Küng: "I'm so glad I'm in the Kingdom."[17]

In the early 1960's expressions of Catholic optimism abounded. Innocence was in bloom, even as the past where it had first taken root was rejected. Irrepressibly hopeful, Catholics like Philip Scharper were primarily more daring than different from those of the previous generation. The genius of American Catholicism, Scharper explained, was "that freedom is not to be feared but fostered, that risk cannot be divorced from decision, that one can safely gamble on the virtue, intelligence and honor of the average man, and, finally, that the past, no matter how splendid, is forever but prelude." The fact that Catholics were now making decisions based on risk rather than conviction and found themselves gambling rather than being certain did not diminish the optimism which linked the generations. As for America, Gary MacEoin wrote in 1965, it remained the land of opportunity where the harmonious advancement of individual and community interests were protected by a sense of limitless plenitude. "When one gets more in this land of expanding horizons," MacEoin offered, "it means there is more for the other." Within a few short years such a statement would sound incredibly presumptuous.[18]

By 1965 Catholics were prepared for the final stage of dispossession. Increasingly free from the formalism that made their certainties firm but impersonal, Catholics were allowing themselves and their thought to be shaped by a new kind of experience. For a time experience all but confirmed their optimism about life, reality, and American society.

Then, suddenly experience soured. The spasm of irrationality that killed John and Robert Kennedy and Martin Luther King confused many. Civil rights reform climaxed in urban rebellion and violence. Governmental activity in the areas of welfare and poverty seemed only to compound difficulties, not solve them. Religious reform soon became boring or led into a quagmire of conflicting and often hostile reactions. Liturgical reform often meant something new, not necessarily something better. Parish life was less constricted but more confusing. Priests and nuns departed without warning, leaving lay Catholics stunned. Conservatives moaned at the destruction of "their" church, liberals yawned and read about the "death of God." A community once proud of its stability watched itself come unglued.

Finally, during the late 1960's and early 1970's the Vietnam War provided the very real presence of ambiguity, despair, confusion, and irrationality. For Catholics it was the first American war which they did not rush into as a group to fight or enthusiastically defend. Catholics were emotionally torn, like everyone else, between defenders, passive critics, and violent and nonviolent resisters. While the defenders were forced to settle for a "victorious defeat," the resisters found themselves exhausted even as the war concluded. The Vietnam War had the effect of wrenching many Catholics from America. Senseless destruction was not easily reconciled with the righteousness of American moralism. By 1970 there was for the first time within the Catholic community a substantial group disaffected with both Catholicism and America. Few Catholics were sure of anything any more. As the radical poet of Catholic resistance, Daniel Berrigan, S.J., wrote in 1970, "the times are rude and descend like a guillotine."[19] The

American Catholic "road to safety, sanity, and salvation" had come upon rocky ways.

The decade of the 1960's was a crucial period for Catholics, as it was for most Americans. Catholics, however, entered the decade differently and had more difficulty escaping. For the most part Catholics had managed to survive for sixty years by paring off intrusions of thought and feeling that had gradually crept into American culture and self-consciousness since 1900. Catholics packed into a decade the conflicting experiences of a half-century. The decade began for them like the century had begun, full of confidence in reform and enthusiasm for ideals. Evolutionary thought was a natural by-product of a progressive world. As the pragmatism James and Dewey had done, many Catholics rejected their own forms of rationalism and formalism. Reality was possibility. Also reminiscent of James and Dewey, they were optimistic that riskiness, experimentation, and adventuresome thought would end well. The pervasive idealism obstructed many of the pitfalls.

Eventually idealism gave way, as it had done in the 1920's, to boredom and disillusionment. Many felt increasingly alienated either by the slowness or rapidity of change in both Church and society. As Catholicism fragmented, there appeared a group of intellectuals comparable to those of the 1920's who described their plight as one of "paradox, tension, and suffering." No longer satisfied with "conventional Catholicism," or with America for that matter, they saw themselves, as Rosemary Reuther related, on the "revolutionary fringe" where some were to catch cold.[20] Whereas once Catholics had been sure of some rock-hard certainties (for example, the rational self capable of free choice, and an understandable universe susceptible of control), many now were no longer sure. As idealism crashed on the rough edges of experience, corruption, and complexity, some, like Michael Novak, dared to enter "the experience of nothingness." As Novak ventured, "no man has a self or an identity; in a society like ours he must constantly be inventing selves." For American Catholics this was a distinctly different kind of thinking.[21]

There was also in the 1960's a sharp increase in the radicalization, passion, and intensity of many Catholics which paralleled similar movements in America in the 1930's. For the first time Catholics vocally rejected America, and Marxism became an option. At the same time there were those who sought to hold on to the fundamentals of Catholicism and American patriotism in opposition even to changes and reforms blessed by orthodoxy. Those not willing to link themselves with fundamentalists were nevertheless anxious to recover some semblance of order and harmony in the midst of chaos and confusion. Intellectually, this recovery was expressed by a regrouping of Thomists who claimed that "real" Thomism was never tried in America. What had passed as Thomism before was an imposter.[22] As the sense of plenitude gave way to the consciousness of limitation, Catholics like Michael Novak rediscovered in the thought of Aquinas a balance between "being and doing" and "story and reason." It was also happily "nonideological."[23] For many other Catholics the urge toward order was expressed in highly emotional ventures. Catholic Pentecostalism became a way of structuring frenzy for some, while many others left the Church to become captivated by rigidly controlled religious sects promising peace, happiness, and a sense of domination.

During the 1960's the experience of a century converged upon Catholics to explode the structure of innocence they had preserved since the period of World War I. Events of the decade accelerated the process of dispossession.[24] Currently, Catholics are conscious of having lost something that even nostalgia cannot recover.[25] They can no longer boast of a "proud and glorious isolation." They are troubled by the same complexities of social, cultural, and religious life that disturb many in contemporary civilization. At the same time, however, Catholics also appear to be uncomfortable in the role of being like everyone else. It is just this ambivalence and uneasiness that may allow creativity to emerge. Catholics today are not only haunted by a tradition of naive optimism and negativism; they are driven by a momentum which that tradition also inspired: the desire to be whole, to be free, and the belief that the promises of hope are not merely tricks of illusion.

Notes

Foreword

1. George Santayana, *Character & Opinion in the United States* (New York: George Braziller, 1955), pp. 30–31.
2. Owen Chadwick, *Freedom and the Historian: An Inaugural Lecture* (Cambridge: at the University Press, 1969), p. 39.
3. Donald T. Miller and Marion Nowak, *The Fifties: The Way We Really Were* (Garden City, N.Y.: Doubleday & Company, 1977); Ronald Berman, *America in the Sixties: An Intellectual History* (New York: Free Press, 1968).
4. Peter Gay and Gerald J. Cavanaugh, eds., *Historians at Work* (New York: Harper & Row, 1972), I, xviii.

Introduction: The Sad Century

1. Ltr., John A. Ryan to Carlton J. H. Hayes, Washington, D.C., February 3, 1942, Carlton J. H. Hayes Papers, Columbia University Library; Carlton J. H. Hayes, "From One Age to Another," *The Commonweal* 21 (November 2, 1934), 11–13.
2. Norman Weyend, S.J., ed., *The Catholic Renascence in a Disintegrating World* (Chicago, 1951); Demetrius B. Zema, "Introduction" to James J. Walsh, *The Thirteenth: The Greatest of Centuries* (New York, 1946).
3. Lionel Trilling, "Whittaker Chambers and 'The Middle of the Journey,' " *The New York Review* 22 (April 17, 1975), 22.
4. Winthrop S. Hudson, *American Protestantism* (Chicago, 1961), p. 128; Robert T. Handy, *A Christian America: Protestant Hopes and Historical Realities* (New York, 1971), pp. 209–210; Sidney Ahlstrom, *A Religious History of the American People* (New Haven, 1972), p. 899.
5. Theodore Maynard, *The Story of American Catholicism* (New York, 1960 [1941]), 2:224; Charles Clayton Morrison, "Is There a Catholic-Protestant Rapprochement," *Christendom* 1 (Autumn 1936), 861; "Thomism and the Rebirth of Protestant Philosophy," ibid., 2 (Winter 1937), 110–111.
6. Reinhold Niebuhr, *The Children of Light and the Children of Darkness* (New York, 1944), pp. 70–73, 132–135, 152–154; Niebuhr, *The Irony of American History* (New York, 1952), pp. 4–7, 71–77.

1: Catholicism: "The Return from Exile"

1. Peter Wust, a German Catholic philosopher, used the phrase "return from exile" in describing a feeling of liberation he thought Catholicism in Germany enjoyed immediately after World War I. See Christopher Dawson, *Essays in Order* (New York, 1931), pp. xvi–xxii.

2. E. L. Woodward, *Three Essays in European Conservatism* (London, 1930).

3. Emmet John Hughes, *The Church and the Liberal Society* (Princeton, N.J., 1944), pp. 203–221; Roger Aubert, *Le Pontificat de Pie IX* (Paris, 1952), pp. 245–261.

4. See Aubert, *Le Pontificat de Pie IX; Pastoral Letter of the Most Reverend Martin John Spalding, D.D.* (Baltimore, 1865); James Hennessey, S.J., *The First Council of the Vatican: The American Experience* (New York, 1963).

5. *Aeterni Patris,* from full text translated in Jacques Maritain, *St. Thomas Aquinas* (New York, 1958 [1931]), pp. 183–214.

6. The published proceedings of these congresses were bound as *Compte rendu Congres Scientifique International des Catholiques.*

7. On Americanism, see Thomas T. McAvoy, C.S.C., *The Great Crisis in American Catholic History* (Chicago, 1957); on Modernism, see Alec R. Vidler, *The Modernist Movement in the Roman Church: Its Origins and Outcome* (Cambridge, 1934), Emile Poulat, *Histoire dogma et critique dans la Crise Modernists* (Paris, 1962).

8. Henry May, *The End of American Innocence* (Chicago, 1964), pp. 372–374.

9. R. R. Palmer, *A History of the Modern World* (New York, 1960), p. 604.

10. "Battle of Lepanto," in *The Collected Poems of G. K. Chesterton* as cited by Marvin O'Connell, *The Counter-Reformation, 1559–1610* (New York, 1974), p. 206.

11. *The Church and the Catholic and the Spirit of the Liturgy* (New York, 1935), p. 11.

12. Eliot, "An Emotional Unity," *The Dial* 84 (February 1928), 111–112.

13. *The Church and I* (Garden City, N.Y., 1974), pp. 94–96.

14. "An Emotional Unity," p. 111.

15. Jacques Maritain, *The Things That Are Not Caesar's* (New York, 1931).

16. Calvert Alexander, S.J., *The Catholic Literary Revival* (Milwaukee, 1935), p. 247.

17. Quotation of Péguy, cited in Frank O'Malley, "The Evangelism of Georges Bernanos," *Review of Politics,* 11 (October 1944), 420; André Gide, *Journals, 1899–1949* (New York, 1967), pp. 95–96.

18. Georges Bernanos, *La France contre les robots* (Paris, 1947), p. 112; O'Malley, "The Evangelism of Georges Bernanos," pp. 403–419.

19. *The Man of Letters in the Modern World* (New York 1955), pp. 13–16.

20. Martin Green, *Yeats' Blessing on Von Hügel* (London, 1967), p. 74.

21. *Sidelights on the Catholic Revival* (New York, 1940), p. 14.

22. *Essays of a Catholic* (London, 1931), pp. 304–305.

23. This was especially true of a number of French Catholic thinkers such as Henri de Lubac, Yves Congar, Jean Daniélou, and Pierre Teilhard de Chardin, who were at the center of an intellectual controversy which resulted in the issuing of *Humani Generis* (1950) by Pius XII; see James M. Connolly, *The Voices of France* (New York, 1961).

24. James A. Weisheipl, O.P., "The Revival of Thomism as a Christian Philosophy," in Ralph M. McInerny, ed., *New Themes in Christian Philosophy* (Notre Dame, Ind., 1968), p. 168.

25. Ibid., pp. 168–170.

26. Owen Chadwick, *From Boussuet to Newman: The Idea of Doctrinal Development* (Cambridge, 1957), p. 169.

27. Maritain, *St. Thomas Aquinas*, p. 11.

28. Charles Péguy, *Temporal and Eternal* (New York, 1958 [1932]); *Blondel-Valensian Correspondence* I: 338, n. 2, as cited in Alexander Dru, "From the *Action Française* to the Second Vatican Council," *The Downside Review* 81 (July 1963), 226.

29. "Medievalism in Toronto," *The Commonweal* 9 (May 1, 1929), 739.

30. Raissa Maritain and Jacques Maritain, *The Situation of Poetry* (New York, 1955 [1938]), p. 37.

31. Maritain, *St. Thomas Aquinas*, pp. 18–19.

32. *A Preface to Metaphysics* (New York, 1971 [1939]), pp. 4–9.

33. Ibid., pp. 10–11.

34. Ibid., p. 14.

35. Ibid., p. 20.

36. John Henry Cardinal Newman, *An Essay on the Development of Christian Doctrine* (London, 1891 [1845]), pp. 185–186.

37. "The Baptism of Aristotle and Marx," *The Nation* 146 (April 9, 1938), 417.

38. "The Future of Thomism," in McInerny, *New Themes in Christian Philosophy*, p. 189.

39. Jacques Maritain, *The Peasant of Garonne* (New York, 1968).

40. *Survivals and New Arrivals* (New York, 1929), p. 178.

41. Maritain, *A Preface to Metaphysics*, p. 1.

42. Jacques Maritain, *Art and Poetry* (New York, 1943), p. 46; Hannah Arendt, "Christianity and Revolution," *The Nation* 161 (September 22, 1945), 289.

43. Editorial, "Trumpet of the Dawn," *The Commonweal* 10 (September 25, 1929), 515.

44. *Contemporary Continental Theology* (New York, 1938), p. 84.

45. *The Situation of Poetry*, pp. 37–38.

2: Michael Williams:
The Romance of American Innocence

1. "Pascendi Domenici gregis" in Colman J. Barry, O.S.B., ed., *Readings in Church History*, 3 vols. (Westminster, Md., 1965), Vol. 3.

2. Charles A. Beard, *Contemporary American History* (New York, 1914), pp. 303–304; Morton White, *Social Thought in America: The Revolt against Formalism* (Boston, 1957); Henry F. May, "The Rebellion of the Intellectuals, 1912–1917," *American Quarterly* 8 (Summer 1956), 114–126.

3. May, *The End of American Innocence;* Loren Baritz, ed., "Introduction," *The Culture of the Twenties* (Indianapolis, 1970), xv–lv; John Higham, "Hanging Together: Divergent Unities in American History," *Journal of American History* 61 (June 1974), 24–28; Henry F. May, "Shifting Perspectives on the Twenties," *The Mississippi Valley Historical Review* 43 (December 1956), 425–426.

4. Michael Williams, *The Catholic Church in Action* (New York, 1934), pp. 2–3.

5. *McClure's* 29 (May 1907), 74–86.

6. See, for example, "The Avenger," *Everybody's* 18 (June 1908), 837–850; "Stolen Song," *McClure's* 34 (November 1909), 112–116; "One in a Million," *Munsey* 49 (September 1913), 966–973; "His Memory," *Harper's Weekly* 55 (May 6, 1911), 16–17.

7. "A Fight in One Round," p. 82.

8. "His Memory," p. 17.

9. "A Fight in One Round," p. 74.

10. Ibid., p. 84.

11. Ibid., p. 86.

12. *The Book of High Romance* (New York, 1926 [1918]), hereafter cited as *High Romance*.

13. Details of Williams' life can be found in *High Romance*; George Shuster, "Michael Williams," *Catholic Press Annual,* 1964, pp. 19–22; Redmond A. Burke, "Michael Williams: Happy Warrior of Catholic Action," *The Catholic Library World* 15 (1944), 263–267; "Michael Williams, Man of Vision," *The Commonweal* 53 (October 27, 1950), 51.

14. *High Romance*, pp. 31, 250.

15. Ibid., pp. 50, 56, 59.

16. Ibid., pp. 59, 69–70.

17. Ibid., pp. 128–129, 108.

18. Ibid., pp. 146–147, 151–153.

19. Ibid., pp. 153–154, 187–188.

20. Ibid., pp. 155–156.

21. Ibid., pp. 218, 241.

22. Santayana, "The Genteel Tradition in American Philosophy," in *Winds of Doctrine and Platonism and the Christian Life* (New York, 1957 [1913]), pp. 186–215.

23. May, "The Rebellion of the Intellectuals," pp. 115–116; White, *Social Thought in America,* pp. 11–46; Alfred Kazin, *On Native Grounds* (New York, 1942), pp. 166–183.

24. *On Native Grounds,* p. 173.

25. Santayana, *Winds of Doctrine,* p. 1.

26. May, *The End of American Innocence,* pp. 9–14.

27. Richard Hofstadter, *The Age of Reform* (New York, 1955), passim; Handy, *A Christian America,* pp. 128–139.

28. May, "The Rebellion of the Intellectuals," pp. 118–121; Samuel Haber, *Efficiency and Uplift: Scientific Management in the Progressive Era: 1890–1920* (Chicago, 1964); Walter Lippmann, *A Preface to Politics* (New York, 1931), p. 200.

29. May, *The End of American Innocence,* pp. 20–29; James Harvey Robinson, "A Journal of Opinion," *The New Republic,* May 8, 1915, pp. 9–10, cited in May, "The Rebellion of the Intellectuals," p. 118.

30. May, *The End of American Innocence,* pp. 30–51; Randolph Bourne, "The Immanence of Dostoevsky," *The Dial* 63 (1917), 25, as cited in May, "The Rebellion of the Intellectuals," p. 122.

31. Joseph Wood Krutch, *The Modern Temper: A Study and a Confession* (New York, 1929), pp. 3–14.

32. May, *The End of American Innocence,* p. 393.

33. Burke, "Michael Williams"; Roger Van Allen, *The Commonweal and American Catholicism* (Philadelphia, 1974).

34. Williams, *High Romance,* pp. 373–380.

35. Williams, "Pan in California," *Catholic World* 109 (April 1919), 30–31.

36. Ibid., p. 31; *High Romance*, p. 380.

37. "Pan in California," pp. 1, 24–25.

38. Ibid., p. 31; *High Romance*, pp. 381–382.

39. *High Romance*, pp. 295–297.

40. "Pan in California," p. 23; *High Romance*, pp. 368–369.

41. *High Romance* p. 399.

42. Ibid., p. 385.

43. Ibid., p. 400; Michael Williams, *American Catholics and the War* (New York, 1921), pp. 444–446.

44. "Pan in California," pp. 23–24, 31.

45. Baritz, *The Culture of the Twenties,* pp. xli–xlii, xlvi–xlvii.

46. *American Catholics and the War,* p. 446; *The Catholic Church in Action,* p. 2.

47. George Santayana, *Character and Opinion in the United States* (New York, 1956 [1920]), p. 89. Michael Williams, *Catholicism and the Modern Mind* (New York, 1928), pp. 102, 106, 122–128.

48. *Catholicism and the Modern Mind,* pp. 299–302.

49. Hemingway, *A Farewell to Arms* (New York, 1929), p. 191.

50. Charles Péguy, *Notre Conjointe sur M. Descartes et la philosophie cartesienne* (Paris, 1935), p. 300; Sister M. Fides Shepperson, "A Comparative Study of St. Thomas Aquinas and Herbert Spencer." Dissertation, University of Pittsburgh, 1923, p. 79; William Turner, "Pragmatism—What Does It Mean?" *Catholic World* 94 (November 1911), 188–189.

51. Granville Hicks, "Hurdles," *The Nation* 128 (January 9, 1929), 48–49.

52. Phelps, *The Commonweal* 8 (October 31, 1928), 668. On Phelps, see May, *The End of American Innocence,* pp. 77–78.

53. *High Romance,* p. 384.

54. See David J. O'Brien, "The Ambiguity of Success," in his *The Renewal of American Catholicism* (New York, 1972), pp. 80–108, for an analysis of Catholic "success" broadly considered.

3: World War I: The Passage into Innocence

1. On the above paragraphs see Thomas T. McAvoy, C.S.C., "The Catholic Minority after the Americanist Controversy, 1899–1917: A Survey," *Review of Politics* 21 (January 1959), 81; McAvoy, *The Great Crisis in American Catholic History.* John Tracy Ellis, *The Life of James Cardinal Gibbons,* 2 vols. (Milwaukee, 1952), was the first real historical study of the period treating Gibbons as well as other figures involved in the many controversies of the time. A more recent study from another perspective is Gerald P. Fogerty, S.J., *The Vatican and the Americanist Crisis: Denis J. O'Connell, American Agent in Rome, 1885–1903* (Rome, 1974); see also Robert D. Cross, *The Emergence of Liberal Catholicism in America* (Cambridge, Mass., 1958); David J. O'Brien, *The Renewal of American Catholicism,* pp. 109–111; Michael V. Gannon, "Before and After Modernism: The Intellectual Isolation of the American Priest," in John Tracy Ellis, ed., *The Catholic Priest in the United States: Historical Investigations* (Collegeville, Minn., 1971), p. 350; Roger Van Allen, *The Commonweal and American Catholicism;* William D. Miller, *A Harsh and Dreadful Love: Dorothy Day and the Catholic Worker Movement* (New York, 1974); Paul B. Marx, O.S.B., *Virgil Michel and the Liturgical Movement* (Collegeville, Minn., 1957); David J. O'Brien, *American Catholics and Social Reform: The New Deal Years* (New York, 1968).

2. Henry F. May, "The Rebellion of the Intellectuals," *American Quarterly* 8 (Summer 1956), 125; May, "Shifting Perspectives on the 1920's," *The Mississippi Valley Historical Review* 43 (December 1956), 425–426; John Higham, "Hanging Together: Divergent Unities in American History," *Journal of American History* 61 (June 1974), 24–28; quotations from Yeats are from his poem "Nineteen Hundred and Nineteen," *The Collected Poems of W. B. Yeats* (New York, 1956), p. 205.

3. An essay which comes nearest to detailing these assumptions, especially in the writing

of John J. Keane and John Ireland, is Thomas E. Wangler, "The Birth of Americanism: Westward the Apocalyptic Candlestick," *The Harvard Theological Review* 65 (July 1972), 415–436.

4. Richard M. Linkh, *American Catholicism and European Immigrants* (New York, 1975); Rudolph H. Vecoli, "Prelates and Peasants: The Italian Immigrant and the Catholic Church," *Journal of Social History* 1 (September 1969), 263.

5. John B. Sheerin, C.S.P., *Never Look Back: The Career and Concerns of John J. Burke* (New York, 1975), pp. 22–23; Ltr., George N. Shuster to Daniel Hudson, Brooklyn, October 4, 1924, Hudson Papers, University of Notre Dame Archives.

6. Peter Guilday Papers, "Diary and Autobiographical File," Archives of the Catholic University of America, cited hereafter as Guilday Papers; dates from which above references are taken are: June 13, 1901; October 6, 1906; November 17, 1906; January 19, 1908; July 8, 1908; September 29, 1907; Ltr., John J. Wynne, S.J., to Guilday, New York, 1919.

7. "Diary," November 8, 10, 16, 1907.

8. Ibid., "Libri Legendi 1905–1909," January 5, 1908, February 8, 1907, May 15, 1908.

9. These conclusions are based on a number of doctoral dissertations done on Catholicism before 1917: Paul J. Schuler, "The Reaction of American Catholics to the Foundations and Early Practices of Progressive Education in the United States, 1898–1917," Notre Dame, 1970; James Addison White, "The Era of Good Intentions: A Survey of American Catholics' Writing Between the Years 1880–1915," Notre Dame, 1957; Edward Roddy, "The Catholic Newspaper Press and the Quest for Social Justice, 1912–1920," Georgetown University, 1961. John Ireland, *The Church and Modern Society* (New York, 1896), pp. 191–192. Washington Gladden, *Recollections* (Boston, 1909), p. 365; Walter Rauschenbusch, *Christianizing the Social Order* (New York, 1912), p. 26.

10. Edgar Lee Masters, "Father Malloy," *The Commonweal* 7 (December 14, 1927), 812–813; quotations from Masters' *Anthology* are taken from the reprint of "Father Malloy" found in this article.

11. Randolph Bourne, *The History of a Literary Radical and Other Papers* (New York, 1956), pp. 159–178.

12. George Santayana, "The Alleged Catholic Danger," in James Ballowe, ed., *George Santayana's America* (Urbana, Ill., 1967), pp. 150–155; the article first appeared in *The New Republic,* January 15, 1916. John Cogley echoed Santayana's judgment: "By World War I American Catholicism had entered a 'triumphalist' phase. . . . It was a period of tremendous expansion, extraordinary stability, and general optimism," *Catholic America* (New York, 1973), p. 79.

13. Handy, *A Christian America,* pp. 151–154; Eldon G. Ernst, *Moment of Truth for Protestant America: Interchurch Campaigns Following World War I* (Missoula, Mont., 1974), pp. 1–35.

14. Philip Gleason, *The Conservative Reformers: German-American Catholics and the Social Order* (Notre Dame, Ind., 1968), p. 172; John Tracy Ellis, *American Catholicism* (Chicago, 1969), pp. 138–139; Thomas T. McAvoy, C.S.C., *A History of the Catholic Church in the United States* (Notre Dame, Ind., 1969), pp. 363–364; Ltr., Peter Guilday to the Very Reverend Monsignor Jackman, Washington, D.C., May 6, 1918, Guilday Papers.

15. James Robinson, "If This Be Treason," *American Mercury* 14 (July 1928), 303; F. Scott Fitzgerald to Mrs. Richard Taylor, n.p., June 10, 1917, in Andrew Turnbull, ed., *The Letters of F. Scott Fitzgerald* (New York, 1963), p. 414. On Fitzgerald's religious frame of mind see Turnbull, *Scott Fitzgerald* (New York, 1962), p. 78. For a more detailed account of Shuster's response to World War I see below, chapter 5. Those Catholics already converted to the spirit of Anglo gentility, like Burke, Guilday, and James Gillis, did feel, as Gillis confessed, "ashamed of some of the things I said in public during the war." But this did not

seem to affect their idealism after the war. In fact, all three were among the more outspoken Catholic idealists in the 1920's. James F. Finley, *James Gillis: Paulist* (New York, 1958), p. 114; Sheerin, *Never Look Back,* pp. 29–31.

16. Edward F. Garesche, S.J., "The Opening Age," *America* 20 (December 1918), 289–290; Ltr., Michael Williams to Peter Guilday, Carmel-by-the-Sea, February 27, 1919, Guilday Papers; Ltr., Joyce Kilmer to Edward F. Garesche, S.J., A.E.F. in France, May 16, 1918, in Robert Cortes Holliday, ed., *Joyce Kilmer,* 2 vols. (New York, 1918), 2:118.

17. Ellis, *American Catholicism*, pp. 141–143. In 1922 *Council* was changed to *Conference* to calm the fears of some bishops who thought the organization might preempt their authority in their own dioceses, and to dispel Roman anxiety over a national church, ibid.

18. Ernst, *Moment of Truth for Protestant America*, pp. 137–180; Editorial, "A Noble Dream," *America* 23 (July 17, 1920), 305; Editorial, "The Interchurch World Movement," *Catholic World* 111 (August 1920), 715–717.

19. J. B. Cuelemans, "Lessons from the War," *America* 23 (July 17, 1920), 297; "Interchurch World Movement," 715–717; Peter Guilday, "Outlines for Sermons and Addresses," 1:389, Guilday Papers.

20. Thomas F. Burke, "American Catholics in the War," *Catholic World* 114 (July 1922), 478; Benedict Elder, "NCWC: The Church in Action," ibid., 111 (September 1920), 724; Peter Guilday, "Outlines for Sermons and Addresses," 1:28, Guilday Papers; "With Our Readers," *Catholic World* 111 (May 1920), 285.

21. Moorhouse F. X. Millar, S.J., "The Origin of Sound Democratic Principles in Catholic Tradition," *Catholic Historical Review,* N.S. 8 (April 1928), 104; Edward R. Pace, "The Development of the Catholic Sense," *The National Catholic Educational Association Bulletin* 17 (November 1920), 354–363; Peter Guilday, "Outlines for Sermons and Addresses," 1:205–206, 221; Guilday, "Address to the Knights of Columbus," Gettysburg, Penn., March 10, 1928, in Sermon and Address File, 27–33, Guilday Papers.

22. Carlton J. H. Hayes, "Obligations to America," *The Commonweal* 1 (December 31, 1924), 200–201; ibid. (January 7, 1925), 227–228; ibid. (January 14, 1925), 255–256; Gerald C. Treacy, S.J., "Catholic Facts and Factors," *America* 30 (February 9, 1924), 405; James M. Gillis, C.S.P., "Editorial Comment," *Catholic World* 116 (October 1922), 137–139, 142–143; ibid. (November 1922), 281–283; Guilday, "Outlines for Sermons and Addresses," 2:394–395, Guilday Papers.

23. Ross Hoffman, *Restoration* (New York, 1934), pp. 132–133, 142–144.

24. Judging from the personal papers of Catholics like Virgil Michel, O.S.B., Peter Guilday, and John LaFarge, S.J., who all had outlines and speeches which delineated the Catholic revival, it seemed to be a favorite source of fascination. Frank Sheed recently wrote of his own experience in America at this time: "Catholic America was fascinated by the Catholic Intellectual Revival. It was in Denver that I first lectured on it. That was in 1933, and in the next dozen years I must have been asked for it at least twenty times a year. But not only did it not produce any great writers as it did in England; it did not produce any great number of readers" (*The Church and I,* p. 160); John A. O'Brien, *The Trek of the Intellectuals to Rome* (New York, 1937).

25. Francis X. Talbot, S.J., "The Future of Thought," *Thought* 14 (December 1939), 527; Thomas McDermott, "The United States," in Stephen J. Brown, S.J., *A Survey of Catholic Literature* (Milwaukee, 1945); p. 125.

26. Francis X. Talbot, S.J., "Catholicism in America," in Harold E. Stearns, ed., *America Now* (New York, 1938), p. 530; Joseph M. Corrigan, "The American Tradition," in *Proceedings of the First National Catholic Social Action Conference* (Milwaukee, 1938), pp. 387–389.

27. Theodore Maynard, "Is Our Age Pagan," *America* 33 (July 18, 1925), 322–324;

James M. Gillis, C.S.P., *False Prophets* (New York, 1925); Ed Willock, "Catholic Radicalism in America," in Philip Gleason, *Catholicism in America* (New York, 1953).

28. Ltr., Mary McGill to Wilfred Parsons, Indianapolis, Ind., October 15, 1927), America Papers, Woodstock Library.

29. Theodore F. MacManus, "The One Thing That Endures," *National Catholic Alumni Federation* Bulletin 3 (August 1928), pp. 71–73, 75.

30. William James, *Pragmatism* (New York, 1907), p. 4. This aspect of James most Catholics agreed with, but of course they felt they had their own way of "seeing."

31. Edward S. Dore, "The Part That Ideas Must Play in Political, Economic, and Spiritual Reconstruction," National Catholic Alumni Federation, *Catholic Thought and National Reconstruction* (Chicago, 1935), p. 95. Louis J. A. Mercier, "Catholic Thought and the Nation," *The Catholic Mind*, 32 (July 22, 1934), 267.

32. Michael Harrington, *Fragments of a Century* (New York, 1973), p. 13.

33. Philip Gleason, "American Catholic Higher Education: A Historical Perspective," in Robert Hassenger, *The Shape of Catholic Higher Education* (Chicago, 1967), pp. 17–19; Harrington, *Fragments of a Century*, p. 10; John Courtney Murray, S.J., "On the Future of Humanistic Education," in Arthur A. Cohen, ed., *Humanistic Education and Western Civilization* (New York, 1964), p. 235; George P. Schmidt, *The Liberal Arts College* (New Brunswick, N.J., 1957), p. 33.

34. Donna Merwick, *Boston Priests, 1848–1910* (Cambridge, Mass., 1973), pp. 123–130. The ideal Fulton set for himself was in the line of other American college presidents; see George P. Schmidt, *The Old Time College President* (New York, 1930).

35. Gleason, "American Catholic Higher Education," p. 46.

36. Peter Guilday, *Graduate Studies* (Washington, D.C., 1924), pp. 10–11, 23–24, 29, 32–33, 35, 52, 84–86, 90, 96.

37. William J. McGucken, S.J., "Conflicting Philosophies of Education," *The Modern Schoolman* 9 (May 1932), 69; McGucken, *The Catholic Way in Education* (Milwaukee, 1934). George Bull, S.J., "Religious Discrimination: What Can We Do About It?" *Catholic Mind* 30 (January, 1932), 11–12; Bull, "The Function of the Catholic College" (1933), in Francis X. Connolly, S.J., ed., *Literature and the Channel of Culture* (New York, 1948), pp. 21–22, 24–25.

38. Bull, "Religious Discrimination," p. 16; "The Function of the Catholic College," pp. 23–24; "The Function of a Catholic Graduate School," *Thought* 13 (September 1938), 365–367, 376–378; "Present Tendencies in Our Educational System," *Jesuit Educational Quarterly* 1 (June 1938), 5–13.

39. Thurber M. Smith, S.J., "A Rejoinder to George Bull," *Thought* 13 (December 1938), 638–643; Martin R. P. McGuire, "Catholic Education and the Graduate School," in Roy J. Deferrari, ed., *Vital Problems of Catholic Education in the United States* (Washington, D.C., 1939), p. 112; Guilday, *Graduate Studies*, p. 96; Stow Persons, "The Academic Mind," *American Minds* (New York, 1958), pp. 187–189.

40. James Hennessey, S.J., "The Distinctive Tradition of American Catholicism," in Philip Gleason, ed., *Catholicism in America* (New York, 1970).

41. Peter Guilday, "The Catholic Information League," *The Catholic Mind* 15 (December 8, 1920), 130.

42. John LaFarge, S.J., "The Effectiveness of Christianity," *Thought* 9 (December 1934), 375. For a complete listing of organizations see *The 1968 National Catholic Almanac* (Paterson, N.J., 1968), pp. 633–640.

43. George N. Shuster, *The Catholic Spirit in America* (New York, 1928), pp. 168–169; Harrington, *Fragments of a Century*, p. 14.

44. William Kane, S.J., *Catholic Library Problems* (Chicago, 1939), pp. 22–24, 130–133, 162–164, 190–191, 201–202.

45. Peter Guilday, "The Origin of the A.C.H.A.," Guilday Papers; "Diary," November 19, 1919, ibid.; "Educational Values of History Teaching," Reference File, ibid.; *On the Creation of an Institute for American Church History* (Washington, D.C., 1924), pp. 7–11, 16–24.

46. Demetrius Zema, S.J., *The Thoughtlessness of Modern Thought* (New York, 1934), pp. 3–8; Zema, "Is Written History an Act of Faith," *The Historical Bulletin* 12 (March 1934), 45–46; see also Marie R. Madden, "A New Program for Catholic Historians," *Catholic Historical Review* 22 (January 1937), 429; Zema, "The Root Ideas of Catholic History," *The Historical Bulletin* 12 (March 1934), 42–43; Ross J. S. Hoffman, "Introduction" to Peter Guilday, ed., *The Catholic Philosophy of History* (New York, 1936).

47. Samuel K. Wilson, S.J., "Current Conditions in American Historiography," *Thought* 12 (March 1937), 17–18.

48. Ross J. S. Hoffman, *Tradition and Progress* (Milwaukee, 1938), pp. 40. 44. American intellectuals' distrust of Catholic culture was also not without a sense of hysteria, as evidenced when a sizable block of historians in the AHA objected to the nomination of Carlton J. H. Hayes for the presidency of the association in 1944. Hayes was eventually elected, becoming the first Catholic to serve as head of the AHA (Arthur Joseph Hughes, "Carlton J. H. Hayes: Teacher and Historian," Dissertation, Columbia University, 1970).

49. "The Society: Some Factual History," in *The Catholic Poetry Society of America: A Congress on Poetry* (New York, 1941), pp. 58–61.

50. Francis X. Talbot, S.J., "The Tenth Anniversary," in ibid., pp. 9–10.

51. Katherine Bregy, "Why Poetry, and Why Catholic," in ibid., pp. 18–19; Theodore Maynard, "The Poets' Need for a Center," in ibid., pp. 20, 22; A. M. Sullivan, "Poetry: The Spirit," in ibid., pp. 37–41.

52. George N. Shuster, "The American Spirit," *Catholic World* 114 (October 1921), 13.

4: The Repossession of Tradition:
Medieval and American

1. *The Leonard Feeney Omnibus* (New York, 1943), p. 1.

2. Finley, *James Gillis: Paulist*, p. 215; see also Thomas T. McAvoy, C.S.C., *A History of the Catholic Church in the United States* (Notre Dame, Ind., 1969), pp. 392–393.

3. Bernard Fay, "Catholic America," *Living Age* 335 (September 1928), 53–56.

4. Cuthbert Wright, *The Story of the Catholic Church* (New York, 1926), pp. 272–274; "Protestant View of the Catholic Forward Movement," *Literary Digest* 63 (December 13, 1919), 34; "After the Fireworks," *American Mercury* 3 (December 1924), 448–449; Editorial, "Tests for Churches," *The Nation* 114 (June 28, 1922), 766. Padraic Colum, "America Today and Tomorrow," *Studies* 16 (September 1927), 393.

5. Gustave Weigel, S.J., "A Quarter Century Review," *Thought* 26 (Spring 1951), 108; Walter Lippmann, Ltr. *The Commonweal* 7 (January 18, 1928), 963; Ltr., Michael Williams to Peter Guilday, New York, October 2, 1922, Guilday Papers; Williams, *Catholicism and the Modern Mind*, pp. 223–238; Editorial, "Ink and America," *The Commonweal* 3 (April 7, 1926), 589–590. James J. Walsh, the popular Catholic medievalist, wrote to Guilday concerning the then anticipated *Commonweal* that "unless the new *Review* caught up all the voices of discontent and unrest in the Church here . . . it stood little chance to last . . . as I see the Catholic situation in the United States, we are a faint figure because we are not being strengthened in our Americanism. Even that word has a bad meaning. If the

Review manages to give little fellows like us that just particular drop of ambrosial confidence, without trying to do it by doué methods, it will be a blessing" (Ltr., James J. Walsh to Peter Guilday, New York, December 19, 1923, Guilday Papers).

6. Editorial, "An Introduction," *The Commonweal* 1 (November 12, 1924), 5.

7. James M. Gillis, C.S.P., "Puritans and Purity," *Catholic News* (New York), May 5, 1934; Haywood Broun, "It Seems to Heywood Broun," *The Nation* 126 (May 9, 1928), 532; H. L. Mencken, "Clerical Notes," *American Mercury* 3 (December 1924), 446.

8. Wright, *The Story of the Catholic Church,* pp. 138–139, 249–250, 283–286; "The Catholic Church and the Modern Mind," *The Atlantic Monthly* 141 (January 1928), pp. 15–21, (February 1928), pp. 158, 166, (April 1928), pp. 539–549, (May 1928), pp. 664–675; Michael Williams, "Response to the Catholic Church and the Modern Mind," *The Atlantic Monthly* 141 (March 1928), 385–394; Virgil Michel, O.S.B., "Catholic Opinion," *The Atlantic Monthly* 141 (March 1928), 396–397.

9. For contemporary attempts at labeling various groups of Catholics see: Francis X. Talbot, S.J., "Catholicism in America" in Stearns, *America Now,* pp. 533–534; Francis X. Connolly, "The Catholic Writer and Contemporary Culture," *Thought* 14 (September 1939), 374–377; John Reardon, S.J., "Active Leadership in American Catholic Culture," *America* 41 (May 6, 1939), 83; James J. Daley, S.J., "Catholic Action among the Cultured," *The Homiletic and Pastoral Review* 35 (August 1935), 1212–1213.

10. Memo, Harold Gardiner to John LaFarge, S.J., n.d., John LaFarge Papers, Woodstock Library, Georgetown University.

11. The quotations below have been digested from the following editorials in *The Commonweal*: "Ink and America," 3 (April 2, 1926), 589–590; "On the Third Threshold," 5 (November 10, 1926), 1–2; "Hope and the Holly Wreath," 5 (December 22, 1926), 169–170; "Unhollowed Hallelujahs," 7 (January 11, 1928), 911–912; "The Burning Bush, 7 (April 25, 1928), 1331–1332; "The Road Ahead," 7 (November 21, 1928), 57–58.

12. George N. Shuster, "After the Revolution," *The Commonweal* 31 (November 2, 1934), 13–15; Russell Wilbur, "A Word About Babbitt," ibid. (January 25, 1935), pp. 364–366.

13. Walter J. Ong, S.J., *Frontiers in American Catholicism* (New York, 1961), p. 53.

14. James J. Walsh, *The Thirteenth: Greatest of Centuries* (New York, 1913), pp. viii, 17; *Catholic News* (New York), May 18, 1929, pp. 2, 6; Mary Marcella Smith, S.M., "James J. Walsh: American Revivalist of the Middle Ages," Dissertation, St. John's University, Brooklyn, N.Y., 1944; John C. Reville, S.J., "Review of *The Thirteenth: Greatest of Centuries,*" *America* 30 (December 29, 1923), 262.

15. Lord's production was described in the *National Catholic Alumni Federation, Bulletin* 3 (August 1928), p. 93; Daniel Lord, S.J., *Played by Ear* (Chicago, 1956).

16. Ralph Adams Cram, "The Place of the Fine Arts in a College Curriculum," *National Catholic Alumni Federation,* Bulletin 2 (February 1927), pp. 67, 69–70; Cram, "Reflections upon Art," *The Commonweal* 10 (June 5, 1929), 120–122; Walter Charles Copeland, "Communications," ibid. (September 25, 1929), p. 533.

17. John Emmett Gerrity, "Communications," *The Commonweal* 10 (October 23, 1929), 647–648; Donald Attwater, "This Talk About Art," ibid. (July 24, 1929), pp. 311–312; Attwater, "How Can Concrete Be Obscene or Natural Stone Chaste?", ibid., 11 (November 13, 1929), 47. In response to Attwater, Cram pointed out that the Catholic Church in Raincy, France was an architectural symbol of Catholic capitulation to modern life. He was afraid that this would lead to changing the liturgy into the vernacular and having the ministers at Mass dress in "morning coats and grey trousers" and conforming its music to the principles of jazz. "Why stop half way," he concluded, "in the surrender of fundamental truths to temporary and probably evanescent fancies?" ("A Commentary on Mr. Attwater," ibid., 10 [September 25, 1929], 533).

18. Editorial, "The Eagerness of Age," *The Commonweal* 5 (March 9, 1927), 477–478.

19. Martin R. P. McGuire, "Medieval Studies in America: A Challenge and Opportunity for American Catholics," *Catholic Historical Review* 22 (April 1936), 17–18; Leo A. Cormican, O.M.I., "Art Values and Life Values," *Thought* 8 (September 1933), 242–243.

20. Hoffman, *Restoration,* pp. 3, 9–12, 35–38, 191. Sylvester McNamara, *American Democracy and Catholic Doctrine* (Brooklyn, N.Y., 1924), pp. 15–34, makes even more outrageous claims for the social and political happiness of the Middle Ages.

21. Hoffman, *Restoration,* pp. 157–159, 179–180; Joseph Wood Krutch, *The Modern Temper: A Study and a Confession* (New York, 1929), pp. 212, 230–232.

22. Hoffman, *The Will to Freedom* (New York, 1935), pp. 67–105, 135–138; Hoffman, *Tradition and Progress,* pp. 23–30.

23. "The Eagerness of Age," p. 478.

24. Leonard Feeney, S.J., "The Brown Derby," *America* 40 (November 24, 1928), 153–154; Editorial, "The Antiphons of Advent," *The Commonweal* 9 (November 28, 1928), 85–86; O'Brien, *American Catholics and Social Reform,* pp. 45–46; James M. Gillis, C.S.P., "Editorial Comment," *Catholic World* 128 (December 1928), 357.

25. Gaillard Hunt, "The Virginia Declaration of Rights and Cardinal Bellarmine," *Catholic Historical Review* 3 (October 1917), 276–289; Merril D. Peterson reviewed the controversy which ensued after Hunt's essay appeared and concluded that there was no direct relationship between Jefferson and Bellarmine but that the "curious" effort to link the two "reflected the desire in certain quarters of the Church for an accommodation between Catholic theology and American Democracy" (*The Jeffersonian Image and the American Mind* [New York, 1960], pp. 306–307).

26. John A. Ryan and Moorhouse F. X. Millar, S.J., *The State and the Church* (New York, 1922), pp. 99–144; John Vincent Rager, *Democracy and Bellarmine* (Shelbyville, Ind., 1926); also, "Catholic Sources and the Declaration of Independence," *The Catholic Mind* 28 (July 8, 1930), 253–268; McNamara, *American Democracy and Catholic Doctrine,* pp. 109–122; William F. Obering, "Our Constitutional Origins," *Thought* 12 (December 1937), 587–618; Peter Guilday, "The Catholic Influence in the Rise of the American Republic, 1776–1815," ms., Reference File, Guilday Papers.

27. For an example of such paralleling see "Catholic Philosophy and the Declaration of Independence" in *National Catholic Almanac, 1950* (Paterson, N.J., 1950), pp. 190–191. After 1950, however, this section was deleted from the *Almanac.* Louis J. A. Mercier, "Catholic Thought and the Nation," *The Catholic Mind* 32 (July 22, 1934), 264; Joseph Husselein, S.J., "Democracy a 'Popish' Innovation," *America* 31 (July 5, 1919); McNamara, *American Democracy,* pp. 5, 73. It caused no little stir among Catholics to have one of their European heroes, Hilaire Belloc, maintain that from its inception American culture was opposed to the Catholic Church. Catholics vigorously replied to the contrary (Hilaire Belloc, "The Church and Anti-Catholic Culture," *Catholic World* 119 [September 1924], 742–745).

28. John M. Lenhart, O.F.M. Cap., "Genesis of the Political Principles of the American Declaration of Independence," *Central Blatt–Social Justice Review* 25 (September 1932), 155–157, and ibid. (October 1932), pp. 187–194; Frederick J. Zwierlein, "Jefferson Jesuits and the Declaration," *America* 49 (July 8, 1933); John F. Wheaton, "The Great Preamble: Did Bellarmine Influence Jefferson? A Look at the Record," *The Commonweal* 42 (July 6, 1945), 284–285.

29. A brief biographical sketch of Millar is R. C. Hartnett, S.J., *Moorhouse F. X. Millar, S.J.;* a bound copy without publisher or date was found in the Fordham University Library. Moorhouse F. X. Millar, S.J., *Unpopular Essays in the Philosophy of History* (New York, 1928), pp. xii–xiii, 7–13, 15–21; "The Great Evasion in History," *America* 23 (September 4, 1920), 463–464; "The Dehumanization of Man," *Thought* 17 (March 1942), 49–68.

30. Millar, *Unpopular Essays,* p. 15; the following articles, all by Millar, appeared in issues of *Thought:* "The Constitution and Related Prejudices," 13 (June 1938), 283–296; "The Dilemma of Democracy," 16 (September 1941), 408–412; "The Philosophy of the Constitution," 13 (March 1938), 67.

31. Millar, "Aquinas and the Missing Link in the Philosophy of History," *Thought* 8 (March 1934), 644–649, 650–651. Browning quote in *The Complete Poetic and Dramatic Works of Robert Browning,* Cambridge Edition (Boston and New York, 1895), p. 391.

32. Millar, "Modern 'Practical Liberty' and Common Sense," in Ryan and Millar, *The State and the Church,* pp. 145–165. In 1922 Millar seemed to be certain of the literal transcription of Jefferson from Bellarmine through Filmore, ibid., pp. 175–178; but in "Bellarmine and the American Constitution" (*Studies* 19 [September 1930], 361), he maintained that he was not trying to prove any "direct" borrowing. Bernard Balyn's *The Ideological Origins of the American Revolution* (Cambridge, Mass., 1967) reviewed a number of sources from classical Rome to English Whigs, but failed to mention medieval or Catholic theorists at all (pp. 22–54). On the other hand, Walter Lippmann in 1927 was quoting Lord Acton in referring to St. Thomas Aquinas as "the first Whig" and praising Catholic thinkers in general for working out a political theory which opposed the "irresistible" pretensions of the state by an appeal to divided and limited powers, ("Autocracy versus Catholicism," *The Commonweal* 5 [April 13, 1927], 627).

33. Ryan and Millar, *The State and the Church,* pp. 163, 171; Millar, "The Philosophy of the Constitution," pp. 48–56; also, "Democracy vs. the Constitution," *Thought* 12 (June 1937), 192–195.

34. Millar, "Democracy vs. the Constitution," pp. 190–191; also "Majority Rule: Assumed Might or Presumed Right," *Thought* 12 (December 1937), 533–539. Catholics, for the most part, as David O'Brien has written, eventually divided or cooled in their support when the Supreme Court judged many of President Roosevelt's programs to be unconstitutional (*American Catholics and Social Reform,* pp. 51–59). As a group, however, Catholics have since World War I tended to support social welfare legislation; see Gerhard Lenski, *The Religious Factor: A Sociological Study of Religion's Impact on Politics, Economics, and Family Life* (Garden City, N.Y., 1961), pp. 135–152.

35. Millar, "Scholasticism and American Political Philosophy," in John Zybura, *Present Day Thinkers and the New Scholasticism* (New York, 1926), p. 323 (hereafter cited as *Present-Day Thinkers*); Ryan and Millar, *The State and the Church,* p. 159.

36. John A. Ryan and Francis J. Boland, *Catholic Principles of Politics* (New York, 1940); see "Preface" on the deletion of Millar's essays, and chapter one, "The Natural Law," on the essential agreement with much of Millar's historical work.

37. Wilfred Parsons, S.J., "The Church in America, 1929," *America* 42 (January 4, 1930), 309; Raoul E. Desvernine, "The New Law and the New Prophets," in National Catholic Alumni Federation, *Catholic Thought and National Reconstruction,* p. 44. Thomas Woodlock offered a parody of the instrumentalist version of the Declaration: "We hold (for the moment) that these truths (which tomorrow may not be true) are (not self-evident but desirable to hold for the present) that all men are (not of course 'created' but just are) equal, that they are endowed by their Creator (we don't of course mean 'God' but whatever process it may be that produced them) with certain (we don't mean inalienable, for everything changes)—and so forth" (*The Catholic Pattern* [New York, 1942], p. 189).

38. Millar, "The Re-education of Mankind," *Thought* 15 (March 1940), 210–214; "Labor and the Common Good," in Fordham University Graduate School, *Labor Law: An Instrument of Social Peace and Progress* (New York, 1940), pp. 1–5.

39. James J. Walsh, *The Education of the Founding Fathers of the Republic* (New York, 1935), pp. 1, 24–28, 33–63, 359–370; Samuel Eliot Morrison encouraged Walsh in this effort, which led to a preliminary essay in *The New England Quarterly* for July 1932. Walsh

also received letters of appreciation from Charles Beard and Herbert Bolton; see Smith, "James J. Walsh: American Revivalist of the Middle Ages." Morrison responded with an address, "The Catholic Tradition in Early Harvard," delivered at the 1935 meeting of the American Catholic Historical Association and reported on by Peter Guilday in *Catholic Historical Review* 22 (April 1936), 58.

40. Walsh, *American Jesuits* (New York, 1934), pp. 102–103.

41. Wilfred Parsons, S.J., "The Threat to Democracy from Within," *National Catholic Alumni Federation,* Bulletin 8 (1937), pp. 38–39. Richard J. Purcell, "Religion in the American Colonies," in National Catholic Alumni Federation, *Man and Modern Secularism: Essays in the Conflict of Two Cultures* (New York, 1940), pp. 14–27.

42. Benjamin L. Masse, "Resurgent Catholicism," *The Modern Schoolman* 13 (November 1935), 18–20; Wilfred Parsons, S.J., "Philosophical Factors in the Integration of American Culture," in Jesuit Philosophical Association of the Eastern States, *Phases of American Culture* (Worcester, Mass., 1942), pp. 15–24. In 1939 Perry Miller similarly noted scholastic patterns in his seminal work *The New England Mind: The Seventeenth Century* (Boston, 1961), 99–107. The scholastic division of education into mental and moral philosophy and its fundamental proposition that reality was "an orderly and intelligible structure" dominated the American academic mind up to the Civil War; see Stow Persons, " Protestant Scholasticism," in *American Minds* (New York, 1958), pp. 187–194.

43. Richard J. Purcell, "Background of the Declaration of Independence," in William J. Kerby Foundation, *Democracy: Should It Survive?* (Milwaukee, 1943), pp. 19–31.

44. See, for example, Richard Hofstadter, *The American Political Tradition* (New York, 1954); Louis Hartz, *The Liberal Tradition in America* (New York, 1958); Daniel Boorstin, *The Genius of American Politics* (Chicago, 1956); Daniel Bell, *The End of Ideology* (New York, 1960).

45. John Courtney Murray, S.J., *We Hold These Truths* (New York, 1960), p. 67.

46. O'Brien, *The Renewal of American Catholicism,* p. 67.

47. On the dissent from Murray see Thomas T. Love, *John Courtney Murray: Contemporary Church-State Theory* (Garden City, N.Y., 1965).

48. T. C. Powers, C.M., "The Catholic Alumni and Catholic Action," *National Catholic Alumni Federation,* Bulletin 5 (July 1931), pp. 7–8.

49. The remaining quotations in this chapter are taken from these essays: Robert C. Pollock, "The Challenge of Secularism to America," in National Catholic Alumni Federation, *Man and Modern Secularism,* pp. 72–82; and "Catholic Philosophy and American Culture," *Thought* 17 (September 1942), 445–463.

50. See *Man and Modern Secularism:* Robert I. Gannon, S.J., "Keynote Address," p. 1; Ross J. S. Hoffman, "The Origins and Development of Secularism," pp. 7–13; Louis J. A. Mercier, "The Reaction Against Secularism," pp. 91–105; Wilfred Parsons, S.J., "The Emancipation of Modern Man Through Modern Faith," p. 123.

51. Two other Catholic attempts to break out of the stranglehold of viewing Catholic thought as a symmetrical design of rational and clear propositions were: Summerfield Baldwin ("The Crucifixion of the Catholic Mind," *The Atlantic Monthly* 140 [August 1927], 178–183), who refers to the Catholic mind as full of inconsistencies, paradoxes, and mysteries which "demand much but cannot guarantee anything." As examples, he points to the variant ways Catholics approach free will, and to the contradiction in their desire to raise man above nature while their attitude on birth control "binds [them] hard and fast to its processes." Russell Wilbur, a priest and a convert to Catholicism, would speak of the essence of the Catholic life as "conflict, struggle" and the only certain facts are those he describes as "intrinsically clear—obscure" in his "A Preface to Catholicism," ibid., 152 (November 1933), 586–591.

52. In 1939 Pollock believed that a "special Providence had enabled Catholicism to

develop in a democratic society, forging 'strong and powerful links between herself and the people.' " Therefore, American Catholics had both the opportunity and responsibility to "become the means of restoring the breath of life to the peoples of the world" ("Catholicism and the American Way," *The Commonweal* 30 [June 20, 1939], 250).

5: George N. Shuster: A Romantic in a Pasture of Logicians

1. George Shuster, "The Crusading Generation," *The Commonweal* 20 (July 20, 1934), 304.

2. Frank J. Sheed, *Theology and Sanity* (New York, 1946), p. 385.

3. George N. Shuster, *The Ground I Walked On* (New York, 1961), p. 23.

4. Van Allen, *The Commonweal and American Catholicism*, pp. 60–67.

5. "An Autobiography," in Vincent P. Lannie, ed., *On the Side of Truth: An Evaluation with Readings* (Notre Dame, Ind., 1974), pp. 13–15, 16, 18, 21; Shuster, "Spiritual Autobiography," ibid., p. 52; this account was first published in Louis Finkelstein, ed., *American Spiritual Autobiographies* (New York, 1948), pp. 25–37; other information is derived from an interview with George Shuster conducted by this writer on May 16, 1974 (hereafter cited as Interview with George Shuster).

6. Shuster, "An Autobiography," p. 15; "Spiritual Autobiography," p. 48.

7. "Spiritual Autobiography," p. 49; George N. Shuster, *The Catholic Church and Current Literature* (New York, 1930), p. 44; Shuster, "Jacques Maritain, Revivalist," *The Bookman* 70 (September 1929), 9–10.

8. Shuster, "An Autobiography," p. 20; "Spiritual Autobiography," pp. 49–50.

9. George N. Shuster, "Catholic Literature as a World Force," *Catholic World* 111 (July 1920), 459; "Spiritual Autobiography," p. 51.

10. "Catholic Literature as a World Force," p. 459; "Spiritual Autobiography," p. 51.

11. John Tracy Ellis, *Documents of American Catholic History* (Chicago, 1967), 2:589.

12. Shuster, "Catholic Literature as a World Force," pp. 454–455, 461–462. In 1964, Shuster referred to "the emancipating impact of that document" on Catholics and the "new terms, free terms" with which the Church spoke to modern America ("Fortieth Anniversary Symposium," *The Commonweal* 80 [November 20, 1964], 273).

13. Kazin, *On Native Grounds,* p. 401.

14. Shuster, "The Crusading Generation," pp. 303–304; "Spiritual Autobiography," p. 49.

15. "The Tragedy of Mark Twain," *Catholic World* 104 (March 1917), 731–732, 736–737.

16. Our Poets in the Streets," *Catholic World* 105 (July 1917), 436–437, 438, 442–443, 445.

17. "The Retreat of the American Novel," *Catholic World* 106 (November 1917), 166, 168–169, 173, 177.

18. Shuster, "An Ancient Vision and Newer Needs," *Catholic World* 106 (March 1918), 740–741; Kazin, *On Native Grounds,* p. 290.

19. "The Crusading Generation," p. 304; "Catholic Literature as a World Force," p. 456; Shuster, *The Catholic Spirit in Modern English Literature* (New York, 1922), pp. 295–296.

20. Shuster, *The Catholic Spirit in America* (New York, 1927), pp. 33–34, 214–217, 223–224; Shuster, "Below the Book," *The Commonweal* 11 (November 13, 1929), 41.

21. *The Catholic Spirit in America,* pp. 217–219, 232–235, 236–237. Alfred Kazin's later interpretations of this period closely parallel Shuster's; see *On Native Grounds,* pp. 207–228, 272–273.

22. *The Catholic Spirit in Modern English Literature,* pp. viii, 1–2. "All Sides of a Question," *The Commonweal* 5 (February 2, 1927), 349.

23. *The Catholic Spirit in America,* pp. 75, 187; *The Catholic Spirit in Modern English Literature,* pp. 320–321, 326, 337–341; 346, 348–350; "Catholic Literature as a World Force," pp. 456–457.

24. *The Catholic Spirit in America,* p. 200; *The Catholic Spirit in Modern English Literature,* p. 347.

25. George Fonsegrive, *L'Evolution des idées dans la France contemporaine* (Paris, 1917), p. 297. On Bergson and French Catholicism see Robert C. Grogin, "Bergson and the French Catholic Revival: 1900–1914," *Thought* 49 (September 1974), 311–322.

26. *The Catholic Spirit in Modern English Literature,* p. 347.

27. Shuster, "The Retreat of the American Novel," pp. 177–178. In 1927 Shuster accused Catholic writers of being "asleep for the last twenty-five years" (Review of George Carver, ed., *The Catholic Tradition in English Literature* (1926) and *Representative Catholic Essays* (1926), *The Commonweal* 5 [February 9, 1927], 338).

28. George N. Shuster, *The Chief Things about Writing* (Notre Dame, Ind., 1920), pp. 49–52; Interview with George Shuster. John O'Hara's literary views can be found in the daily journal he edited at Notre Dame, *Religious Bulletin* 1 (March 7, 1924–March 23, 1924), n.p. Shuster also found himself bearing the brunt of Catholic "indignation" that forced the cancellation of a series for *America* on contemporary Catholic novelists, which he began with a study of Compton Mackenzie (Interview with George Shuster). Continuing his plight, his first major book, *The Catholic Spirit in Modern English Literature* (1922), was criticized quite strongly by Francis X. Talbot, S.J., who thought too much space was given to writers like Walter Pater, Oscar Wilde, and Taine, while not enough was given to "Catholic" authors per se (" 'The Catholic Spirit' in Literature," *America* 27 [July 15, 1922], 304–305).

29. "All Sides of a Question," pp. 350–351; "The Life of Literature," *America* 30 (February 16, 1924), 436.

30. *The Catholic Spirit in America,* p. 116; *The Catholic Church and Current Literature,* pp. 42–43; Paul R. Messbarger, *Fiction with a Parochial Purpose: Social Uses of American Catholic Literature, 1884–1900* (Boston, 1971), pp. 65–70.

31. "All Sides of a Question," p. 350; *The Catholic Spirit in America,* pp. 168, 170–171.

32. *The Catholic Church and Current Literature,* p. 41.

33. Ibid., p. 42.

34. Ibid., pp. 43, 101; *The Catholic Spirit in America,* pp. 116–118.

35. Shuster, "Sigrid Undset and the Nobel Prize," *The Commonweal* 9 (December 26, 1928), 227–228; Mary E. McGill, "An Iconoclast Ventures," *Sign* 8 (April 1929), 531; Shuster, *The Catholic Spirit in America,* p. 117, and *The Catholic Church and Current Literature,* p. 44.

36. Shuster, "Catholics and Other People," *American Scholar* 6 (Summer 1937), 290.

37. Camile McCole, "Humanism's Challenge to Catholicism," *America* 43 (May 24, 1930), 165; Louis J. A. Mercier, *The Challenge of Humanism* (New York, 1933), pp. 120, 178–182; Jerome Kobell, O.F.M., "Catholicism and the New Humanism," in Franciscan Educational Conference, *Catholic English Literature* (Washington, D.C., 1940), pp. 328–331.

38. "The High Lights of Humanism," *The Commonweal* 9 (April 17, 1929), 674–675; "The Crusading Generation," p. 304.

39. *The Catholic Spirit in America,* pp. 51–61; Emerson himself was not above recognizing, even at a time when the Church was held in rather low esteem by his contemporaries, that Catholicism might offer a person an object of attachment which might fulfill personal potentialities. He wrote in his journal of a young girl converting to Catholicism with approval as long as it meant that the Church provided her with a "power to call out the slumbering religious sentiment." What he objected to was the simple transferring from "this icehouse of Unitarianism, all external, into an icehouse again of external" (E. W. Emerson and W. E. Forbes, eds., *The Journals of Ralph W. Emerson,* 10 vols. [Boston, 1909–1914], 6:217–218.

40. "After the Revolution," *The Commonweal* 21 (November 2, 1934), 15; "The American Spirit," *Catholic World* 114 (October, 1921), 13; *The Catholic Spirit in America,* p. 296.

41. *The Catholic Spirit in America,* p. 274; "A Catholic Defends His Church," *The New Republic* 97 (January 4, 1939), 248; "The Conflict among Catholics," *The American Scholar* 10 (Winter, 1940–41), 5–16. In 1939, Shuster's sense of separation from the Catholic community was brought to a head because of his neutrality on the Spanish Civil War. Also in that year Shuster published his only novel, *Look Away,* which was accused, according to him, by the pious and even the more urbane Harold Gardiner of *America* of being a "naturalistic novel" (Interview with George Shuster). Sister Mary Gonzaga Udell, O.P., *A Theory of Criticism of Fiction in Its Moral Aspects According to Thomistic Principles* (Washington, D.C., 1941), p. 108.

6: Literature: A Bastion of Tranquillity

1. Robert Penn Warren, "Bearers of Bad Tidings: Writers and the American Dream," *The New York Review,* March 20, 1975, pp. 17–19. See Robert E. Spiller, Willard Thorp, et al., *Literary History of the United States* (London, 1963), pp. 809–826, for a discussion of the "defenders of ideality."

2. Irving Howe, "Literature of the Latecomers: A View of the Twenties," *Saturday Review/World,* Golden Anniversary Issue, August 10, 1974, pp. 33, 36.

3. William Charvat, *The Origins of American Critical Thought, 1810–1835* (New York, 1961), pp. 170–172.

4. Henry Brownson, ed., *The Works of Orestes Brownson,* 20 vols. (Detroit, 1887), 19:295, 335, 191–192, 321.

5. Brother Azarias, *Essays Philosophical* (Chicago, 1896), pp. 156–159; *An Essay Contributing to a Philosophy of Literature* (Philadelphia, 1906), pp. 14–16, 233–234, 244; *Books and Reading* (New York, 1896), p. 53; *Phases of Thought and Criticism* (New York, 1892), p. 57; *Essays Miscellaneous* (Chicago, 1896), p. 15.

6. Maurice Francis Egan, *Lectures on English Literature* (New York, 1889), pp. 41–60; *Studies in Literature* (St. Louis, 1899), p. 50; *Confessions of a Book Lover* (New York, 1922), pp. 134–140; *Modern Novels and Novelists* (New York, 1888), pp. 138, 299, 120–121. When Egan died in 1924 John C. Reville, S.J., recalled Egan's books favorably: they did not "betray bitterness [or] revolt against life," but rather they breathed a "thoroughly Catholic" philosophy of life which was "a cheery, sunny optimism" ("Maurice Francis Egan," *America* 30 [January 26, 1924], 348–349).

7. For a complete discussion of Catholic literary expression at the end of the century see Messbarger, *Fiction with a Parochial Purpose.* Messbarger observes that despite his "aggressive disassociation" the "American Catholic was in many ways by 1900 a veritable caricature of the American" (p. 79).

8. R. P. "Novel Writing as a Science," *Catholic World* 42 (1885), 287, 289. Messbarger cites this review and suggests that its "language formed a veritable refrain" in Catholic journals of the period (*Fiction with a Parochial Purpose,* p. 66). After World War I Catholics regularly pointed to Mabie as indicating the right approach to literature where "our minds are enlarged, our hearts are thrilled and our whole being is permeated with a joy exalted and serene" (Brother Leo, *English Literature* [Boston, 1928], p. 12).

9. Louise Imogen Guiney, "Wilful Sadness in Literature," *Patrins* (Boston, 1897); see also *Goose-Quill Papers* (Boston, 1885), p. 115.

10. John Lancaster Spalding: "University Education Considered in its Bearings on the Higher Education of Priests," *Memorial Volume of the Third Plenary Council of Baltimore* (Baltimore, 1885), pp. 75–102; "Religion and Art," in *Essays and Reviews* (New York, 1877), pp. 306–313; *Religion and Art and Other Essays* (Chicago, 1905), pp. 80, 87; "Believe and Take Heart," in Joyce Kilmer, ed., *Dreams and Images* (New York, 1917), p. 245.

11. Earls, *Manuscripts and Memories* (Milwaukee, 1935), p. 161.

12. Woodlock, *The Catholic Pattern,* pp. 168–170; James Edward Tobin, ed., "Introduction" in Thomas Woodlock, *Thinking It Over* (New York, 1947), p. ix.

13. William Butler Yeats, "Nineteen Hundred and Nineteen," *The Collected Poems of W. B. Yeats* (New York, 1956), p. 207.

14. The discussion of the Catholic novel in Europe is the result of the reading of the following works: Albert Lonnenfeld, "Twentieth Century Gothic Reflections on the Catholic Novel," *The Southern Review* 1, N.S. (April 1965), 388–405; Richard Griffiths, *The Reactionary Revolution: The Catholic Revival in French Literature, 1870–1914* (New York, 1965); Melvin J. Freedman, ed., *Vision Obscured: Perceptions of Some Twentieth-Century Catholic Novelists* (New York, 1970).

15. James J. Daley, S.J., *A Cheerful Ascetic* (Milwaukee, 1932); Ltr., Joyce Kilmer to Charles O'Donnell, n.p., n.d., Charles O'Donnell Papers, University of Notre Dame Archives. *Joyce Kilmer,* edited with a memoir by Robert Cortes Holiday, 2 vols. (New York, 1918), 2:54; Ltr., Kilmer to Howard W. Cook, A.E.F. France, June 28, 1918, ibid., 2:109–110; Ltr., Kilmer to Aline Kilmer, A.E.F. France, April 27, 1918, ibid., 2:204. Many Catholics objected that John Dos Passos and Stephen Crane found only ugliness on the battlefield. As one put it, there were "inspiring" qualities: "the perfection of organization; the soul of discipline; the strength in cooperation; the will of one man translated into millions of bayonets and bullets wielded by millions of men; the intricacy of thought; and the fervor of purpose" (Elbridge Colby, "Ugliness in Modern Fiction," *America* 26 [March 11, 1922], 449).

16. Henry May, *The End of American Innocence,* p. 7; Henry A. Lappin, "The Passing of W. D. Howells," *Catholic World* 111 (July 1920), 445–453; John C. Reville, S.J., "William Dean Howells," *America* 23 (May 22, 1920), 112–113; Brother Leo, "Howells and His Godfather," ibid., 20 (February 15, 1919), 478; Marshall Lochbiler, S.J., "The Trend of American Literature," *Catholic World* 131 (April 1930), 30; John J. Burke, C.S.P., "With Our Readers," ibid., 115 (July 1922), 569.

17. Francis X. Talbot, S.J., "Poetry of Late," *America* 34 (November 21, 1925), 139; Conde B. Pallen, "Free Verse," ibid., 24 (April 2, 1921), 579; Michael Earls, S.J., *Under College Towers* (New York, 1926), p. 57.

18. Francis X. Talbot, S.J., "The Trend towards Whitman," *America* 31 (June 14, 1924), 214; Sister M. Eleanore, C.S.C., "The Subject Matter of the New Poetry," ibid., 33

(May 16, 1925), 115–116; Talbot, "Poetry of Late," p. 139; Aline Kilmer, "Frost—Early and Late," *The Commonweal* 9 (February 20, 1929), 461; Thomas J. Gerrard, "The Art of Paul Claudel," *Catholic World* 104 (January 1917), 471–474; 483.

    19. J. R. N. Maxwell, S.J., "A Decade of American Catholic Poets," *America* 43 (September 6, 1930), 526–527; Francis X. Connolly, "A Room for the Poets," ibid., 44 (December 13, 1930), 240; "A Manifesto on Poetry," in John Gilland Brunini, ed., *Return to Poetry* (New York, 1947), pp. 5–7; John Duffy, C.S.S.R., "Individualism in Poetry," in Brunini, ed., *Return to Poetry,* pp. 40–41.

    20. Sister M. Eleanore, C.S.C., "The Pessimistic Craze in Modern Fiction," *America* 31 (July 12, 1924), 308–309; "The Alleged Pessimism of the American Novel," ibid. (July 19, 1924), pp. 332–333; James Gillis, "Sursum Corda," *The Catholic News* (New York), February 6, 1932.

    21. Edythe H. Browne, "The Catholic Triumfeminate," *America* 30 (May 24, 1924), 138–139; Eleanore, "The Alleged Pessimism of the American Novel," p. 333; Maurice Francis Egan, "Our Literature and Our Life," *America* 25 (September 3, 1921), 474–475; Blanche Mary Kelly, "The Romance of Reality," ibid., 28 (November 18, 1922), 105; Austin O'Malley, "The Novel and the Romance," ibid., 25 (May 21, 1921), 102–104; John B. Kennedy, "The Need for More Nonsense," ibid., 30 (December 8, 1923), 188–189.

    22. Williams, "Catholicism and American Literature" and "The Sinclair Lewis Industry," in *Catholicism and the Modern Mind,* pp. 217–218, 222, 245; Editorial, "America and Sinclair Lewis," *The Commonweal* 9 (April 24, 1929), 705.

    23. J. V. Cunningham, "*The Commonweal* and Literature," *The Commonweal* 15 (December 2, 1931), 130–133; Editorial, "Fancy's Thoroughfare," ibid., 8 (July 25, 1928), 304; André Gide, *Journals, 1889–1949,* p. 340.

    24. Francis X. Talbot, S.J., "On Literary Self-Complacency, *America* 32 (April 11, 1925), 618; Robert A. Parsons, S.J., "Catholic Literature's Dilemma," ibid., 49 (January 11, 1930), 339–340. Harold C. Gardiner, S.J., "Catholic Fiction: A Reader Hazard," ibid., 45 (September, 1941), 607–608.

    25. Information on Talbot is in America Papers, Woodstock Library, Georgetown University, Washington, D.C.

    26. Talbot, "Our Abject Book Poverty," *America* 41 (May 18, 1929), 139–140; "On Literary Self-Complacency," p. 618; "A School of Critics," *America* 42 (November 16, 1929), 140; "Novelists and Critics: Both Catholic," ibid. (November 2, 1929), p. 93.

    27. For Catholic reactions to Norris and other Catholic writers, see *America* 40 (March 23, 1929), 583; ibid., 41 (April 20, 1929), 48; Louis F. Doyle, S.J., "Novels Called Catholic," ibid., 35 (August 7, 1926), 403–404; also, Ltr., Mary Mannix to Daniel Hudson, San Diego, January 1, 1920, Daniel Hudson Papers, Archives, University of Notre Dame. Hudson was the editor of *Ave Maria,* a Catholic publication of Notre Dame, Indiana. In 1914 Howells praised Norris' fiction as "art for truth's sake and goodness' sake, and mostly for hope's sake" ("A Number of Interesting Novels," *North American Review* 200 [1914], 912, as cited by May, *The End of American Innocence,* p. 17).

    28. Agnes Repplier, "The Novel Reader," *America* 34 (January 23, 1926), 356–357; Elizabeth Jordan, "The Romantic Novel," ibid. (February 13, 1926), pp. 428–430; Kathleen Norris, "Religion and Popular Fiction," ibid. (March 13, 1926), p. 526; Lucille Borden, "Why 'Catholic' Novels," ibid. (April 3, 1926), pp. 597–598; Sister M. Eleanore, C.S.C., "A Plea for Salutary Sentimentalism," ibid., 35 (May 15, 1926), 107–108; Edith O'Shaughnessy, "The True Book of Adventure," ibid., pp. 116–117.

    29. Talbot, "A School of Critics," p. 140; "Three Principles for Novels," *America* 42 (February 1, 1930), 412–413; "Why Catholic Novels," p. 334.

    30. Ltr., Francis X. Talbot, S.J., to Mary E. Kerwin, New York, October 11, 1940,

American Papers. For criticism of Talbot for his sponsoring the lecture tour of Sigrid Undset, see his correspondence, especially Ltr., Most Reverend Daniel J. Gerche, Bishop of Tucson, Ariz., to Francis X. Talbot, Tucson, January 8, 1937; Ltr., same to same, Tucson, September 11, 1940; Ltr., John Menton to Talbot, New York, April 1, 1941, America Papers.

31. Ltrs. Talbot to Elizabeth Jordan, New York, October 7, 1938; Jordan to Talbot, New York, October 10, 1938; Talbot to Jordan, New York, December 18, 1939, America Papers.

32. Parsons, "Catholic Literature's Dilemma," pp. 339–340; "The Freedom of the Catholic Novelist," *America* 42 (March 8, 1930), 532; James F. Kearney, "Alfred Noyes, 'Victorian,' " ibid., 22 (September 19, 1925), 547. McCole, "On the Need for Catholic Criticism," ibid., 46 (February 6, 1932), 437.

33. Editorial, "Is There a Catholic Novel?" *The Commonweal* 19 (March 30, 1932), 593; Jack English, "Can a Catholic Write a Novel?" *American Mercury* 31 (January 1934), 94.

34. Robert C. Broderick, "The Position of the Catholic Fictionist," *The Ave Maria* 49 (February 4, 1939), 130; Charles M. Carey, C.S.C., "Catholic Novel Writing," ibid, 47 (March 5, 1938), 299; Blanche Mary Kelly, *The Sudden Rose* (New York, 1939), pp. 67, 170, 178.

35. John Hugo, "The Realism of Values," *Thought* 9 (December 1934), 391, 393, 397–398; Thomas J. Fitzmorris, "The Formula for the Great American Catholic Novel," *America* 53 (August 19, 1935), 425–426.

36. Harold C. Gardiner, S.J., *Tenets for Readers and Reviewers* (New York, 1945), p. 18; Francis X. Connolly, "Re-Affirmation of Poetic Values," in Brunini, *Return to Poetry,* pp. 13–14; C. J. Eustace, *Romewards* (New York, 1933), p. 236; Camile John McCole interpreted the popularity of Margaret Mitchell's *Gone With the Wind* (1936) as indicative of a "literary hunger" for a "character who is not a puppet" but one "who dominates his environment" (*Lucifer at Large* [New York, 1937], p. 295).

37. Brother Leo, a professor of literature at St. Mary's College in California, was active in preaching such a return. See his *The Catholic Tradition and Modern Life* (San Francisco, 1931); *The Catholic Tradition in Literature* (Washington, D.C., 1939); Francis Beauchesne Thorton, ed., *Return to Tradition* (Milwaukee, 1948); Michael Williams, *A Book of Christian Classics* (New York, 1943 [1933]). Williams was rather apologetic for invoking "the ghost of dead glories" but felt that his generation was looking for a set of ideals amid the "welter of confusing ideas" which might lead them "to ecstasy and to order" (p. xiii).

38. Francis X. Connolly, "For Catholic Puritans," *America* 44 (October 25, 1930), 68; "Intention in the Modern Novel," *Thought* 9 (September 1934), 256–257, 258, 260.

39. Connolly, "Intention in the Modern Novel," pp. 256, 257, 258–259, 260. On Connolly's regard for Bull see Connolly's *Literature: The Channel of Culture* (New York, 1948), pp. 3, 21; "Poetry and Politics," in Brunini, *Return to Poetry,* p. 131.

40. Connolly, "The Novel in America Today, *Thought* 15 (December 1940), 592–594, 596–599, 600–602, 605.

41. Connolly, "The Catholic Writer and Contemporary Culture," *Thought* 14 (September 1939), 374, 377, 379, 380, 381–382; "Catholic Fiction: Two Reactions," *America* 65 (September 13, 1941), 635.

42. Connolly, "Towards a Respectable Anarchy," in Brunini, *Return to Poetry,* pp. 261–262; Connolly and Tobin, *To An Unknown Country* (New York, 1942), pp. 14–16.

43. Marshall Lochbiler, S.J., "The Trend of American Literature," p. 34; Thomas Woodlock, "The Visible Church," *National Catholic Welfare Conference Bulletin* 11 (October 1929), 13–14, 35–39; Bakewell Morrison, S.J., Review of Louis J. A. Mercier's *The Challenge of Humanism, Thought* 9 (June 1934), 173; Editorial, "The Centennial Genera-

tion," *The Commonweal* 8 (October 31, 1928), 644; Leo R. Ward, C.S.C., "The Futile Decade," *America* 43 (July 12, 1930), 334–335.

44. William Franklin Sands, "Catholics and the New Humanism," *Thought* 5 (June 1930), 18; Wilfred Parsons, S.J., "What Is This New Humanism?" *America* 43 (April 12, 1930), 20–21; Howard Morrison, "A Philosophy for a Humanist," *The Modern Schoolman* 8 (March 1931), 46–47; Edward Drummond, "The Future of Humanism," ibid. (May 1931), pp. 74–76; Aloysius R. Caponigri, "The Grecian Fount of the New Humanism," ibid., 10 (March 1933), 63–64.

45. Irving Babbitt, *Democracy and Leadership* (New York, 1924), p. 186; Fulton Sheen, "The New Pelagianism," in *Old Errors and New Labels* (New York, 1931), pp. 213–229; Calvert P. Alexander, "Scholasticism and the New Humanism," *The Modern Schoolman* 6 (January 1930), 27.

46. Louis J. A. Mercier, *The Challenge of Humanism*, pp. 108–109, 117, 178–182; "Humanism and Natural Religion," in *Proceedings of the American Catholic Philosophical Association* 10 (December, 1934), 37–38, 49–50.

47. Kazin, *On Native Grounds*, pp. 426–442; Mercier, *The Challenge of Humanism*, pp. 80–81; Leo L. Ward, C.S.C., "The New Humanism and Standards," in Charles A. Hart, ed., *Aspects of the New Scholastic Philosophy* (New York, 1932), pp. 66–68, 75–76; Jerome Kobel, O.F.M. Cap., "Catholicism and the New Humanism," Franciscan Educational Conference, *Catholic English Literature* (Washington, D.C., 1940), pp. 330–331.

48. Francis P. Donnelly, "Imagination and Emotion in Literature," *Catholic World* 111 (May 1920), 223–228; Feeney, "Clean Literature," in *Leonard Feeney Omnibus*, p. 228; Leonard Callahan, O.P., in *The Theory of Esthetic According to the Principles of St. Thomas Aquinas* (Washington, D.C., 1927), spoke continually of "sane emotionalism," "sane rationalism," "sober objectivism," pp. 118–119; Paul F. Speckbough, C.P.P.S., *Some General Canons of Literary Criticism Determined from an Analysis of Art* (Washington, D.C., 1936), pp. 91–102; Sister Mary Gonzaga Udell, O.P., *A Theory of Criticism of Fiction in Its Moral Aspects According to Thomistic Principles* (Washington, D.C., 1941), pp. 72, 77–78, 104–106, 117.

49. John Chamberlain, "Which Way Writing," *The Commonweal* 9 (April 17, 1929), 682; Ward, "The New Humanism and Standards," p. 81.

50. Theodore Maynard, "The Rise and Fall of American Humanism," *Studies* 24 (December 1935), 588; Russell Wilbur, "A Word about Babbitt," *The Commonweal* 21 (January 25, 1935), 365.

51. Ltr., Elizabeth Jordan to Francis X. Talbot, S.J., New York, November 13, 1931, America Papers.

52. Martin Joseph Quigley, *Decency in Motion Pictures* (New York, 1937), pp. 18, 27–28, 31, 42–47. Quigley believed, as did most Catholics of this era, that "the function of art is primarily to ennoble" as well as having a responsibility to uphold the standards of society (pp. 9–15). For an example of American liberal reaction to Catholic involvement in American culture, see "Is There a Catholic Problem," *New Republic* 97 (November 16, 1938), 32–33.

53. *Decency in Motion Pictures*, pp. 52, 76–86; Lord, *Played by Ear*, pp. 259–305; *The National Legion of Decency: Thirty Years of Christian Witness; a Review and Preview* (Washington, D.C., 1964). Walter Kerr, "Movies," in *Catholicism in America*, p. 209.

54. Charvat, *The Origins of American Critical Thought*, pp. 7–26; the 1930 code is reproduced in Quigley, *Decency in Motion Pictures*, pp. 52–70.

55. Sister Mariella Gable, O.S.B., *This Is Catholic Fiction* (New York, 1948), p. 13. Gable observes that Powers symbolized the passage of Catholic writing from "immaturity" and self-conscious defensiveness (pp. 28–29). She also points to the developing appreciation

for Graham Greene by Catholics as "a most healthy condition" because in Greene "we now have the question before the answer" (p. 37).

56. John V. Hagopian, *J. F. Powers* (New York, 1968), pp. 1–26.

57. Alfred Kazin, "Gravity and Grace," *The New Republic* 34 (April 30, 1956), 19–20; Martin Green, "J. F. Powers and Catholic Writing," in *Yeats' Blessing on von Hügel* (London, 1967), pp. 92–122.

58. J. F. Powers, "Lions Hearts Leaping Does," in *The Prince of Darkness* (New York, 1958), pp. 33–56; "Prince of Darkness," ibid., pp. 152–193; "Look How the Fish Live," *The Reporter* 17 (October 31, 1957), 36–42, recently reprinted in *Look How the Fish Live* (New York, 1975).

59. Sister M. Kristen Malloy, O.S.B., "The Catholic and Creativity: J. F. Powers," *American Benedictine Review* 15 (March 1964), 63–64.

60. George Scouffas, "J. F. Powers: On the Vitality of Disorder," *Critique* 2 (Fall 1958), 41–58; Malloy, "The Catholic and Creativity," p. 76. Indicative of the changing mood of Catholics in the 1960's was Michael Novak's impatience with Powers' good but merely "descriptive" writing. Novak complained of the lack of a "prophetic note" which he saw in European novelists such as Georges Bernanos who wrote of "the word of God [as] a white-hot iron" ("Prophecy and the Novel," *The Commonweal* 77 [February 22, 1963], 568).

7: F. Scott Fitzgerald: The Other Side of Innocence, the Far Side of Catholicism

1. *The Catholic Church and Current Literature*, p. 11.

2. Ibid., pp. 27–31.

3. Ibid., pp. 21, 32–33.

4. John Pick, "The Renascence in American Catholic Letters" in Norman Weyand, S.J., ed., *The Catholic Renascence in a Disintegrating World* (Chicago, 1951), p. 161.

5. Alexander, *The Catholic Literary Revival*, pp. 225–226.

6. Thomas McDermott, "The United States," in Stephen J. Brown, S.J., *A Survey of Catholic Literature* (Milwaukee, 1945), p. 148.

7. Charles M. Carey, C.S.C., "Catholic Novel Writing," *The Ave Maria* 47 (March 5, 1938), 299. Hemingway's Catholicism was of a European, especially a "Mediterranean" type, as Morely Callaghan observed (*That Summer in Paris* [New York, 1963], p. 95). A more extended but on the whole rather confusing description of Hemingway's beliefs is Julanne Isabelle, *Hemingway's Religious Experience* (New York, 1964), pp. 52–61.

8. James F. Kearney, S.J., *Psychology in the New Literature* (Chicago, 1931), pp. 67–69; Kearney, "The Lost Ideal," *America* 35 (July 24, 1926), 355–356; R. Danna Skinner, "Eugene O'Neill's *Dynamo*," *The Commonweal* 9 (February 27, 1929), 489–490; Elizabeth Jordan, "Mr. O'Neill's Dramatic Stunt," *America* 38 (February 25, 1928), 490–491.

9. Joseph A. Daley, S.J., "A Catholic Looks at Eugene O'Neill," *The Catholic Mind* 32 (February 8, 1934), 53–60. The cause of Daley's surprise was a letter from O'Neill to George Jean Nathan and quoted by Joseph Wood Krutch in his "Introduction" to *Eugene O'Neill, Nine Plays* (New York, 1959); Ltr. Daniel Lord, S.J., to Martin Quigley (St. Louis) December 27, 1933; Ltr. Eugene O'Neill to Martin Quigley, New York, January 7, 1934, copies in America Papers, Woodstock Library, Georgetown University.

10. Brother Leo, *New York World Telegram*, June 15, 1934, p. 18; Ltr. R. Danna Skinner

to Wilfred Parsons, S.J., New York, January 16, 1934; Ltr. Martin Quigley to Brother Leo, New York, April 30, 1934, America Papers; in this letter Quigley denounces Leo's attack on O'Neill as "sensational" and a "trespass beyond the legitimate bounds of dramatic criticism" and "Christian tolerance."

11. Lionel Trilling, *The Liberal Imagination* (New York, 1950), pp. 251–252; Jackson R. Bryer, *The Critical Reputation of F. Scott Fitzgerald* (New York, 1967).

12. Arthur Mizener, *The Far Side of Paradise* (Boston, 1951), pp. 60–61.

13. F. Scott Fitzgerald, "Pasting It Together," *The Crack-Up,* ed. by Edmund Wilson (New York, 1945 [1936]), p. 84.

14. *This Side of Paradise* (New York, 1954 [1920]), p. 304.

15. Wilson, *The Shores of Light* (New York, 1952), pp. 30–31.

16. Malcolm Cowley, *The Literary Situation* (New York, 1952), p. 153.

17. Ltr., Archbishop Austin Dowling to Msgr. Charles O'Hern, June 3, 1921, St. Paul, Minn., F. Scott Fitzgerald Papers, Princeton University Library. This is a letter of introduction so that Fitzgerald might have an audience with the Pope while visiting Rome. Dowling refers to Fitzgerald as an "author of talent and of wide celebrity."

18. William V. Shannon, *The American Irish* (New York, 1963), p. 236.

19. "Cross-Country St. Paul: Home of the Saints," *Partisan Review* 16 (July 1949), 714–721.

20. "The American Republic," in Ireland, *The Church and Modern Society,* 2:116–118.

21. James Addison White, "The Era of Good Intentions: A Survey of American Catholics Writing Between the Years 1880–1915," Ph.D. dissertation, University of Notre Dame, 1957; Messbarger, *Fiction with a Parochial Purpose.*

22. Henry F. May, "The Rebellion of the Intellectuals, 1912, 1917," *American Quarterly* 8 (Summer 1956), 114–126.

23. Ltr., Fitzgerald to Edmund Wilson, August 15, 1919, in Turnbull, *The Letters of F. Scott Fitzgerald,* p. 325.

24. Mizener, *The Far Side of Paradise,* p. 85.

25. Frederick J. Hoffman, *The Twenties* (New York, 1962), p. 134; Kent Krueter and Gretchen Krueter, "The Moralism of the Later Fitzgerald," *Modern Fiction Studies* 7 (Spring 1961), 71–81.

26. Ernst Boyd, *Portraits: Real and Imaginery* (New York, 1970 [1924]), pp. 220–221.

27. Ltr., Fitzgerald to Frances Fitzgerald Lanahan, November 4, 1939, *The Crack-Up,* p. 306.

28. *The Great Gatsby* (New York, 1958 [1925]), pp. 1–2.

29. Turnbull, *Scott Fitzgerald,* p. 270.

30. *This Side of Paradise,* p. 136.

31. Fitzgerald, "Benediction," *Flappers and Philosophers* (New York, 1959 [1920]), p. 153.

32. "The Crack-Up," *The Crack-Up,* p. 69.

33. *High Romance,* p. 264.

34. *This Side of Paradise,* p. 303.

35. Ltr., Wilson to Fitzgerald, August 9, 1919, quoted in Mizener, *The Far Side of Paradise,* p. 84.

36. "Homage to the Victorian," review of Shane Leslie, *The Oppidian, New York Tribune,* May 14, 1922, Section IV, p. 6.

37. "The Ordeal" in John Kuehl, ed., *The Apprentice Fiction of F. Scott Fitzgerald, 1909–1917* (New Brunswick, N.J., 1965), pp. 81–87.

38. "Absolution" in Arthur Mizener, ed., *The Fitzgerald Reader* (New York, 1963), p. 76.

39. Shane Leslie, *Dublin Review* 167 (October, November, December, 1920), 286–287.

40. Ltr., Shane Leslie to Fitzgerald, New York City, January 23, 1919, Fitzgerald Papers.

41. Cardinal Gibbons' appreciation of Fay can be found in his Introduction to the memorial volume, Sigourney W. Cyril Fay, *The Bride of the Lamb and Other Essays* (New York, 1922).

42. Mrs. Winthrop Chandler, *Autumn in the Valley* (Boston, 1936), p. 80; Ltr., Sigourney Fay to Fitzgerald, Rome, n.d. [c. 1918], Fitzgerald Papers.

43. *The Bride of the Lamb*, pp. 85–86. Fay was introduced to Bergson while the latter was teaching at Columbia University (Chandler, *Autumn in the Valley*, pp. 124–125).

44. *The Bride of the Lamb*, pp. 34–42.

45. *This Side of Paradise*, p. 26.

46. Ltr., Fitzgerald to Mr. Delbos, Camp Sheridan, Ala., n.d. (c. January 1919), Fitzgerald Papers; "The Crack-Up," *The Crack-Up*, p. 69.

47. *This Side of Pardise*, p. 286.

48. Ltr., Peter Guilday to Bishop Thomas J. Shahan, Washington, D.C., January 19, 1921, Guilday Papers. The essays eventually appeared as *The Bride of The Lamb and Other Essays* with an introduction by Cardinal Gibbons.

49. T. S. Eliot, "An Emotional Unity," *The Dial* 84 (February 1928), 112.

50. *This Side of Paradise*, pp. 226–227. This "cool" quality of Catholicism has struck other American writers. Nathaniel Hawthorne wrote in his journals of the "blessed convenience" of Catholics' having "a cool, quiet, silent, beautiful place of worship in even the hottest and most bustling street" where they could leave the troubles of the world, purify themselves with water, and lay the "whole dark burden at the foot of the cross . . . coming forth in the freshness and elasticity of innocence (Newton Arvin, *The Heart of Hawthorne's Journals* [Boston, 1929], 277–278); Ernest Hemingway also has Lieutenant Henry in *A Farewell to Arms* (1927) attracted to a priest because of his dry, clean mind (Isabelle, *Hemingway's Religious Experience*, p. 32).

51. *This Side of Paradise*, p. 136.

52. Ibid., pp. 114–115.

53. "The Crack-Up," *The Crack-Up*, pp. 71–72.

54. *The Great Gatsby*, p. 4.

55. Ltr., Fitzgerald to Frances Fitzgerald Lanahan, No. 4, 1939, *The Crack-Up*, p. 305.

56. John M. Kennedy, Jr., "The Great Gatsby," *The Commonweal* 2 (June 3, 1925), 110; *America* 33 (May 30, 1925), 166.

57. *The Great Gatsby*, p. 2.

58. *The Liberal Imagination*, p. 245.

59. "The Note Books," *The Crack-Up*, pp. 209, 202.

60. Ltr., Fay to Fitzgerald, Deal Beach, N.J., June 6, 1918, Fitzgerald Papers.

61. "Handle with Care," *The Crack-Up*, p. 76.

62. Ltr., Fitzgerald to John Grier Hibbon, Westport, Conn., June 3, 1920, *The Letters of F. Scott Fitzgerald*, p. 462.

63. Ltr., Fitzgerald to Frances Fitzgerald Lanahan, n.d., *The Crack-Up*, p. 306.

64. Francis Downing, "The Disenchantment of Scott Fitzgerald," *The Commonweal* 53 (November 10, 1950), 117.

65. Thomas Keneally, *Three Cheers for the Paraclete* (New York, 1970), as cited by Gary Wills, "Catholic Faith and Fiction," *The New York Times Book Review*, January 16, 1972, p. 2.

8: The American Reconstruction of Thomism I:
The Road to Safety, Sanity and Salvation

1. James, *Pluralistic Universe* (New York, 1909), p. 176.
2. Francis Augustine Walsh, "Trends in American Thought," *Proceedings of the American Catholic Philosophical Association* 4 (1928), 94–95; (hereafter referred to as *Proceedings ACPA*).
3. Ernan McMullin, "Philosophy in the United States Catholic College," in McInerny, *New Themes in Christian Philosophy*, p. 372.
4. W. Norris Clarke, S.J., "The Future of Thomism," in ibid., p. 192.
5. Jess A. Mann, "Neoscholastic Philosophy in the United States of America in the Nineteenth Century," *Proceedings ACPA* 33 (1959), 127.
6. Collins, *Crossroads in Philosophy* (Chicago, 1969), p. 309.
7. Roger Aubert, "Aspects divers du neo-Thomisme sous le pontificat de Leon XIII," in *Aspetti della cultura Catolica nell' eta' di Leone XIII* (Rome, 1961), p. 152.
8. Robert J. Henle, S.J., "The New Scholasticism," *Thought* 13 (September 1938), 475.
9. Brownson, *The Convert: Or, Leaves from My Experience* (New York, 1857), p. 174. *Brownson's Quarterly Review* L.S. 3 (1875), 260, 490–491.
10. Azarias, *Essays Philosophical*, pp. 156–159.
11. John Gemeiner, *Medieval and Modern Cosmology* (Milwaukee, 1891).
12. Biographical information on Pace is in the unpublished notes of Ryan, who planned to write his biography, Edward Pace Papers, Archives of the Catholic University of America; see also Miriam Theresa Rooney, "Fifty Years Ago," *New Scholasticism* 19 (October 1945), 353–368; James Hugh Ryan, "Edward Aloysius Pace, Philosopher and Educator," in Hart, *Aspects of the New Scholastic Philosophy*, pp. 1–9; James Hugh Ryan, "Edward A. Pace: Commemorative Appreciation," *New Scholasticism* 12 (April 1938), 207.
13. Royce, "Pope Leo's Philosophical Movement and Its Relations to Modern Thought," *Boston Evening Transcript*, July 29, 1903, p. 14.
14. *Programma dei Modernisti* (Turin, 1911), quoted by John Zybura in his Introduction to Rudolph G. Bandas, *Contemporary Philosophy and Thomistic Principles* (Milwaukee, 1932), p. 2.
15. "Pope Leo's Philosophical Movement and Its Relations to Modern Thought," p. 14.
16. English text in Maritain, *St. Thomas Aquinas*, p. 218.
17. James A. Weisheipl, O.P., "The Revival of Thomism as a Christian Philosophy," in McInerny, *New Themes in Christian Philosophy*, pp. 180–181.
18. Canon 1366, par. 2, found in Maritain, *St. Thomas Aquinas*, p. 172. English translations of *Studiorium Duceni* and *Humani Generis* also found in Maritain, Appendix III.
19. Joseph L. Perrier, *The Revival of Scholastic Philosophy in the Nineteenth Century* (New York, 1909), pp. 3–4; Zybura, *Present Day Thinkers and the New Scholasticism* (St. Louis, 1926), pp. 116–125; Morton White, "Jacques Maritain: Philosopher in the Service of His Church," in *Pragmatism and the American Mind* (New York, 1973), refers to Maritain as a "technician . . . in the pay of an institutionalized religion," pp. 239–240; Anton Pegis, "Thomism as a Philosophy," in *St. Thomas Aquinas and Philosophy: The McAuley Lectures, 1960* (West Hartford, Conn., 1960), pp. 15–16.
20. Edward A. Pace, "Philosophy in the University," 1895, p. 5, Edward Pace Papers.
21. John B. Hogan, *Clerical Studies* (Boston, 1898), p. 59. John Talbot Smith, *The Training of a Priest* (New York, 1897), p. 276.
22. J. B. Ceulemans, "Le movement philosophique en Amerique," *Revue neo-scholastique de philosophie,* 16 (November 1909), 617–618.

23. M. J. Ryan, "How Are We to Make Scholasticism Popular," *American Ecclesiastical Review* 39 (September 1908), 229.

24. Ltr., William Kerby to Charles O'Donnell, November 19, 1921, O'Donnell Papers, cited in David Joseph Arthur, "The University of Notre Dame, 1919–1933: An Administrative History," Dissertation, University of Michigan, 1973, p. 56.

25. Gustave Weigel, S.J., "A Quarter Century Review," *Thought* 26 (Spring 1951), 108.

26. Cotter, "Scholastic Philosophy," *Thought* 1 (December 1926), 434.

27. Celestian J. Steiner, S.J., "The Seminar Idea," *The Modern Schoolman* 1 (January 1925), 1, 4.

28. John Reardon, "The Seventh Age," *The Modern Schoolman* 1 (January 1925), 10, 12.

29. John Reardon, "A Vision of Empire," *The Modern Schoolman* 1 (January 1925), 8.

30. Editorial, "The Coming of St. Aquinas," *The Modern Schoolman* 1 (February 1925), 7–8.

31. John J. O'Brien, S.J., "Remove the Bushel," *The Modern Schoolman* 2 (March 1926), 7.

32. *Proceedings ACPA* 1 (1926), 9.

33. W. Norris Clarke, S.J., "The Future of Thomism," p. 191.

34. Ernan McMullin, "Presidential Address: 'Who Are We,' " *Proceedings ACPA* 41 (1967), 4.

35. Edward A. Pace, "What a Philosophical Organization Can Do," *Proceedings ACPA* 1 (1926), 16.

36. James A. McWilliams, "The Philosophical Congress at Notre Dame," *The Modern Schoolman* 3 (January 1927), 49.

37. James H. Ryan, "Football and Philosophy," *The Commonweal* 5 (January 26, 1927), 322.

38. Virgil Michel, "Why Scholastic Philosophy Lives," *The Philosophical Review* 36 (March 1927), 169.

39. Perry, *Philosophy of the Recent Past* (New York, 1926).

40. Krutch, *The Modern Temper,* pp. 185–232; Walter Lippmann, *A Preface to Morals* (New York, 1931), p. 327.

41. Bertrand Russell, *Mysticism and Logic* (London, 1921), p. 54.

42. Alfred North Whitehead, *Science and the Modern World* (Cambridge, Mass., 1926), p. 291.

43. Russell, *A History of Western Philosophy* (New York, 1945), pp. xiii–xiv.

44. James Hugh Ryan, "American Philosophy during 1926," *New Scholasticism* 1 (April 1927), 171; "The Sixth International Congress of Philosophy," ibid. (January 1927), p. 78.

45. John O. Riedl, "Philosophy and the Social Sciences," *Proceedings ACPA* 11 (1935), 1–6.

46. John S. Zybura, "The Perennial Vitality and Timeliness of the Philosophy of St. Thomas," Introduction to Bandas, *Contemporary Philosophy and Thomistic Principles,* p. 31.

47. James Hugh Ryan, "The New Scholasticism and Its Contribution to Modern Thought," in Zybura, *Present Day Thinkers,* p. 344.

48. Walsh, "Trends in American Thought," pp. 94–95.

49. T. O'R. Boyle, "A Neo-Scholastic Appreciation of Modern Tendencies in Theodicy," *Proceedings ACPA* 5 (1930), 87–88.

50. Francis E. McMahon, "Modern Tendencies in Metaphysics," ibid., p. 47.

51. Zybura, *Present Day Thinkers,* p. iv.

52. Charles Hart, "Is There a Catholic Philosophy," *Proceedings ACPA* 10 (1934), 160.

53. Riedl, "Everyman's Philosophy, *Proceedings ACPA* 11 (1935), 186–187.

54. James A. McWilliams, "Presidential Address," *Proceedings ACPA* 8 (1932), 17.

55. "The New Scholasticism and Its Contribution to Modern Thought," p. 344.
56. Michel, "Why Scholastic Philosophy Lives," p. 173.
57. "What a Philosophical Organization Can Do," p. 18.
58. John A. Staunton, *Scholasticism: The Philosophy of Common Sense* (Notre Dame, Ind., 1937), p. 7; see the "Foreword" by Charles Miltner.
59. Zybura, "The Perennial Vitality and the Timeliness of the Philosophy of St. Thomas," pp. 28, 32–33; Zybura, "Introduction" to Gerardo Bruni, *Progressive Scholasticism* (St. Louis, 1929), pp. xxxii–xxxiii. James H. Ryan consciously contrasted James's "will-to-believe" with the Thomist epitaph, "the intellect-which-knows" ("The New Scholasticism and Its Contribution to Modern Thought," p. 363).
60. John A. O'Brien, *The New Knowledge and the Old Faith* (New York, 1935), p. 12. See also James M. Gillis, *False Prophets* (Chicago, 1927) for an attack on the "pessimism" of a whole range of contemporary thinkers.
61. Alphonse M. Schwitalla, "The Relation of Biology to Neo-Scholasticism," *Proceedings ACPA* 1 (1925), 55–56.
62. In Hart, *Aspects of the New Scholastic Philosophy*, p. 30; Ltr., Shields to Michel, n.d., Northport, Long Island, Michel Papers, Archives of St. John's Abbey, Collegeville, Minn.

9: The American Reconstruction of Thomism II: The Intuitions of Innocence

1. Daniel Lord, S.J., *Armchair Philosophy* (New York, 1918), pp. 4, 7, 123; "Has Philosophy Failed," *America* 36 (January 15, 1927), 327–328.
2. Miltner, "Foreword" to Staunton, Scholasticism; *The Philosophy of Common Sense*, p. 5. One energetic student went so far as to maintain that "where Scholastic principles dominate, progress is inevitable" (Sister M. Regis Grace, "Possibility of Progress and Scholastic Philosophy," M.A. Thesis, University of Notre Dame, 1924, p. 28).
3. John F. McCormick, S.J., "Presidential Address," *Proceedings ACPA* 5 (1929), 20.
4. James A. McWilliams, S.J., "Presidential Address," *Proceedings ACPA* 8 (1932), 6, 16–17. A year before, Gerard B. Phelan of the Institute of Medieval Studies in Toronto, concluded in his address that Scholastic philosophy "is not only regarded by all thoughtful persons as a very respectable system but it is also bringing intellectual satisfaction to many whose mental outlook has been perturbed by the disarray of contemporary philosophical thinking" ("Presidential Address," *Proceedings ACPA* 7 (1931), 27–28).
5. James Hugh Ryan, "Presidential Address: Problems Facing the New Scholasticism," *Proceedings ACPA* 6 (1930), 20–23.
6. Anton C. Pegis, ed., *Essays in Modern Scholasticism in Honor of John F. McCormick* (Westminster, Md., 1944), p. 2.
7. McCormick, "America," *The Modern Schoolman* 10 (May 1933), 95–97; also, "The Student and Philosophy," ibid., 17 (March 1940), 51–53.
8. Ltrs. Scott to Parsons, New York, January 31, 1930; Parsons to Scott, New York, February 7, 1930; Parsons to Scott, New York, January 30, 1930, America Papers, Woodstock Library.
9. A. C. Coyle, "Vital Scholasticism," *The Modern Schoolman* 15 (March 1938), 51; Leonard A. Waters, "Schoolmen Outside the Schools," ibid., 14 (November 1936), 3.
10. John O. Riedl, "Everyman's Philosophy," *Proceedings ACPA* 11 (1935), 183–187; Francis A. Walsh, "Philosophy and the Plain Man," ibid., 10 (1934), 154–157.

11. James A. McWilliams, *Philosophy for the Millions,* (New York, 1942), pp. 11–12, 26.

12. Zybura, "Introduction," Bruni, *Progressive Scholasticism,* p. xxxiv.

13. O'Grady, "Thomism as a Frame of Reference," *The Thomist* 1 (July 1939), 213–236.

14. Norbert C. Hoff, "Emergent Evolution of C. Lloyd Morgan and J. C. Smuts," *Proceedings ACPA* 11 (1935), 90; the discussion on Newman can be found in ibid., pp. 141–152.

15. Fulton Sheen, *God and Intelligence in Modern Philosophy* (New York, 1925). In the introduction Chesterton speaks in his usual robust fashion: "In this book, as in the modern world generally, the Catholic Church comes forward as the one and only real champion of Reason" (p. vii); Ernst Sutherland Bates, *The Commonweal* 3 (July 13, 1926), 264–265.

16. Wyndham Lewis, *Time and Western Man* (New York, 1928), p. 372.

17. Ltr., Sheen to Pace, Louvain, Belgium, February 19, 1921, Edward Pace Papers.

18. *God and Intelligence,* pp. xii, 8.

19. Sheen, *Religion Without God* (New York, 1928), pp. 190–191.

20. These books include: *The Life of All Living* (New York, 1929); *Old Errors and New Labels* (New York, 1931); *Moods and Truths* (New York, 1932); *Philosophy of Science* (Milwaukee, 1934); *The Mystical Body of Christ* (New York, 1935); *The Moral Universe* (Milwaukee, 1936); *The Cross and the Crisis* (Milwaukee, 1937); *Liberty, Equality, and Fraternity* (New York, 1938); *Freedom under God* (Milwaukee, 1940); *For God and Country* (New York, 1941).

21. Fulton Sheen, "Religion and Values," *New Scholasticism* 2 (January 1928), 39–43; *The Life of All Living,* pp. 205, 211–216.

22. "Religion and Values," p. 45; *Old Errors and New Labels,* p. 19.

23. Sheen, "New Physics and New Scholasticism," *New Scholasticism* 3 (July 1929), 241–252; *God and Intelligence,* p. 71; *Philosophy of Science,* pp. xxii–xxiii, 182–184.

24. Fulton Sheen, "Introduction" to Edward F. Murphy, S.S.J., *New Psychology and Old Religion* (New York, 1933), pp. viii–ix. Charles Bruehl, "Psychoanalysis," *Catholic World* 116 (February 1923), 587–588; James F. Kearney, S.J., *Psychology in the New Literature* (Chicago, 1931).

25. *For God and Country,* pp. 38, 47–48.

26. Butler, "The Role of a Philosopher of Education in a Democratic State," *Proceedings ACPA* 13 (1937), 16–17.

27. Dillon, "Philosophy and Life," *Proceedings ACPA* 12 (1936), 172.

28. Horace C. Longwell, "The Significance of Scholasticism," *The Philosophical Review* 37 (May 1928), 223–224; John Loewenberg, "Fifty Years of Thomism," *The Commonweal* 11 (January 8, 1930), 274.

29. Samuel C. Craig, *The Revival of Theology in the Roman Catholic Church* (Philadelphia, 1938), pp. 13–19; John Clarence Petrie, "Wanted: A Protestant Scholasticism," *Christian Century* 45 (August 1928), 977–978; John Line, "Catholic Theology and Modern Culture," *Christendom* 1 (Summer 1936), 737.

30. For Perry's and Dewey's views toward Scholastic philosophy see Zybura, *Present Day Thinkers,* pp. 5–6, 29–31. Henry Nelson Wieman, "Modern Catholic Philosophy," *Journal of Religion* 7 (May 1927), 317.

31. McWilliams, "Editor's Notes," *The Modern Schoolman* 21 (November 1943), 51. The two worlds did meet in a joint session of the American Catholic Philosophical Association and the American Philosophical Association, Eastern Division, in New York City, December 30, 1937. At this meeting Louis J. A. Mercier discussed "dualistic humanism" in the light of contemporary monistic philosophies, implying that the latter had led to disastrous social consequences. Branch Blanshard of Swarthmore College replied to Mercier's charges by implying that Catholicism itself would seem to be condoning to-

talitarianism, especially in Fascist Italy. *Proceedings ACPA* 13 (1937), 132. The meeting left bitter memories, especially among Catholics. In 1955 Charles A. Hart, secretary of the ACPA, was still referring to Blanshard's "vitriolic attack" as an example of the hostility separating Thomism from professional American philosophers (ibid., 29 [1955], 48).

32. "The Return to Reality," *The Commonweal* 11 (February 12, 1930), 410–411.

33. For an account of Michel's life and various pursuits see Paul B. Marx, O.S.B., *Virgil Michel and the Liturgical Movement* (Collegeville, Minn., 1957).

34. Virgil Michel, "The Mission of Catholic Thought," *American Catholic Quarterly Review* 46 (1921), 661; Michel, "Our Modern Civilization," *The Acolyte* 5 (June 1, 1929), 6.

35. Ltrs. Michel to Abbot Alcuin Deutsch, O.S.B., Rome, March 19, 1924; Michel to Norbert Gerthen, O.S.B., Rome, July 4, 1924, in Michel Papers, Archives of St. John's Abbey, Collegeville, Minn., as cited in Marx, *Virgil Michel and the Liturgical Movement,* pp. 26–27.

36. Ltrs., Michel to Deutsch, Louvain, March 14, 1925, and April 25, 1925, cited in Marx, pp. 35–36.

37. "Philosophy at the End of an Era" went unpublished. The manuscript version was missing from the Michel Papers at St. John's Abbey when I visited there. The above summary is taken from Marx, *Virgil Michel and the Liturgical Movement,* pp. 335–337.

38. Ltr., Cunningham to Michel, Ithaca, New York, April 14, 1936. Michel's response is in a letter from Michel to Cunningham, Ithaca, New York, May 14, 1936, Michel Papers.

39. Virgil Michel, "Towards a Vital Philosophy," *New Scholasticism* 11 (April 1937), 130–133, 137–138.

40. Ibid., 133–138.

41. Ltr., Michel to Robert E. Brennan, O.P., Collegeville, Minn., November 11, 1938, Michel Papers.

42. "The Mansions of Thomistic Philosophy," appeared in *Thomist* 1 (1939). "Troubadour of Truth," in Robert Brennan, O.P., *Essays in Thomism* (New York, 1942), pp. 3–24; a manuscript version of "Thomas Aquin: Then and Now," was located in Michel Papers.

43. John K. Ryan, "The Problem of Truth," in Brennan, *Essays in Thomism,* pp. 74–75; Ltr., Ryan to Michel, Washington, D.C., November 20, 1936, Michel Papers.

44. For examples see James V. Mullaney's review of four Thomistic publications (including Brennan's *Essays in Thomism*), *Thought* 18 (September 1943), 554–556. Mullaney concluded his reflections with the following advice: "zeal is to be tempered by prudence. Silence for those who have only enthusiasm to offer. . . ." Joseph F. Collins' review of the 1942 *Proceedings* of the ACPA, *The Modern Schoolman* 21 (March 1944), 181–182. A review of articles appearing in *Proceedings ACPA, Thought, The Modern Schoolman, New Scholasticism,* and *Thomist* from 1945 to the present indicates the specialized essay replacing general philosophical comment.

45. Becker, "Some Generalities That Still Glitter," *Yale Review* 29 (1940), 665–667.

46. Francis E. McMahon, "Metaphysics and Culture," *Proceedings ACPA* 16 (1940), 126–128; Walter Lippman, "Man's Image of Man," ibid., 17 (1941), 67–68, 74–75.

47. McMahon, "Metaphysics and Culture," p. 128.

48. Anton Pegis, "Law and Liberty," *New Scholasticism* 16 (October 1942), 315–316.

49. Simon, "Liberty and Authority," *Proceedings ACPA* 16 (1940), 88–90.

50. Charles A. Hart, "An American Center of the New Scholastic Philosophy," *Proceedings ACPA* 29 (1955), 47; Rudolph Allers, *New Scholasticism* 13 (October 1939), 377–378, 381. One young Catholic philosopher, James Collins, was at least bringing to American attention the horizons Thomists were exploring in Europe; see his "The German Neo-Scholastic Approach to Heidegger," *The Modern Schoolman* 21 (March 1944), 143–152; and "For Self-Examination of Neo-Scholastics," *The Modern Schoolman* 21 (May 1944), 231–233.

51. Collins, *Crossroads in Philosophy*, p. 280; Charles A. Hart, "An American Center of the New Scholastic Philosophy," p. 49; Sister Helen James John, S.N.D., *The Thomist Spectrum* (New York, 1966).

52. George Santayana, in Zybura, *Present Day Thinkers*, p. 76. Collins, "Oligati's Conception of Modern Philosophy," *Thought* 18 (September 1943), 479.

10: Conclusion: The Dispossession

1. Ltr., Dawson to Tate, London, August 27, 1940, Tate Collection, Princeton University Library. Tate became a convert to Catholicism in 1948. Indicative of the temper of those times, the young Marshall McLuhan, who was to become the guru of the electronic media of the 1960's, wrote that Tate's conversion was comparable to Newman's in England a century earlier. McLuhan sought to link the Catholic cause with Tate's southern traditionalism. "The South can recover itself," McLuhan wrote, "only as it becomes Catholic." This seemed possible because America appeared after World War II to be returning "willy-nilly, to the Age of Jefferson, encyclopedism, and world awareness. Now is the time to baptize the world and ideal of Thomas Jefferson, and to begin the rout of Hamilton" (Ltr., McLuhan to Tate, Toronto, Canada, December 23, 1948, ibid).

2. Wilfred Sheed, "America's Catholics," *The New York Review* 21 (March 7, 1974), 20; Garry Wills, *Bare Ruined Choirs* (Garden City, N.Y., 1972), pp. 15–16, 32.

3. Herberg, *Protestant-Catholic-Jew* (Garden City, N.Y., 1955), p. 160.

4. Connolly, "1950—Crisis and Challenge," *Thought* 25 (March 1950), 17–19.

5. Hart, "An American Center of the New Scholastic Philosophy," *Proceedings ACPA* 29 (1955), 46–47; Charles A. Fecher, *The Philosophy of Jacques Maritain* (New York, 1969 [1953]), p. 342; Leo R. Ward, *Catholic Life U.S.A.* (St. Louis, 1959), p. 2.

6. Ong, *Frontiers in American Catholicism*, pp. 2–3.

7. Francis X. Connolly, "The Complete Twentieth Century Man," *Thought* 24 (March 1949), 10–14; Trilling, *The Liberal Imagination*, p. 20.

8. Thomas Merton, *The Secular Journal* (New York, 1959), pp. 190, 28, 118–119, 183.

9. Robert Lowell, *Lord Weary's Castle* (New York, 1946); Frank O'Malley, "The Blood of Robert Lowell," *Renascence* 2 (Fall 1949), republished in the Twenty-Fifth Anniversary Issue of *Renascence* 25 (Summer 1973), 190–195; Harry Stiehl, "Achievement in American Catholic Poetry," *Ramparts* 1 (November 1962), 38.

10. Daniel Callahan, ed., *Generation of the Third Eye* (New York, 1965), pp. 7–12.

11. O'Gorman, in *Generation of the Third Eye*, pp. 174–184. By the 1970's O'Gorman was dissatisfied with the transformation of Catholicism in the 1960's. He found it "morbidly uninteresting" and "dull" with "no processions, no incense, no sin . . ." ("Catholicism Past," *The Atlantic Monthly* 231 [June 1973], 93).

12. Ellis, *American Catholics and the Intellectual Life* (Chicago, 1956), p. 57. For the reaction following Ellis, see Frank L. Christ and Gerard E. Sherry, eds., *American Catholicism and the Intellectual Ideal* (New York, 1961).

13. Thomas O'Dea, *The American Catholic Dilemma* (New York, 1962), pp. 127–137; Edward Wakin and Joseph F. Scheuer, *The De-Romanization of the American Catholic Church* (New York, 1970 [1966]), pp. 270–275. Philip Gleason, "The Crisis of Americanization," in Philip Gleason, ed., *Contemporary Catholicism in the United States* (Notre Dame, Ind., 1969), pp. 19–24.

14. Leslie Dewart, *The Future of Belief: Theism in a World Come of Age* (New York, 1966);

Eugene Fontinell, "Religious Truth in a Relational and Processive World," *Cross Currents,* Summer 1967, p. 314. Anton C. Pegis, "In Search of St. Thomas Aquinas," *The McAuley Lectures* (West Hartford, Conn., 1966), p. 1; W. Norris Clarke, S.J., "The Future of Thomism," in McInerny, *New Themes in Christian Philosophy,* p. 192.

15. Michael Novak, *A New Generation: American and Catholic* (New York, 1964), p. 11.

16. Michael Novak, "American Catholicism after the Council," *Commentary,* August 1965, p. 52; "The Revolution of 1976," *The Commonweal* 76 (July 14, 1967), 441; Daniel Callahan, "Christianity Is, Finally, More Than Ethics," *The National Catholic Reporter,* May 14, 1969, cited in David J. O'Brien, *The Renewal of American Catholicism* (New York, 1972), p. 157.

17. Sister Helen James John, S.N.D., in Callahan, *Generation of the Third Eye,* p. 97.

18. Philip Scharper, "Speculations," *The Critic* 23 (February–March, 1965), 43: Gary MacEoin, *New Challenges to American Catholics* (New York, 1965), p. 43.

19. Berrigan, "On 'The Dark Night of the Soul,' " *The New York Review,* October 22, 1970.

20. Douglas Cole, in Callahan, *Generation of the Third Eye,* p. 57; Rosemary Reuther, ibid., pp. 186–194.

21. Novak, *The Experience of Nothingness* (New York, 1970), p. 1.

22. James A. Weisheipl, O.P., "Thomism as a Christian Philosophy," in McInerny, *New Themes in Christian Philosophy,* pp. 184–185; Ralph M. McInerny, *Thomism in an Age of Renewal* (Garden City, N.Y., 1966), pp. 176–191. James Hitchcock, *The Decline and Fall of Radical Catholicism* (New York, 1971).

23. Novak, " 'Coming Out' For Tommaso," *The Commonweal* 100 (March 8, 1974), 8. Novak was also a part of Catholic social and political regrouping, see his *The Rise of the Unmeltable Ethnics: Politics and Culture in the Seventies* (New York, 1972).

24. In 1964 Michael Novak, sensing that American Catholics had missed much of the experience which surrounded the wars of the twentieth century, suggested to a group of Catholics that they "recapitulate this history of the last several generations. . . . We ought to live through it until we understand it, until we sympathize with it, until we feel it, until it has become a part of us: this critique of religion, this purification if you will" (*The National Catholic Reporter,* May 12, 1965, as cited by Wakin and Scheuer, *The De-Romanization of the American Catholic Church,* p. 305).

25. Andrew Greeley and William McCready, "The End of American Catholicism," *America* 127 (October 28, 1972), 334–338; John Tracy Ellis, "American Catholicism in an Uncertain and Anxious Time," *The Commonweal* 98 (April 27, 1973), 177–184.

Bibliography

General

Ahlstrom, Sidney. *A Religious History of the American People.* New Haven, Conn.: Yale University Press, 1972.

Alexander, Calvert, S.J. *The Catholic Literary Revival.* Milwaukee: The Bruce Publishing Company, 1935.

Arvin, Newton. *The Heart of Hawthorne's Journals.* Boston: Houghton Mifflin Company, 1929.

Aubert, Roger. *Le Pontificat de Pie IX.* Paris: Bloud et Gay, 1952.

Azarias, Brother. *Books and Reading.* New York: Cathedral Library Association, 1896.

―――. *An Essay Contributing to a Philosophy of Literature.* Philadelphia: J. J. McVey, 1906.

―――. *Essays Miscellaneous.* Chicago: D. H. McBride and Company, 1896.

―――. *Essays Philosophical.* Chicago: D. H. McBride and Company, 1896.

―――. *Phases of Thought and Criticism.* New York: Houghton Mifflin Company, 1892.

Babbitt, Irving. *Democracy and Leadership.* New York: Houghton Mifflin Company, 1924.

Ballowe, James, ed. *George Santayana's America.* Urbana, Ill.: University of Illinois Press, 1967.

Balyn, Bernard. *The Ideological Origins of the American Revolution.* Cambridge, Mass.: Harvard University Press, 1967.

Bandas, Rudolph G. *Contemporary Philosophy and Thomistic Principles.* Milwaukee: The Bruce Publishing Company, 1932.

Baritz, Loren, ed. *The Culture of the Twenties.* Indianapolis, Ind.: The Bobbs-Merrill Company, 1970.

Barry, Colman J., O.S.B., ed. *Readings in Church History,* 3 vols. Westminster, Md.: Newman Press, 1965.

Beard, Charles. *Contemporary American History.* New York: The Macmillan Company, 1914.

Bell, Daniel. *The End of Ideology.* New York: Free Press, 1960.

211

Belloc, Hilaire. *Essays of a Catholic.* London: Sheed and Ward, 1931.

————. *Survivals and New Arrivals.* New York: The Macmillan Company, 1929.

Bernanos, Georges. *La France contre les robots.* Paris: R. Laffort, 1947.

Boorstin, Daniel. *The Genius of American Politics.* Chicago: University of Chicago Press, 1956.

Bourke, Vernon T. *Thomistic Bibliography, 1920–1940.* St. Louis: B. Herder, 1945.

Bourne, Randolph. *The History of a Literary Radical and Other Papers.* New York: S. A. Russell, 1956.

Boyd, Ernst. *Portraits: Real and Imaginary.* New York: AMS Press, 1970.

Brennan, Robert, O.P. *Essays in Thomism.* New York: Sheed and Ward, 1942.

Broderick, Francis C. *Right Reverend New Dealer: John A. Ryan.* New York: The Macmillan Company, 1963.

Brown, Stephen J., S.J. *A Survey of Catholic Literature.* Milwaukee: The Bruce Publishing Company, 1945.

Brownson, Henry, ed. *The Works of Orestes Brownson,* 20 vols. Detroit: T. Nourse, 1887.

Brownson, Orestes. *The Convert: Or, Leaves from My Experience.* New York: E. Dunigan and Brother, 1857.

Bruni, Gerardo. *Progressive Scholasticism.* St. Louis: B. Herder, 1929.

Brunini, John Gilland. *Whereon to Stand.* New York: Harper Brothers, 1946.

————, ed. *Return to Poetry.* New York: Declan X. McMullan Company, 1947.

Bryer, Jackson R. *The Critical Reputation of F. Scott Fitzgerald.* New York: Archon Books, 1967.

Callahan, Daniel, ed. *Generation of the Third Eye.* New York: Sheed and Ward, 1965.

Callahan, Leonard. *The Theory of Esthetic According to the Principles of St. Thomas Aquinas.* Washington, D.C.: Catholic University of America Press, 1927.

Callaghan, Morely. *That Summer in Paris.* New York: Coward, McCann, 1963.

Catholic Poetry Society of America. *A Congress on Poetry.* New York: Catholic Poetry Society of America, 1941.

Catholicism in America, A Series of Articles from The Commonweal. New York: Harcourt, Brace and Company, 1953.

Chadwick, Owen. *From Boussuet to Newman: The Idea of Doctrinal Development.* Cambridge: Cambridge University Press, 1957.

Chandler, Mrs. Winthrop. *Autumn in the Valley.* Boston: Little Brown and Company, 1936.

Charvat, William. *The Origins of American Critical Thought.* New York: A. S. Barnes and Company, 1961.

Christ, Frank L., and Gerard E. Sherry. *American Catholicism and the Intellectual Ideal.* New York: Appleton, 1961.

Cogley, John. *Catholic America.* New York: The Dial Press, 1973.

Cohen, Arthur A., et al., eds. *Humanistic Education and Western Civilization: Essays for Robert M. Hutchins.* Essay Index Reprint Series. New York: Arno, 1964.

Collins, James. *Crossroads in Philosophy.* Chicago: Henry Regnery and Company, 1969.

Confrey, Burton. *The Moral Mission of Literature and Other Essays.* Manchester, N.H.: Magnificat Press, 1939.

Connolly, Francis X. *Literature: The Channel of Culture.* New York: Harcourt, Brace and Company, 1948.

————, and James Edward Tobin. *To An Unknown Country.* New York: Cosmopolitan Science and Art Service, 1942.

Connolly, James M. *The Voices of France.* New York: The Macmillan Company, 1961.

Cowley, Malcolm. *The Literary Situation.* New York: Viking Press, 1952; Penguin, 1958.

Craig, Samuel C. *The Revival of Theology in the Roman Catholic Church.* Philadelphia: Board of Christian Education of the Presbyterian Church in the United States of America, 1938.

Cross, Robert D. *The Emergence of Liberal Catholicism in America.* Cambridge, Mass.: Harvard University Press, 1958.

Daley, James J., S.J. *A Cheerful Ascetic.* Milwaukee: The Bruce Publishing Company, 1932.

Dawson, Christopher. *Essays in Order.* New York: Sheed and Ward, 1931.

DeFerrari, Roy J., ed. *Vital Problems of Catholic Education in the United States.* Washington, D.C.: Catholic University of America Press, 1939.

Delfgaauw, Bernard. *Twentieth Century Philosophy.* Albany, N.Y.: Magi Books, 1969.

Dewart, Leslie. *The Future of Belief: Theism in a World Come of Age.* New York: Herder and Herder, 1966; Seabury (Crossroad Books), 1968.

Earls, Michael, S.J. *Manuscripts and Memories.* Milwaukee: The Bruce Publishing Company, 1935.

————. *Under College Towers.* New York: The Macmillan Company, 1926.

Egan, Maurice Francis. *Confessions of a Book Lover.* New York: Doubleday, Page and Company, 1922.

————. *Lectures on English Literature.* New York: William H. Sadlier, 1899.

————. *Modern Novels and Novelists.* New York: William H. Sadlier, 1888.

————. *Studies in Literature.* St. Louis: B. Herder, 1899.

Ellis, John Tracy. *American Catholics and the Intellectual Life.* Chicago: The Heritage Foundation, 1956.

————. *American Catholicism.* Chicago: University of Chicago Press, 1969.

————. *Documents of American Catholic History,* 2 vols. Chicago: Henry Regnery Company, 1967.

———. *The Life of James Cardinal Gibbons,* 2 vols. Milwaukee: The Bruce Publishing Co., 1952.

———, ed. *The Catholic Priest in the United States: Historical Investigations.* Collegeville, Minn.: St. John's University Press, 1971.

Ernst, Eldon C. *Moment of Truth for Protestant America: Interchurch Campaigns Following World War I.* Missoula, Mont.: Scholar's Press, 1974.

Eustace, C. J. *Romewards.* New York: Benziger Brothers, 1933.

Evans, Joseph W., ed. *Jacques Maritain: The Man and His Achievement.* New York: Sheed and Ward, 1963.

Farrell, Walter. *A Companion to the Summa,* 4 vols. New York: Sheed and Ward, 1938.

Fay, Sigourney W. Cyril, *The Bride of the Lamb and Other Essays.* New York: Encyclopedia Press, 1922.

Fecher, Charles A. *The Philosophy of Jacques Maritain.* New York: Greenwood Press, 1969.

Feeney, Leonard. *The Leonard Feeney Omnibus.* New York: Sheed and Ward, 1943.

Finkelstein, Louis, ed. *American Spiritual Autobiographies.* New York: Harper and Row, 1948.

Finley, James F. *James Gillis: Paulist.* New York: Hanover House, 1958.

Fitzgerald, F. Scott. *The Crack-Up.* ed. Edmund Wilson. New York: New Directions, 1945.

———. *Flappers and Philosophers.* New York: Charles Scribner's Sons, 1959.

———. *The Great Gatsby.* New York: Charles Scribner's Sons, 1958.

———. *This Side of Paradise.* New York: Charles Scribner's Sons, 1954.

Fogarty, Gerald P., S.J. *The Vatican and the Americanist Crisis; Denis J. O'Connell, American Agent in Rome, 1885–1903.* Rome: Gregorian University Press, 1974.

Fonsegrive, George. *L'Evolution des idées dans la France contemporaine.* Paris: Bloud et Gay, 1917.

Fordham University Graduate School. *Labor Law: An Instrument of Social Peace and Progress.* New York: Fordham University Press, 1940.

Franciscan Educational Conference. *Catholic English Literature.* Washington, D.C.: The Franciscan Educational Conference, 1940.

Freedman, Melvin J., ed. *Vision Obscured: Perceptions of Some Twentieth-Century Catholic Novelists.* New York: Fordham University Press, 1970.

Gable, Sister Mariella, O.S.B. *This Is Catholic Fiction.* New York: Sheed and Ward, 1948.

Gardiner, Harold C., S.J. *American Classics Reconsidered.* New York: Charles Scribner's Sons, 1958.

———. *Fifty Years of the American Novel.* New York: Charles Scribner's Sons, 1951.

———. *Tenets for Readers and Reviewers.* New York: America Press, 1945.

Gide, André. *Journals 1889–1949*. New York: Penguin Modern Classics, 1967.

Gillis, James M., C.S.P. *False Prophets*. New York: The Paulist Press, 1925.

Gladden, Washington. *Recollections*. Boston: Houghton Mifflin Company, 1909.

Gleason, Philip. *Catholicism in America*. New York: Harper and Row, 1970.

————. *The Conservative Reformers: German-American Catholicism and the Social Order*. Notre Dame, Ind.: University of Notre Dame Press, 1968.

————, ed. *Contemporary Catholicism in the United States*. Notre Dame, Ind.: University of Notre Dame Press, 1969.

Gemeiner, John. *Medieval and Modern Cosmology*. Milwaukee: J. H. Yewdale and Sons, 1891.

Green, Martin. *Yeats' Blessing on Von Hügel*. London: Longmans, Green and Company, 1967.

Griffiths, Richard M. *The Reactionary Revolution: The Catholic Revival in French Literature, 1870–1914*. New York: Frederick Ungar Publishing Company, 1965.

Guardini, Romano. *The Church and the Catholic and the Spirit of the Liturgy*. New York: Sheed and Ward, 1935.

Guilday, Peter. *Graduate Studies*. Washington, D.C.: Printed privately, 1924.

————. *On the Creation of an Institute for American Church History*. Washington, D.C.: Printed privately, 1924.

————, ed. *The Catholic Philosophy of History*. P. J. Kenedy and Sons, 1936.

Guiney, Louise Imogen, *Goose-Quill Papers*. Boston: Roberts Brothers, 1885.

————. *Patrins*. Boston: Copeland and Day, 1897.

Gurr, John, S.J. *The Principle of Sufficient Reason in Some Scholastic Systems, 1750–1900*. Milwaukee: Marquette University Press, 1959.

Haber, Samuel. *Efficiency and Uplift: Scientific Management in the Progressive Era, 1890–1920*. Chicago: University of Chicago Press, 1964.

Hagopian, John V. *J. F. Powers*. New York: Twayne Publishers, 1968.

Handy, Robert T. *A Christian America; Protestant Hopes and Historical Realities*. New York: Oxford University Press, 1971.

Harrington, Michael. *Fragments of a Century*. New York: Saturday Review Press, 1973.

Hart, Charles A., ed. *Aspects of the New Scholastic Philosophy*. New York: Benziger Brothers, 1932.

Hartz, Louis. *The Liberal Tradition in America*. New York: Harcourt Brace, 1958.

Hassenger, Robert. *The Shape of Catholic Higher Education*. Chicago: University of Chicago Press, 1967.

Hemingway, Ernest. *A Farewell to Arms*. New York: Charles Scribner's Sons, 1927.

Hennessey, James, S.J. *The First Council of the Vatican: The American Experience*. New York: Herder and Herder, 1963.

Herberg, Will. *Protestant-Catholic-Jew*. Garden City, N.Y.: Doubleday and Company, 1960.

Hitchcock, James. *The Decline and Fall of Radical Catholicism*. Garden City, N.Y.: Doubleday and Company, 1971.

Hoffman, Frederick J. *The Twenties*. New York: Collier Books, 1962.

Hoffman, Ross. *Restoration*. New York: Sheed and Ward, 1934.

————. *Tradition and Progress*. Milwaukee: The Bruce Publishing Company, 1938.

————. *The Will to Freedom*. New York: Sheed and Ward, 1935.

Hofstadter, Richard. *The Age of Reform: From Bryan to F.D.R.* New York: Alfred A. Knopf, 1955.

————. *The American Political Tradition*. New York: Random House (Vintage), 1954.

Hogan, John B. *Clerical Studies*. Boston: Marlier, Callanan and Company, 1898.

Holliday, Robert Cortes, ed. *Joyce Kilmer*. 2 vols. New York: Doran, 1918.

Hopkins, Gerard Manley. *Poems*. London: Oxford University Press, 1935.

Horton, Walter Marshall. *Contemporary Continental Theology*. New York: Harper and Brothers, 1938.

Hudson, Winthrop S. *American Protestantism*. Chicago: University of Chicago Press, 1961.

Ireland, John. *The Church and Modern Society*. New York: McBride, 1896.

Isabelle, Julanne. *Hemingway's Religious Experience*. New York: Vantage Press, 1964.

James, William. *Pluralistic Universe*. New York: Longmans, Green and Company, 1909.

————. *Pragmatism*. New York: Longmans, Green and Company, 1907.

Jesuit Philosophical Association of the Eastern States. *Phases of American Culture*. Worcester, Mass.: Holy Cross College Press, 1942.

John, Sister Helen James, S.N.D. *The Thomist Spectrum*. New York: Fordham University Press, 1966.

Kane, William, S.J. *Catholic Library Problem*. Chicago: Loyola University Press, 1939.

Kazin, Alfred. *On Native Grounds*. New York: Reynal and Hitchcock, 1942.

Kearney, James F., S.J. *Psychology in the New Literature*. Chicago: Loyola University Press, 1931.

Kellogg, Gene. *The Vital Tradition: The Catholic Novel in a Period of Convergence*. Chicago: Loyola University Press, 1970.

Kelly, Blanche Mary. *The Sudden Rose*. New York: Sheed and Ward, 1939.

Kilmer, Joyce, ed. *Dreams and Images*. New York: Boni and Liveright, 1917.

Krutch, Joseph Wood. *The Modern Temper: A Study and a Confession*. New York: Harcourt Brace, 1929.

————, ed. *Eugene O'Neill: Nine Plays*. New York: Random House, 1959.

Kuehl, John, ed. *The Apprentice Fiction of F. Scott Fitzgerald*. New Brunswick, N.J.: Rutgers University Press, 1965.

Lannie, Vincent P., ed. *On the Side of Truth: An Evaluation with Readings*. New edition of George Shuster work, q.v.

Lenski, Gerhard. *The Religious Factor: A Sociological Study of Religion's Impact on Politics, Economics, and Family Life*. Garden City, N.Y.: Doubleday and Company, 1961.

Leo, Brother Francis Meehan. *The Catholic Tradition and Modern Life*. San Francisco: Alumni Association of St. Mary's College, 1931.

———. *The Catholic Tradition in Literature*. Washington, D.C.: Catholic University of America Press, 1939.

———. *English Literature*. Boston: Ginn and Company, 1928.

———. *Living Upstairs: Reading for Profit and Pleasure*. New York: E. P. Dutton and Company, 1942.

———. *Religion and the Study of Literature*. New York: Schwartz, Kirwin and Fauss, 1923.

Lewis, Wyndham. *Time and Western Man*. New York: Harcourt, Brace and Company, 1928.

Linkh, Richard M. *American Catholicism and European Immigrants*. New York: Center for Migration Studies, 1975.

Lippmann, Walter. *A Preface to Morals*. New York: The Macmillan Company, 1931.

———. *A Preface to Politics*. Ann Arbor, Mich.: University of Michigan Press, 1962.

Lord, Daniel, S.J. *Armchair Philosophy*. New York: America Press, 1918.

———. *Played by Ear*. Chicago: Loyola University Press, 1956.

Love, Thomas T. *John Courtney Murray: Contemporary Church-State Theory*. Garden City, N.Y.: Doubleday and Company, 1965.

Lowell, Robert. *Lord Weary's Castle*. New York: Harcourt Brace, 1944.

McAvoy, Thomas T., C.S.C. *The Great American Crisis in American Catholic History, 1895–1900*. Chicago: Henry Regnery Company, 1957.

———. *A History of the Catholic Church in the United States*. Notre Dame, Ind.: University of Notre Dame Press, 1969.

McCole, Camile John. *Lucifer at Large*. New York: Longmans, Green and Company, 1937.

McCormick, John, S.J. *St. Thomas and the Life of Learning*. Milwaukee: Marquette University Press, 1937.

MacEoin, Gary. *New Challenges to American Catholics*. New York: P. J. Kenedy and Sons, 1965.

McGucken, William J. *The Catholic Way in Education*. Milwaukee: The Bruce Publishing Company, 1934.

McInerny, Ralph M. *Thomism in an Age of Renewal*. Garden City, N.Y.: Doubleday and Company, 1966.

————, ed. *New Themes in Christian Philosophy*. Notre Dame, Ind.: University of Notre Dame Press, 1968.

McLean, George F. *An Annotated Bibliography of Philosophy in Catholic Thought, 1900–1964*. New York: Frederick Ungar Company, 1967.

————, ed. *A Bibliography of Christian Philosophy and Contemporary Issues*. New York: Frederick Ungar Company, 1967.

McMahon, Francis E. *A Catholic Looks at the World*. New York: Vanguard Press, 1945.

McNamara, Sylvester. *American Democracy and Catholic Doctrine*. Brooklyn, N.Y.: International Catholic Truth Society, 1924.

McWilliams, James A. *Philosophy for the Millions*. New York: The Macmillan Company, 1942.

Maritain, Jacques. *Art and Poetry*. New York: The Philosophical Library, 1943.

————. *The Peasant of Garonne*. New York: Holt, Rinehart and Winston, 1968.

————. *A Preface to Metaphysics*. New York: Books for Libraries, 1971.

————. *St. Thomas Aquinas*. New York: Meridian Books, Inc., 1958.

————. *The Things That Are Not Caesar's*. New York: Charles Scribner's Sons, 1931.

Maritain, Raissa, and Jacques Maritain. *The Situation of Poetry: Four Essays on the Relations between Poetry, Mysticism, Magic and Knowledge*. New York: The Philosophical Library, 1955.

Marx, Paul B., O.S.B. *Virgil Michel and the Liturgical Movement*. Collegeville, Minn.: St. John's University Press, 1957.

May, Henry F. *The End of American Innocence: A Study of the First Years of Our Own Time, 1912–1917*. New York: Franklin Watts (New Viewpoints), 1964.

Maynard, Theodore. *The Story of American Catholicism*. 2 vols. Garden City, N.Y.: Doubleday and Company, 1960.

————. *The World I Saw*. Milwaukee: The Bruce Publishing Company, 1938.

Meehan, Francis. See Leo, Brother.

Mercier, Louis J. A. *American Humanism and the New Age*. Milwaukee: The Bruce Publishing Company, 1948.

————. *The Challenge of Humanism*. New York: Oxford University Press, 1933.

Merton, Thomas. *The Secular Journal*. New York: Farrar, Straus and Giroux, 1959.

Merwick, Donna. *Boston Priests, 1848—1910*. Cambridge, Mass.: Harvard University Press, 1973.

Messbarger, Paul R. *Fiction with a Parochial Purpose: Social Uses of American Catholic Literature, 1884–1900*. Boston: Boston University Press, 1971.

Millar, Moorhouse, F. X., S.J. *Unpopular Essays in the Philosophy of History*. New York: Fordham University Press, 1928.

Miller, Perry. *The New England Mind: The Seventeenth Century.* Boston: Beacon Press, 1961.

Miller, William D. *A Harsh and Dreadful Love: Dorothy Day and the Catholic Worker Movement.* Garden City, N.Y.: Doubleday and Company, 1974.

Mizener, Arthur. *The Far Side of Paradise.* Boston: Houghton Mifflin Company, 1951.

————, ed. *The Fitzgerald Reader.* New York: Charles Scribner's Sons, 1963.

Monroe, N. Elizabeth. *The Novel and Society.* Chapel Hill, N.C.: University of North Carolina Press, 1941.

Murphy, Edward F., S.S.J. *New Psychology and Old Religion.* New York: Benziger Brothers, 1933.

Murray, John Courtney. *We Hold These Truths: Catholic Reflections on the American Proposition.* New York: Sheed and Ward, 1960; Garden City, N.Y.: Doubleday and Company (Image), 1964.

National Catholic Almanac. Paterson, N.J.: St. Anthony's Guild, various years.

National Catholic Alumni Federation. *Catholic Thought and National Reconstruction.* Chicago: National Catholic Alumni Federation, 1935.

————. *Man and Modern Secularism: Essays in the Conflict of Two Cultures.* New York: National Catholic Alumni Federation, 1940.

Newman, John Henry Cardinal. *An Essay on the Development of Christian Doctrine.* London: Longmans, Green and Company, 1891.

Niebuhr, Reinhold. *The Children of Light and the Children of Darkness.* New York: Charles Scribner's Sons, 1944.

Novak, Michael. *The Experience of Nothingness.* New York: Harper and Row, 1970.

————. *The Rise of the Unmeltable Ethnics: Politics and Culture in the Seventies.* New York: The Macmillan Company, 1972.

————, ed. *A New Generation: American and Catholic.* New York: Herder and Herder, 1964.

Obering, William F., S.J. *The Philosophy of Law of James Wilson.* Washington, D.C.: Catholic University of America Press, 1938.

O'Brien, David J. *American Catholics and Social Reform: The New Deal Years.* New York: Oxford University Press, 1968.

————. *The Renewal of American Catholicism.* New York: Oxford University Press, 1972.

O'Brien, John A. *Evolution and Religion.* New York: The Century Co., 1932.

————. *The New Knowledge and the Old Faith: The Bearing of Modern Science on Christianity.* New York: Paulist Press [1935].

————. *The Trek of the Intellectuals to Rome.* New York: Paulist Press, 1937.

O'Connell, Marvin R. *The Counter-Reformation, 1559–1610.* New York: Harper and Row, 1974.

O'Dea, Thomas. *The American Catholic Dilemma: An Inquiry into the Intellectual Life.* New York: Sheed and Ward, 1962.

Ong, Walter J., S.J. *American Catholic Crossroads*. New York: The Macmillan Company, 1959.

————. *Frontiers in American Catholicism*. New York: The Macmillan Company, 1961.

Pallen, Conde. *As Man to Man*. New York: The Macmillan Company, 1927.

Palmer, R. R. *A History of the Modern World*. New York: Alfred A. Knopf, 1960.

Pegis, Anton C. *Essays in Modern Scholasticism in Honor of John F. McCormick*. Westminster, Md.: Newman Press, 1944.

————. *St. Thomas Aquinas and Philosophy*. The McAuley Lectures, 1960, West Hartford, Conn. Milwaukee: Marquette University Press, 1964.

Péguy, Charles. *Notre Conjointe sur M. Descartes et le philosophie cartesienne*. Paris: Gallinard, 1935.

————. *Temporal and Eternal*. New York: Harper and Row, 1958.

Perrier, Joseph. *The Revival of Scholastic Philosophy in the Nineteenth Century*. New York: Columbia Univesity Press, 1909.

Perry, Ralph Barton. *Philosophy of the Recent Past*. New York: Charles Scribner's Sons, 1926.

Persons, Stow. *American Minds*. New York: Holt, Rinehart and Winston, 1958.

Peterson, Merril D. *The Jeffersonian Image and the American Mind*. New York: Oxford University Press, 1960.

Poulat, Emile. *Histoire dogma et critique dans la Crise Moderniste*. Paris: Casterman, 1962.

Powers, J. F. *Look How the Fish Live*. New York: Random House (Ballantine), 1975.

————. *The Presence of Grace*. New York: Atheneum, 1962.

————. *The Prince of Darkness*. Garden City, N.Y.: Doubleday and Company, 1958.

Quigley, Martin Joseph. *Decency in Motion Pictures*. New York: The Macmillan Company, 1937.

Rager, John Vincent. *Democracy and Bellarmine*. Shelbyville, Ind.: Quality Print, Inc., 1926.

Rauschenbusch, Walter. *Christianizing the Social Order*. New York: The Macmillan Company, 1912.

Regan, Richard J., S.J. *American Pluralism and the Catholic Conscience*. New York: The Macmillan Company, 1963.

Rooney, Miriam Theresa. *Lawlessness, Law, and Sanction*. Washington, D.C.: Catholic University of America Press, 1937.

Russell, Bertrand. *A History of Western Philosophy*. New York: Simon and Shuster, 1945.

————. *Mysticism and Logic*. London: Longmans, Green and Company, 1921.

Ryan, John A., and Francis J. Boland. *Catholic Principles of Politics*. New York: The Macmillan Company, 1940.

———, and Moorhouse F. X. Millar, S.J. *The State and the Church*. New York: The Macmillan Company, 1922.

Santayana, George. *Character and Opinion in the United States*. New York: George Braziller, 1956.

———. *The Winds of Doctrine and Platonism and the Spiritual Life*. Magnolia, Mass.: Peter Smith, 1958.

Schmidt, George P. *The Liberal Arts College*. New Brunswick, N.J.: Rutgers University Press, 1957.

———. *The Old Time College President*. New York: Columbia University Press, 1930; New York: AMS Press, 1970.

Shannon, William V. *The American Irish*. New York: The Macmillan Company, 1963.

Sheed, Frank. *The Church and I*. Garden City, N.Y.: Doubleday and Company, 1974.

———. *Sidelights on the Catholic Revival*. New York: Sheed and Ward, 1940.

———. *Theology and Sanity*. New York: Sheed and Ward, 1946.

Sheen, Fulton. *The Cross and the Crisis*. Milwaukee: The Bruce Publishing Company, 1937.

———. *For God and Country*. New York: P. J. Kenedy and Sons, 1941.

———. *Freedom under God*. Milwaukee: The Bruce Publishing Company, 1940.

———. *God and Intelligence in Modern Philosophy*. New York: Longmans, Green and Company, 1925.

———. *Liberty, Equality and Fraternity*. New York: The MacMillan Company, 1938.

———. *The Life of All Living*. New York: The Century Company, 1929.

———. *Moods and Truths*. New York: The Century Company, 1932.

———. *The Moral Universe*. Milwaukee: The Bruce Publishing Company, 1936.

———. *The Mystical Body of Christ*. New York: Sheed and Ward, 1935.

———. *Old Errors and New Labels*. New York: The Century Company, 1931.

———. *Philosophy of Science*. Milwaukee: The Bruce Publishing Company, 1934.

———. *Religion without God*. New York: Longmans, Green, and Company, 1928.

Sheerin, John B., C.S.P. *Never Look Back: The Career and Concerns of John J. Burke*. New York: Paulist Press, 1975.

Shuster, George N. *The Catholic Church and Current Literature*. New York: The Macmillan Company, 1930.

———. *The Catholic Spirit in America*. New York: Dial Press, 1927.

———. *The Catholic Spirit in Modern English Literature*. New York: The Macmillan Company, 1922.

————. *The Chief Things about Writing.* Notre Dame, Ind.: University of Notre Dame Press, 1920.

————. *The Ground I Walked On.* New York: Farrar, Straus and Giroux, 1961; Notre Dame, Ind.: University of Notre Dame Press, 1969.

————. *On the Side of Truth: An Evaluation with Readings.* Vincent P. Lannie, ed. Notre Dame, Ind.: University of Notre Dame Press, 1974.

Simple, Henry Churchill, S.J. *American Liberty Enlightening the World.* New York: G. P. Putnam and Sons, 1920.

Sixth International Congress of Philosophy. *Proceedings.* New York: Longmans, 1927.

Smith, John Talbot. *The Training of a Priest.* New York: William H. Young and Company, 1897.

Spalding, John Lancaster. *Essays and Reviews.* New York: Catholic Publishing Company, 1877.

————. *Religion and Art and Other Essays.* Chicago: A. C. McClurg and Company, 1905.

Speckbough, Paul F., C.P.P.S. *Some General Canons of Literary Criticism Determined from an Analysis of Art.* Washington, D.C.: Catholic University of America Press, 1936.

Staunton, John A. *Scholasticism: The Philosophy of Common Sense.* Notre Dame, Ind.: University of Notre Dame Press, 1937.

Stearns, Harold E., ed. *America Now.* New York: Charles Scribner's Sons, 1938.

Talbot, Francis X., S.J. *Fiction by Its Makers.* New York: America Press, 1928.

Thorton, Francis Beauchesne, ed. *Return to Tradition.* Milwaukee: The Bruce Publishing Company; 1948.

Tobin, James Edward, ed. *Thinking It Over.* New York: Declan X. Mullen Company, 1947.

Trilling, Lionel. *The Liberal Imagination.* New York: Viking Press, 1950.

Turnbull, Andrew. *Scott Fitzgerald.* New York: Charles Scribner's Sons, 1962.

————, ed. *The Letters of F. Scott Fitzgerald.* Charles Scribner's Sons, 1963.

Udell, Sister Mary Gonzaga, O.P. *A Theory of Criticism of Fiction in Its Moral Aspects According to Thomistic Principles.* Washington, D.C.: Catholic University of America Press, 1941.

Van Allen, Roger. *The Commonweal and American Catholicism.* Philadelphia: Fortress Press, 1974.

Vann, Gerald, O.P. *Saint Thomas Aquinas.* New York: Benziger Brothers, 1941.

Vidler, Alec R. *The Modernist Movement in the Roman Church: Its Origins and Outcome.* Cambridge: Cambridge University Press, 1934.

Wakin, Edward, and Joseph F. Scheuer. *The De-Romanization of the American Catholic Church.* New York: The New American Library, 1970.

Walsh, James J. *American Jesuits.* New York: The Macmillan Company, 1934.

————. *The Education of the Founding Fathers of the Republic.* New York: Fordham University Press, 1935.

————. *Health Through Will Power.* Boston: Little, Brown and Company, 1920.

————. *The Thirteenth: Greatest of Centuries.* New York: Catholic Summer School Press, 1913.

Ward, Leo R. *Catholic Life U.S.A.* St. Louis: B. Herder, 1959.

Weyand, Norman, S.J. *The Catholic Renascence in a Disintegrating World.* Chicago: Loyola University Press, 1951.

White, Morton. *Pragmatism and the American Mind: Essays and Reviews in Philosophy and Intellectual History.* New York: Oxford University Press, 1973.

————. *Social Thought in America: The Revolt against Formalism.* Boston: Beacon Press, 1957.

Whitehead, Alfred North. *Science and the Modern World.* Cambridge, Mass.: Harvard University Press, 1926.

William J. Kerby Foundation. *Democracy: Should It Survive?* Milwaukee: The Bruce Publishing Company, 1943.

Williams, Michael. *American Catholics and the War.* New York: The Macmillan Company, 1921.

————. *The Book of High Romance.* New York: The Macmillan Company, 1926.

————. *The Catholic Church in Action.* New York: The Macmillan Company, 1934.

————. *Catholicism and the Modern Mind.* New York: Dial Press, 1928.

————. ed. *A Book of Christian Classics.* New York: Liveright Publishing Corporation, 1943.

———— and Upton Sinclair. *Good Health and How We Found It.* New York: Frederick A. Stokes, 1909.

Wills, Garry. *Bare Ruined Choirs.* Garden City, N.Y.: Doubleday and Company, 1972.

Wilson, Edmund. *The Shores of Light.* New York: Farrar, Straus, and Giroux, 1952.

Woodlock, Thomas. *The Catholic Pattern.* New York: Simon and Schuster, 1942.

Woodward, E. L. *Three Studies in European Conservativism.* London: Constable and Company, 1929.

Wright, Cuthbert. *The Story of the Catholic Church.* New York: Charles and Albert Boni, 1926.

Yeats, William Butler. *The Collected Poems of W. B. Yeats.* New York: The Macmillan Company, 1956.

Zema, Demetrius, S.J. *The Thoughtlessness of Modern Thought.* New York: Fordham University Press, 1934.

Zybura, John. *Contemporary Goodlessness.* St. Louis: B. Herder, 1924.

————. *Present Day Thinkers and the New Scholasticism.* St. Louis: B. Herder, 1926.

Archives

America Papers, Woodstock Library, Georgetown University, Washington, D.C.

> Francis X. Talbot, S.J. Papers
> John LaFarge, S.J. Papers

Archives of the Catholic University of America, Washington, D.C.

> Peter Guilday Papers
> Edward A. Pace Papers
> John A. Ryan Papers

Archives of the University of Notre Dame, Notre Dame, Indiana.

> Charles O'Donnell Papers
> Daniel Hudson Papers
> The Jacques Maritain Center

Archives of St. John's Abbey, Collegeville, Minnesota.

> Virgil Michel Papers

Columbia University Library, New York.

> Carlton J. H. Hayes Papers

Library of Congress, Washington, D.C.

> T. Lawson Riggs Family Papers

Princeton University Library, Princeton, New Jersey.

> The Allen Tate Collection
> F. Scott Fitzgerald Papers

St. Louis University, Philosophy Department, St. Louis, Missouri.

> Two collections of letters (1923 and 1940) of prominent American philosophers eliciting their views of the revival of neoscholastic philosophy.

Dissertations and Theses

Arthur, David Joseph. "The University of Notre Dame, 1919–1933: An Administrative History." Dissertation, University of Michigan, 1973.

Clements, Robert Brooke, "The *Commonweal*, 1924–1938: The Williams-Shuster Years." Dissertation, University of Notre Dame, 1972.

Doherty, Robert E. "The American Socialist Party and the Roman Catholic Church, 1901–1917." Dissertation, Teachers College, Columbia University, 1959.

Drummond, Edward J. "A Critical History of Catholic Literary Criticism in America: Studies in Brownson, Azarias, and Egan, with an Essay for Catholics." Dissertation, University of Iowa, 1942.

Fay, Sigourney W. Cyril. "The Sources and Development of the Christian Doctrine of the Supernatural." Thesis, Catholic University of America, 1913.

Grace, Sister M. Regis. "Possibility of Progress and Scholastic Philosophy." Thesis, University of Notre Dame, 1924.

Hughes, Arthur Joseph. "Carlton J. H. Hayes: Teacher and Historian." Dissertation, Columbia University, 1970.

McKeown, Elizabeth. "War and Welfare: A Study of American Catholic Leadership." Dissertation, University of Chicago, 1972.

Roddy, Edward. "The Catholic Newspaper Press and the Quest for Social Justice, 1912–1920." Dissertation, Georgetown University, 1961.

Schuler, Paul J. "The Reaction of American Catholics to the Foundations and Early Practices of Progressive Education in the United States." Dissertation, University of Notre Dame, 1970.

Shepperson, Sister M. Fides. "A Comparative Study of St. Thomas Aquinas and Herbert Spencer." Dissertation, University of Pittsburgh, 1923.

Smith, Mary Marcella, S.M. "James J. Walsh: American Revivalist of the Middle Ages." Dissertation, St. Johns University, Brooklyn, 1944.

Walsh, John P. J. "The Catholic Church in Chicago and the Problems of an Urban Society, 1893–1915." Dissertation, University of Chicago, 1948.

White, James Addison. "The Era of Good Intentions: A Survey of American Catholics' Writing Between the Years 1880–1915." Dissertation, University of Notre Dame, 1957.

Periodicals

America
The Catholic World
The Commonweal
The Modern Schoolman
National Catholic Alumni Federation Bulletin
National Catholic Educational Association Bulletin
The New Scholasticism
Spirit
Thought

Interview

Author with George N. Shuster. May 16, 1974.

Index